Up
The Country

Up The Country

A SAGA OF PIONEERING DAYS

Miles Franklin

BEAUFORT BOOKS
Publishers
New York

TO THE OLD HANDS AFFECTIONATELY DEDICATED

Library of Congress Cataloging-in-Publication Data
Franklin, Miles, 1879–1954.
  Up the country.

  I. Title.
PR9619.3.F68U6 1987 823 87-1035
ISBN 0-8243-0417-2

This edition first published in 1984 by Angus & Robertson
Publishers, London and Sydney.
Published in the United States by Beaufort Books
Publishers, New York.
Printed in the U.S.A.
First American Edition 1987

10 9 8 7 6 5 4 3 2 1

PUBLISHER'S NOTE

Up the Country was first published in 1928 by Blackwood of Edinburgh. Its author was the mysterious "Brent of Bin Bin". Two years later its sequel, *Ten Creeks Run*, by the same gentleman, appeared, carrying forward the saga of the Mazere, Stanton, Poole and Healey families to the middle of the 1890s. A third book in this great story, *Back to Bool Bool*, was published in 1931.

As is now known but was a very well-guarded literary secret for over 30 years, Brent of Bin Bin was a pseudonym of the extraordinarily gifted Miles Franklin. *Up the Country*, *My Brilliant Career* and *All That Swagger* were the only three novels of her prolific output to enjoy any kind of real success during her own lifetime.

After George Robertson rejected *My Brilliant Career*'s sequel, *The End of My Career*, Miles turned her back on Australian publishing until the very end of her life. Believing that there was a prejudice against women writers, she took refuge in a bewildering array of pseudonyms, of which Brent of Bin Bin is the most famous.

However, a few years before her death she came to an agreement with Angus & Robertson that its distinguished editor, Beatrice Davis, would prepare for publication the six Brent of Bin Bin books (the other three never having previously achieved publication).

A new edition of *Up the Country* appeared in 1951, the author's note from which is appended to this edition. As is clear from material now in the Mitchell Library, Beatrice Davis worked from a copy of the Blackwood edition, to which Miles had made numerous changes. Undoubtedly the author was not always easy to work with and haste was necessary; the published book is in fact spoiled by simple literals, puzzling inconsistencies and straggling loose ends. No attempt was made to subdue the floridity and syntactical eccentricity that are the hallmarks of Miles Franklin at her worst.

Many of this author's aficionados, such as Professor Colin Roderick, regard *Up the Country* as her finest work and it was well received in Australia when originally published by Blackwood. *The*

Bulletin thought of it as likely to become an Australian classic and it went through four impressions between 1928 and 1931. Nonetheless, its reissue in 1951 was not successful and the whole series was subsequently allowed to go out of print.

In fact, although the 1951 published version is often clotted by overblown verbiage and the last fifty pages are a disappointing anti-climax, the basic story of this wonderful book, which Miles embroidered from the family history of her maternal grandmother, is an authentic and moving account of pioneering life in the second half of the nineteenth century. When we discovered that there was an earlier manuscript version of this book amongst the Franklin papers held by the antiquarian booksellers, Berkelouw's, which told the story in simpler, fresher, more direct language, we became interested in re-editing this version to restore this book to its rightful place in the hearts of a new generation of readers.

The Berkelouw manuscript, which may be the version rejected by both Duckworth and Chatto & Windus in 1927, has been edited more severely than Miles Franklin herself would ever have allowed. At the same time the unmistakable Franklin style has been retained. We have also taken the liberty of deleting her long, anti-climactic ending. We believe this results in a book with a strong narrative and considerable vitality. Some would judge what we have done a literary impertinence, but if it brings this wonderful book the attention it so richly deserves it will have achieved our intention.

1984

PROLOGUE
THREE RIVERS, 1852

It was the night, remembered long after by the old hands, of the greatest flood ever seen up the country.

After a thirsty January with rain long overdue, the showers that began on Saturday at noon were wholeheartedly welcomed by the graziers, even in the valley of Bool Bool which, situated at the lower edge of the wild, mountainous regions of south-eastern New South Wales and veined by scores of rivers and a thousand crystal creeks, had never been known to go dry.

"The rain," remarked Philip Mazere Senior, master of the property known as Three Rivers, complacently on Saturday evening, "is just in the nick of time to save the harvest and top up the stock for the autumn."

But on Monday morning his old friend Brennan, of The Gap, squinting shrewdly at the heavens, exclaimed, "By the pipers, we've had enough for this time of year! It had better leave off now." For there was danger of it flattening the tall, tasselled maize that adorned the flats of Three Rivers farm and those near by, and which was said to grow taller there than anywhere else in the world.

On Monday afternoon, coach-driver Cornstalk Bill, Parramatta born and so named for his lanky height, came in from Gundagai with the mail. He had left his vehicle, which, with more regard to courtesy than accuracy was called a coach, at Billings' Half Way House on the

1

other side of the Yarrabongo River and had finished the trip on horseback.

"My oath!" said he, flinging off his steaming oilskin in the great kitchen of Three Rivers and shaking the water from his wide-brimmed cabbage-tree hat with its bobbing cork fly-chasers. "Another hour and I'd never have got through with the mail bags. Ole Boomerang was almost swimmin' as it was, and in the Bulgoa we was carried near half a mile below the crossin', the current was that swift."

There were various reasons for Bill's appearance at Three Rivers. Foremostly Ellen, the servant woman, was a grass widow far from decrepit whose unfortunate squint militated hardly at all against her in the undersupplied market of marriageable women. Further, Bill was agent for Miss Rachel, whose wedding to Mr Simon Labosseer was to be celebrated the next day. When the trousseau materials had originally arrived from Sydney, it had been found that the ribbon to be put on or puffed out or sewed up, or something as recondite or as indispensable to one of the bridal costumes, was missing. The little general stores up the country, though prodigies for their era, were unequal to remedying the deficiency, and it had been necessary to send all the way to Sydney again, with Cornstalk Bill as an important link in the chain of messengers. As this was the last day upon which the ribbon could arrive in time for the wedding, the bride had been on tenterhooks waiting for the trusty Bill, who had no more than reached the kitchen before Emily, the third daughter of the house, a handsome girl nearing sixteen and chief bridesmaid on the morrow, appeared, representing her sister.

"Good afternoon, Miss Emily! I got it," Bill announced. "At least I got somethin' in here. I thought I'd have to tie it on me head crossin' the Bulgoa."

"Was the river so very high?" she asked, eagerly awaiting the parcel that was making a bulge inside his shirt.

"It's a banker, miss, an' risin' fast. If that young man of Miss Rachel's doesn't turn up with the parson within half an hour, there won't be no weddin' tomorrer, nor the next day, nor the next."

"He's a pretty good swimmer," said Emily in her pleasant way.

"He'll have to be a fish, if you arsk me, with the river a mile wide at Gundagai by now — an' wot about the poor ole Bishop?"

"We'll just have to get a balloon or build a raft," said Emily gaily, departing with her spoils. "Thank you, Bill. Ellen will give you something to eat."

2

"She might and then again she mightn't! Go an' drain yourself off on the verandah. This ain't a fish pond, you know, especially not for sharks," said Ellen tartly, but with a sufficiently flirtatious glance that Bill, going out obediently, felt encouraged to stand near enough to the door to converse.

"Where's the Boss?" he inquired, lowering his voice. The master of Three Rivers was known as a real old John Bull, with a temper to match.

"He went over to the flats this mornin' to see how the crops an' stock are farin'."

"He won't get back except by boat if he don't cross back pretty soon. By this time tomorrer the melons will be well on the way to Gundagai, if I know anythin'."

"Which you don't, if you want my opinion," retorted Ellen, going out to look with him across the rich flats, grey with rain. From the rise on which Three Rivers homestead was placed in the fork of the Yarrabongo and Bulgoa rivers, eastward across the Yarrabongo stretched one of the most fertile valleys in the colony. The boast of its inhabitants was that the soil was so rich that the melon and pumpkin vines wore out their produce dragging it after them.

"Must have rained a dooce of a lot higher up," observed Bill.

"It doesn't look like givin' over," said Ellen. "Don't you think Mr Labosseer'll be able to get the parson here?"

"He won't get himself here, if you arsk me. Aw, Labosseer's such an old codger! I don't know why Miss Rachel chose him when there's plenty of nice young fellers who'd be glad to be in his shoes."

"She likes 'em a bit grown up, not these young things just weaned," said Ellen, feeling the authority of her twenty-six years against his twenty-two.

Bill's reply was drowned out by an influx of children. They were led by Fannie and Rhoda, the youngest members of the Mazere family, aged four and a half and two respectively. (Though their mother fervently hoped that they might be the last of her brood, she was still not able to feel out of the woods at the age of forty-four in that era where there was no circumvention of natural fecundity save affliction more devastating than child-bearing itself.) Next came Georgie Stanton, aged three, firstborn of the eldest Mazere girl, Isabel. Her second, a bantling of twelve months, was taking his afternoon nap.

Isabel and her husband, George, had a run at Mungee, about thirty miles distant. They had arrived at Three Rivers on horseback

3

on Saturday, just before the rains started, the husband carrying Georgie before him on the pommel and his wife holding the baby in her arms. George's younger brother, Jack, who had been helping with fencing at Mungee, accompanied them. A sturdy old piebald packhorse was laden with their wardrobe and other requirements, including an axe, a quart pot, a gun and jingling hobble chains that made music as they went. Eliza, their servant lass, rode a safe old brumby in the rear. Her employers could not safely leave her behind at Mungee, not with miscellaneous men abounding like prey and not another member of her own sex within thirty miles.

Richard, the second Mazere son, had likewise arrived on Saturday for the wedding. He had come from Nanda, twenty miles in the opposite direction, carrying his infant of eleven months and bringing his wife, Amelia, and her servant girl, all on horseback, to swell the numbers.

"Oh, Bill, I saw what you brought for Rachel," cried flaxen-haired little Rhoda, pretty as a valentine and adored by all.

"I've seen it too. Did you bring me something?" asked the more practical Fannie.

"Did I promise the little girls lollipops?" said Bill, fumbling in his pockets. "I do declare, they must've melted in the Bulgoa!" Anxiety and expectancy mingled on the little faces as Bill, with solemn face, turned out his pockets one by one.

"Aw, he's only gammoning!" said Joseph Mazere, aged seven and the youngest son of the house, who had come into the kitchen with his Man Friday, otherwise Mick Slattery, son of Ellen, aged six and a half. In their wake was little Philip, grandson of old Mazere. Charlotte, his mother, had been a member of the Three Rivers household for some time, having gone there for the birth of her son. Her husband, also called Philip, had gone off to the first gold rush at the Ophir about a year before. Ellen and Charlotte had their grass widowhood as a bond, the difference in their situations being that at intervals Charlotte received letters from her spouse, whereas Ellen heard nothing from her Charlie and did not know if she could rest easy in the rumours of his demise, which more than one candidate for the absentee's conjugal prerogatives was anxiously persuading her to do.

When the old hands up the country tell their yarns of long ago, they are prone sometimes to be garrulous and to hold up the main theme

4

of their narrative to prospect up its tributaries; at this their audience impatiently exclaims, "Gosh, he's like the possums when he starts to spin a yarn!" For possums, when excited by the barking of dogs at the foot of the trees in which they have refuge, will run up and down every branch in turn before returning to the main trunk. So now, while the waters rush and swell in the Jenningningahma, the Nanda, the Bulgoa, the Mungee, the Yarrabongo and a score of water channels thereabout, the good example of the dear old hands must be followed, and the branches of this history explored by the fruitful method of possuming.

CHAPTER I

1

The surname Mazere was a corruption of de Mazières, a name borne originally by a branch of the great Huguenot family of d'Abzac. The family tree boasted such dignitaries as the Archbishop of Naronne and, later, when the family was driven out of France during the religious persecution of the seventeenth century, the Bishop of Canchester in England added to its distinction.

Philip Mazere Senior therefore considered himself something of an aristocrat and was outraged when he learned that Philip, his firstborn, had lost his heart to Charlotte Pool. She was a member of a wild brood that had a run on a slope of the Bogong Mountains, by the wide windy plains of Maneroo where the streams, snow-fed from old Kosciusko, sing their icy way with a music that is meet accompaniment to the poetry of their names.

It was generally felt that Charlotte's father, old Boko Pool, must have been "sent out" to the colonies, and further, that his offence could have been no mere trifle. He was well over six feet tall, with unkempt jet-black hair and beard, and only one eye, which lent a sinister expression to his wild, forbidding appearance. It was further rumoured by Larry Healey of Little River, who enjoyed nothing better than to put about scandal concerning his neighbours, that while transportation might have changed his place of residence, it had not

6

altered his black heart. It was said that he preferred the society of blacks to white men, that he ate snakes and goannas with Aboriginal relish, and that his first child had just escaped being born out of wedlock. Rumour had its way with him unchallenged for he never set foot in his neighbours' houses nor asked them into his. In a day when the very blacks were extended hospitality in the kitchens of the homesteads, this alone would have rendered him conspicuous.

However, as Charlotte grew towards maturity, tall and comely, a brown-skinned, bright-eyed beauty, the opposite sex did not await invitation and, since they constituted the bulk of society, the Pools no longer lacked company. Men of various ages came in droves and, among them by chance one evening came young Philip Mazere, slender of form, blue-eyed, gentle of manner and enamoured of adventure. He came seeking his father's shorthorn bull, a celebrated beast sired by imported stock, which had escaped from Three Rivers and had been tracked as far as Billy-go-Billy up towards the head of the Jenningningahma River. Steering for Gowandale, Philip had gone astray and at dusk fetched up at the Pool homestead where he stayed the night. The next day old Pool and his eldest son, Bert, both intrepid bushmen, enthusiastically entered into the business of helping Philip recover the bull. They were the best-suited of all the Maneroo settlers for the undertaking and it occupied them for ten days, with Pool's Creek as their headquarters.

It was inevitable that the shy and untutored Charlotte should be intrigued by this genial young man's correctness, inculcated in a well-regulated home that was modelled on a squire's hall of the old country. He actually carried sleeping attire about with him and a toothbrush, accoutrements derided by the men but which earned him favour with Charlotte, who was astonished by such refinements in a man.

At the age of thirteen, Charlotte had taken charge of a family of six younger brothers and sisters. She had the comfort of her mother, though constantly suffering and virtually bed-ridden, for only two years more, when Mrs Pool was laid to rest, with her two last, prematurely born, near Pool's Creek. After that, Charlotte was without an adviser.

But her courage and ability, far in excess of her years, and astonishing in view of her lack of opportunities, earned her a respect that made the neighbours wonder if Healey's gossip about old Pool wasn't ill-founded. And in those days no young man would have had the strength to visit the sins of the father even on a hangman's daughter, had she youth and comely form. So it was that Pool's alleged past was let drop by the next generation.

2

There was an uproar at Three Rivers when Mazere Senior learned that his firstborn had, after the way of his sex, looked below him.

"Never, never, will I have that baggage here!" he roared.

"Who ever said she was such a thing?" inquired his wife mildly, but alert and skilled in the rising gale.

"She's a hussy, you fool woman. What else can she be — the daughter of that old lag — and you know what her mother's morals must have been."

"Poor soul! She might be let rest in her grave. And what does it matter when the first child came, as it's in the grave with her?"

"The only time I ever saw her, she seemed a shingle short."

"You might have a whole roof short if you'd had thirteen children, and half of them not surviving."

"You'd like to drag your own son down to convict level! You'd —"

"Since when has Charlotte been a convict?"

"I'm not talking of the hussy — the old gorilla's the one I mean! Don't pretend to misunderstand me, Rachel," shouted Mazere.

"And Philip is not marrying the old gorilla, as I have ever heard," returned his wife.

"Who ever got anything but foolishness and equivocation in return for trying to reason with a woman! They've nothing inside their heads! The devil's invention, the lot of them! If he marries that hussy he'll never have a shilling of mine, and if you countenance him, I'll turn you out with him."

"You'd be very glad to turn me in again," said Mrs Mazere imperturbably.

"If he marries her, I change my will. Take note of that!"

The changing fortunes of the new district of Bool Bool and the unfailing increase of Mazere's family and property necessitated the drafting of a new will or codicils at least yearly, so this threat failed to impress Mrs Mazere. And Philip would have been a puling specimen at variance with his generation and environment if, in weighing a slice of his father's run against that rare prize of a beautiful maid, the scales had not gone down with a bump.

Old Pool liked Philip's courteous, kindly ways and Philip found Pool most obliging and capable. Further than this the young man knew not what Pool thought, for he kept his usual silence and let matters take their course. And the course from which Philip would not be deflected was that up past Billy-go-Billy and on to the Pool homestead at Maneroo. Those were the days when certain horses, known as ''ninety milers'', were capable of ninety miles on Saturday and ninety again on Sunday night — and what miles! So steep in the ascent that the rider abandoned his saddle and was towed up by his beast's tail, so sheer in the descent that the horse's hind legs often propped far ahead of his forefeet. Girth-galls and backs sore enough to wring pity from the Inquisition were familiar, but wind unbreakable and splendid bottled hoofs that had been moulded by the granite ridges of the area carried young love along the marked-tree bridle tracks around precipitous sidelings where the leaping, lilting Jenningningahma has its source amid the Bogongs and beyond, up and on to the roof of Australia.

3

Old Mazere held fast to his determination when Philip announced his intention of marrying Charlotte, and promptly executed his threat of disinheritance. But Mrs Mazere stood by her firstborn, always the best-loved of her children, reasonable and affectionate mother though she was to them all. Had not Philip held her almost a night with his head in her lap, sobbing that he could not forgo Charlotte?

"Mamma," he said, "I wish you could know how good she is. There is nothing she cannot do. She has reared the younger ones all by herself, and, Mamma, she is so good and true."

Mrs Mazere announced her intention of accompanying the bridegroom to the wedding, it being the year that Fannie was due to be weaned.

"If you defy me, you never enter my door again," raged her husband in one of his volcanic eruptions that are part of the history of the little town of Bool Bool.

"That's hardly for you to decide," maintained Mrs Mazere stoutly.

"Since when am I not the master of this house? You seem determined to fill it with colonial riff raff..!"

This confirmed the determination of Mrs Mazere, _née_ Rachel

9

Freeborn. She herself was a colonial of humble but godfearing, honest, free-settler origin. Her name itself was a proud heritage earned by her family in far-off, if obscure, days. Her husband's disparagement of things colonial, with which he sometimes consciously but more often unintentionally belaboured his wife who had not known the amenities and glories of the old country, raised in her a clansman's feeling towards Charlotte Pool.

"That hussy, she'd set her snares for the son of a gentleman, would she —"

"By the time she's had six or seven children, she'll have discovered that one man is about the same as another. They all wear a woman out and there's no peace — whether they're gentlemen or jockeys."

"If you persist in this foolishness, I'll beat you and tie you up," shouted Mazere, beside himself with anger.

The family cowered out of sight, the little ones being shooed off to bed by their seniors. Richard and younger brother Hugh spoke of keeping guard outside their parents' door, ready to rush in and restrain Papa should Mamma really be in danger, for she had the secret and spontaneous loyalty of every child. The girls were not so apprehensive. Mamma had her proven methods of bringing Papa to heel.

"Mamma will come out on top," said Rachel, as she and Emily stole away to bed, whispering softly of marrying the first man who asked them and setting up homes of their own, as Isabel had done already, in order to be free of Papa.

"Might get someone worse," said Emily dolefully.

"Couldn't," said Rachel.

"Might be as bad though."

"Not if he's nice and quiet."

"Ho! Ho! Like Simon Labosseer," jibed Emily. "Is he still waiting for you?"

"Don't be silly!" said Rachel, smiling to herself, and comfortably went to sleep.

Papa, of course, was vanquished. Mamma accompanied Philip to his wedding without her doors being closed behind her. Mazere never admitted knowledge of Mamma's visit to Maneroo, and it was not etiquette to speak of it in his hearing. To save face he went to Gundagai to sit on the Bench and during his absence, Mamma, it was officially stated, went to Mungee to be with Isabel, who was expecting a baby.

10

4

Charlotte might have been rather overwhelmed by the arrival of the lady of Three Rivers, a showplace famous for amenities unknown elsewhere up the country, had not Mrs Mazere immediately allied herself with the Pools and taken from Charlotte the burden of entertaining the clergymen and the more important guests. On her arrival she had seen at a glance all the courageous little subterfuges by which Charlotte had contrived to conceal the deficiencies of the household and to do honour to the occasion. Her heart warmed to this brave young creature who, though besieged with admirers and without guidance, had nevertheless chosen her Philip. She was the only other person in all the world who rated Philip Mazere Junior so highly, the only other who had for him the same unbroken loyalty.

The self-reliant but isolated heart of the girl burgeoned at the overtures of Mrs Mazere. For, though Philip had tried to soften the situation with such predictions as, "Oh, the old man will come round, he always does. His bark's worse than his bite," he could not hide from the girl the violence of the family storm caused by the contemplated union. Old Mazere had a voice like a bass drum and no modulations save from forte to fortissimo when he was in a rage, and all the bush telegraph had been on the qui vive to report him, especially the rivals of Philip. They pointed out to Charlotte that she might do better than espouse a disinherited young man who was not especially renowned for thrift. Much troubled, Charlotte had offered to release Philip, and it was then that he had enlisted his mother's support.

But disinheritance did not weigh heavily with the native-born, heirs to a whole new world where dozens of opportunities beckoned to the experienced and energetic. Ex-convicts were becoming leaders of the squattocracy and bosses of the bureaucracy — to what might not a Mazere aspire? So Charlotte's qualms, never very strong when weighed against her love for this man, vanished after a little persuasion on Philip's part.

In the little parlour, Mrs Mazere opened her valises of gifts gathered with an understanding of what would be welcome to a motherless girl living far up the country. To Charlotte's confused delight, she brought forth articles of fine linen and finer needlecraft, fashioned with such exquisite neatness and such invisible stitching that the girl, reverently touching the articles, was lost in wonder. Mrs Mazere was renowned for her needlework. In later years the

11

christening robe she made for her grandchildren became an heirloom brought out to stimulate the energies of young sewers whose fingers lagged. It was shown under glass at church bazaars and, now, when the grandchildren for whom it was made have grandchildren of their own, the work of the old fingers, knotted with pioneer labours sufficient to make half a dozen women quail today, resides in the needlework section of the Bool Bool museum.

Charlotte had already collected a trousseau of sorts by dint of great enterprise and loyal co-operation on the part of the sisters of the coach-drivers travelling the route between Cooma, Yass and Queanbeyan. Many of the articles, she now realised, were a trifle flashy by comparison with the Mazere offerings, and she did not quite know how to receive these bride's gifts which should, by convention, have come from her side.

"They're lovely, Mrs Mazere. It is very good of you. I'd like to pay you for them," she stammered, the red flushing her clear sunburned skin, her effort to keep back her tears, half of pleasure, half of wounded independence, rendering her tall, long-limbed young body a trifle stiff and forbidding.

"Pay me, my dear child! You are a brave good girl to think of such a thing. But there never can be any talk of payment between you and me. From now on, you are my own dear daughter, dear as my own, the wife of my dear boy. Ah me, it seems only yesterday that he was a little thing in my arms, and I not quite your age, and here he is setting up on his own!"

At that, Charlotte's rare tears fell and Mrs Mazere put her arms about her. They fell on their knees spontaneously and Mrs Mazere offered up a little prayer of supplication that God should bless His dear children, that they should walk in His ways all their life in good health, happiness and prosperity.

"My dear," she said as they rose, "it is all in God's hands. If your trust is in Him you can never be dismayed, no matter what may come to you."

Thus began a deep and unassailable friendship between the two women. The simple prayer opened again for the girl the fount of ultimate refuge. She had always said her prayers nightly, as taught by her mother, but it had become a perfunctory ritual. Mrs Mazere reillumined the ceremony. And further, Mrs Mazere had unconsciously performed another ceremony of deep significance to the girl. From that hour on, Charlotte moved with a new confidence through the responsibilities and vigorous industry that her wedding entailed. Mrs Mazere, not the clergyman, had made Charlotte a Mazere for all time. She, all unconsciously, like a king when he elevates his son's commoner bride, had conferred royal or Mazere rank upon the bride. There was a new light in Charlotte's eyes, a peace and surety in her heart and movements. Little it mattered now how intransigent old Mr Mazere's attitude might be; let it beat like the waves upon Gibraltar.

5

The day after the wedding Mrs Mazere set out for her daughter Isabel's at Mungee, a good seventy miles away over the spur of the Great Dividing Range in a slightly south-western direction from Bool Bool. The bride and groom were to escort her and spend a couple of nights at Mungee as a wedding holiday.

If Mrs Mazere had had to supplement Charlotte's bridal deficiencies, the Pools had to fill gaps in Philip Mazere's resources, which were limited owing to his father's disinheriting propensity. This they willingly did. Bert, Charlotte's eldest brother, a youth of seventeen and already one of the most resourceful, daring and accomplished bushmen in those parts, was to conduct the party. Bert, who had never had a collar and rarely a shoe on him till Charlotte's wedding, was only a shade less knowledgeable in bush lore than the Aborigines, from whom he had received some tuition. To lose, drown, freeze or frighten him in all the south-eastern portion of the unconquered continent which had cradled him and been his playground was considered inconceivable. Any stream swimmable by a horse he could ford by that means, he could bottom holes that most men were afraid to bathe in, he could snare if not shoot anything that ran on the earth or flew above it, and he could seize deadly serpents by the tail and dash out their life on a tree trunk — or if no tree or stick was at hand, he could despatch them with whip or surcingle. And though these and a score of other accomplishments were common to all bushmen worthy of the name, Bert's prowess was already legendary.

Out of consideration for Mrs Mazere, two days were to be given to the journey. Charlotte, in natural circumstances riding like a boy, was as equal to her ninety miles in one sitting as any Bert or Philip, but the gentility of her new status and of becoming a Mazere as well

13

meant demotion to a lady's two-horned saddle and a flowing Queen Victoria riding habit that had to be held up nearly every mile of the way owing to boggy passages or scrub. Now she rode as sedately as the mother of a large family.

Bert and his heelers chased the packhorses ahead of the riders. One pack contained the tents, another the personal valises, and perched on top of Mrs Mazere's packhorse, Curlew, was an ingenious cage containing a little bantam hen. This was one of the things the Pools had and the Mazeres had not. The tireless Bert carried in his hand a clutch of bantam eggs packed in paper and tied in a coloured handkerchief. The eggs could not be carried by packhorse, because they might have become addled. If a broody hen were forthcoming at Mungee, it was proposed to hatch from these a spouse to assist in increase and multiplication.

"Let us each take a turn with the eggs. You'll be tired, Bert," said Mrs Mazere.

"No fear! I'll sling 'em round my neck when I want to use my gun." He had a finely kept gun on top of one of the packs, and powder and shot flasks attached to his saddle. While the Mazere establishment could be relied upon to send forth sleeping apparel and fine linen, the Pool abode could be depended upon to produce the best firearms, spurs, bits and bridles, and was never without a charge of ammunition or wadding and caps.

The beginning of the journey was across open tussock land alive with the purling streams from which twenty rivers take their rise. From a height on the Pool run, a quartette of these streams could be seen forking away in the flashing, exhilarating sunshine of the perfect November morning.

Kish-swisk! went the horses' hoofs, well above the fetlocks in the bogs of the springheads, the mountain horses plunging in confidently. But one old packhorse who had been raised down the country was feeling his way like a pedestrian on thin ice until he was pushed in by Bert.

"Look at old Cootamundra — scared he'll sink! His great boats of hoofs ought to keep him up though!"

Across virgin country by bridle tracks well known to their leader, the party progressed enjoyably, cantering girth-deep in flowers on the plains and slowing up on the ridges that were crowned with snow gums, blackbutt, ribbon gums and taller eucalypts. At noon they halted to boil the billy at Dead Horse Flat, so named because of the number of carcases found there after a particularly severe winter. A number of the skeletons still remained among the flowers and tussocks. The tiny flat, like a lawn amid the timber, lay in the bend of a creek bordered with shrubs all in bloom, and their perfume mingled with a music that might have been learned in paradise.

While Bert eased all the animals of pack or saddle and let them have a mouthful of grass, Philip made the fire and Charlotte produced the tucker bags. Mrs Mazere was made to rest in state. They lunched heartily on meats from yesterday's feast and then, after Mrs Mazere was persuaded to take a sleep and while Bert saddled up again, Charlotte and Philip took a lovers' stroll through the fields of flowers.

With her multifarious activities and vigorous brood of children, with scarce a twelvemonth between some of them, it was long since Mrs Mazere had had a holiday, and right royally she appreciated it. The inauguration of Charlotte into her family thus began with a pleasant adventure, the memory of which ever lingered with her. It was like one of the "larks" of her brief girlhood, before the pack-saddle of marriage in pioneer conditions settled heavily on her withers.

On they rode through the long afternoon, the dazzling sunshine beaming down in golden shafts between the tall tree tops and glancing off their mighty trunks, snow white, lily graceful, strong as steel, a hundred feet without a branch, regal as marble pillars — Nature's sublime cathedral, a hundred miles square.

"We'll give Flea Creek the slip, I reckon," observed Bert as the afternoon shadows began to lengthen. "I camped there one night when I was after cattle and was eaten alive." Riding on ahead of the party, he reached a break in the ranges and selected another stream similarly lovely but, mercifully, without fleas. By the time the rest of the party came in, he had the camp fires blazing. Here, under the lee of mighty granite rocks rearing up like the ruins of a mediaeval castle, Philip Mazere pitched his snow-white bridal tent between two stately saplings standing like pages to the forest monarchs about them. For a couch, he chopped soft springy boughs of the ti-tree, laden with starry perfumed bloom like a cascade of fine lace in a bridal veil, and then scattered some purple aromatic senna amongst the boughs. The saddle seats were placed for pillows, and then were spread the brave red blankets of the pioneer.

What bridal bower or tour could equal this, when all the world seemed young!

The tents had been brought in honour of the ladies and the bridal nature of the journey. On their own, Philip and Bert would have covered the distance without camping at all or, if compelled to camp, would have simply wrapped themselves in blankets or coats. If it rained and no cave was available, a sheet of stringybark tomahawked from the nearest tree and raised on rocks would make a shelter.

Bert erected Mrs Mazere's tent at a little distance from the bridal tent on a site carefully selected as free from ants' nests and snake holes.

"You know, that old parson is a silly old codger," Bert confided to Mrs Mazere as he cut the ti-tree for her couch. "When I was fetching him to the weddin', I left him to unsaddle the horses and make the fire, and I'm jiggered if he wasn't sitting on a bulldog ants' nest when I came back. I got them off of his pants before they got inside or crikey, wouldn't he have jumped into the middle of next week!"

"He has not had much colonial experience," observed Mrs Mazere, laughing.

For supper, Bert prepared a treat in hot johnny cakes which he cooked on the coals. The dogs regaled themselves on kangaroo rats. At dusk Bert stole a little higher up the creek to a swamp, returning with a fine black duck whose satin green wing feathers were soon decorating the hats of the party. Then, after he had taken a look at the horses, tied up one or two of the dogs and made up a number of fires to keep away dingoes, he surrounded himself with his pack-saddles and stores and stretched out near a tent fly at the flap of Mrs Mazere's tent to be close by in case she should want him. The little bantam hen was set between himself and her, for fear of a marauding native cat.

The little party lay secure from visitors, for the straggling remnants of the Aboriginal tribes had not yet returned south from their winter retreats. The world was their own, and what a world! A thousand miles of unspoiled forest distilled an aromatic fragrance chaste as a puritan heaven, and above the regal tree tops the white stars blazed like diamonds. Across the dome spread the great white way where long ago an old woman had gone to heaven, spilling her pail of milk as she went.

6

Bert's breathing soon announced the dreamless slumber he had earned, but Mrs Mazere lay awake awhile, contemplating the significance of the milestone she had reached. A murmur of voices came from the young couple's tent and she felt a great tenderness towards them as she thought of all that lay before them. It came gradually, thank heaven. She felt particularly tender towards Charlotte, for in her experience God's will towards women was hard and unrelenting. But Charlotte had the good fortune to be starting off with her own dear gentle boy. She herself had been rushed into marriage at the age of seventeen. Not with her consent would any of her own daughters marry before eighteen, and if the deed could be warded off till they were twenty-one, so much the better.

It seemed but yesterday that Philip was a little blue-eyed, bald-headed thing whimpering as he first nuzzled for her breast and now . . . she pulled up with a jerk. It was many years since his christening had made his father "Old Philip". She recalled the shock with which she had first heard her husband spoken of as "the old man", but he was six years her senior and she had soon settled down again. Now, since yesterday, she had become *old* Mrs Mazere. *Old Mrs Mazere.* Mrs Mazere Senior on envelopes, but by word of mouth — old Mrs Mazere.

She sat up on her couch. Old! No more children! Old. . . stiff. . . helpless!

The time had fled like the mists from Three Rivers flats on a winter morning when the sun came up. Time seemed to be bolting downhill, out of control. Another twenty-five years and she would nearly have completed man's allotted span. What then would it matter whether one had borne ten or twenty children, or if one's spouse had been bad-tempered or easygoing? Taking him on the whole, Philip Senior had not been so bad. He was a good provider, not mean with his money, healthy, honest, energetic, sober, always in the lead. . . "God give me strength to bear what may come to me in the future as Thou hast done hitherto, for Jesus Christ's sake. Amen," she whispered and, turning on her couch, she too slept soundly, leaving the early-summer night to the exquisitely eerie wail of the curlews and the jingle of hobbles and bells, as the horses grazed around the camp.

7

Bert was up at daybreak to light the fires and fill the quart pots and then, while the women made their toilets at the stream, he and Philip caught and saddled the horses. For breakfast Bert produced the duck, which he had roasted overnight in earth under one of the fires, a dodge

17

he had learned from the blacks. Very appetising the bird was too, in that early morning air that almost had a hint of frost.

Then on again: over peaks, through gullies of treeferns, maidenhair fern, musk and sassafras, round dizzy sidelings, conquering ridge on ridge of the last spur of the meridional range and attaining the more open country where Isabel and George Stanton had their home.

They were not so lucky in the weather today. After reading the sky, Bert hurried them through tucker time in twenty minutes, just long enough to ease the packhorses and old Wellington, Mrs Mazere's hack, who was mud-fat and a little galled. At about four o'clock, he herded the women into the hollow trunk of an old forest giant left by an ancient fire, and stood before them to prevent their skirts from being splashed. An hour later and Bert observed, "It's turning into a steady pelter — I think we'd better push on." This was agreed to, and in his role as conductor of a ladies' party, Bert triumphed in bringing forth a couple of umbrellas which he had concealed in one of the packs.

"I've already tried old Wellington with one, just to be sure. I even took him over a fence with one, sitting sideways."

Bert's performance after the wedding, wearing a blanket to represent a habit and holding an unfurled umbrella aloft as he ran Mrs Mazere's Wellington over jumps, had been one of the most laughter-provoking pranks of the festivities.

"I got the tip from the parson, an' if he can ride with an umbrella, surely a woman can."

With skirts bunched around them, serge shoulder capes and the umbrellas for shelters, the women rode comfortably dry in the steady rain and enjoyed the novelty. The Mungee country being open with a well-defined bridle track, they progressed without delay, and the Stanton dogs loudly heralded their approach at about sundown.

The rain had given up for some time and Isabel came down to the home sliprails to meet them. The women dismounted to walk back with her while the men took the caravan on for the quarter of a mile to the house. It was the first visit of both Mrs Mazere and Charlotte to Mungee and they looked about with absorbed interest. Primaeval trees, imperial as any that ever guarded an emperor's avenue, still abounded on one side of the way, while on the other was a young orchard already in bearing and extensive flower and vegetable gardens.

George Stanton had taken up his run only four years before, but already there was a comfortable homestead. Amid the timber on the rich flats bordering two creeks there were potato and maize clearings. A three-acre wheat field had been cleared, the stumps of the lately deposed forest giants giving the appearance of tombstones. Native flowers bloomed in glorious luxuriance. Sheds and yards came into view. Plump hens and turkeys were going to roost and the heartening clamour of geese mingled with the raucous good-night laughter of the kookaburras. A stockman was driving in the milking cows in order to pen the calves for the night, and a shepherd could be seen with his hurdles on a further ridge.

The house consisted of the usual four rooms, two larger ones and two little lean-tos behind, with a passage right through and a straight verandah before. Set at a safe distance, in case of fire, was a building of similar design, with the front apartments being apportioned as kitchen and store room and the skillions as rooms for station hands. The buildings were all of slabs which were placed horizontally upon adzed wall-plates set in the earth and which ran between stout red-gum corner posts. Only the front room of the residence proper had a boarded floor, the others being of stamped earth. The roofs were of bark.

In an age of famous housewives, the Mazere women were especially renowned and the Stanton home bore witness to Isabel's skills. The verandah was enlivened with an extensive collection of pot plants, the little windows were adorned with lace curtains. Curtains and valances of dimity enlivened the home-made four-poster bed, and there were counterpanes of patchwork and crocheted antimacassars. The living room was wallpapered in one of the wild and woolly designs of the forties, though the walls of the other rooms were still covered with the *Gazette* or *The Illustrated London News*.

George Stanton was ambitious for a nice home and proud to have one of the Three Rivers girls in his, but he knew the best way to get on was to attend first to the things on which the home depended — clearing, fencing, building yards and developing good stock. This was only a temporary residence until he got time to build a better. He was reputed to have a head on him and it was predicted that he would get on.

He was a tall, quiet, thin young man, son of a settler who had preceded Mazere of Three Rivers in the district by a good ten years.

His father had set him up on land that had belonged traditionally to a tribe of Aborigines. Advised by Mazere, young Stanton had dealt peaceably with the blacks, buying the land for some gaily coloured shirts, tomahawks, negro head and such commodities.

The dwindling remnants of the tribe still returned each year in summer and Isabel was generous with them. She persuaded George to give them a beast or a sheep or two for their corroborees, and she herself contributed garments to the gins, whom she sometimes employed in odd jobs about the house and garden. George found the men a great stand-by for the routine jobs of washing sheep and rounding up stray beasts, and for all the procedures of mustering and branding. The tribe was permitted to camp in their old haunt under the mighty river gums where the Mungee slept in a bottomless pool about half a mile below the homestead.

Mungee being the Aboriginal word for fish, the Mungee Creek got its name from that hole; it was thought that the fish bred there, they were so plentiful. In fact, the Mungee was really a river and a tributary of the Yarrabongo, which was a channel for countless crystal streams to reach the Murrumbidgee and thence to the Murray and the Great Australian Bight a thousand miles distant.

That night, happy faces shone in the glow of the home-made tallow candles that were held in tall brass candlesticks, polished until they were mirrors. Even chance callers lent a glow to the daily routine in the vast solitude of pioneering days, and real visitors were a carnival.

Everything was comfortable and ship-shape for the night. Bert's dogs, which had speedily come to issues with those of Mungee, were tethered in a number of kennels placed around the fowl house; a few dogs were drafted each night as sentinels against the native cats which could devastate a fowl roost of twenty or thirty birds in one attack. The bantam had been fed and let out to stretch her legs and, now in her cage again, was honoured by a lodging in the kitchen lest her larger relatives should put upon her before being properly introduced. There was plenty of accommodation for all — horses, dogs and men. Bert's packs were stacked on the verandah, and the side saddles hung over a crossbeam of the kitchen. Bert was not permitted to erect a tent; he was to sleep on the home-made sofa in the front room when the others had retired. The bride and groom were to be placed in state in the four-poster while the host and hostess retreated to one of the skillions; Mrs

Mazere was to share the other with the servant girl.

The talk after the meal was all about George's doings. He had several men at work splitting timber for rails and slabs. He thought of starting his grand new weatherboard house with shingled roof in the winter.

"Fencing is the thing that is going to save us," he ventured. "I reckon if I could fence all my run and let the sheep out like the cattle, there would be no scab."

"I noticed some trees coming along that would split out two or three hundred rails easy," said Bert.

"You must point them out to me," said George.

As she listened, Mrs Mazere wished that Philip could have been on the way to owning so thriving an establishment, but she loyally stifled comparisons. It was not to be expected that her dear gentle boy could be as sharp for the main chance as one of old skinflint Stanton's brood. Anyway, with a brave girl like Charlotte to stand by him, he would soon be on his feet, and, she told herself, his father would relent presently.

The young people were easily persuaded to stay a couple of days and might have dallied longer, but for the imminence of Isabel's first travail. Philip and George had much to say, being friends from George's courting days; Isabel was come again a little girl to her mother's knee in face of the approaching event, and Bert and Charlotte, drinking in the Stanton-Mazere amenities with avidity, were inspired to a campaign of emulation.

On Monday, the young people started back over the ranges to Maneroo. The cavalcade was lessened by the absence of Mrs Mazere's hack, Wellington, and her packhorse Curlew, as well as Plover, another packhorse that Bert had sold to George; it was enlarged by fruit trees, rose slips and many plants for the orchard and garden which Charlotte was anxious to start at Pool's Creek, as well as Isabel's gifts to her. Like her mother, Isabel had taken to Charlotte, the Stanton insistence on principle and social standing in neighbours not being as rigid as that of Mazere Senior. It was George who said in the general handshaking, with no lack of cordiality, "Always be a shakedown here for you, Bert, any time you come this way."

8

Her first grandchild, a boy, was four weeks old before he, Mrs Mazere

21

and the new parents left Mungee so as to be back in time for Christmas at Three Rivers.

"Well, Mamma, I'm very glad to see you back," said her husband with unforced geniality on her arrival. "If you had stayed away a week longer, I should have been advertising for another old woman to keep me company."

If she had stayed much longer, he would have gone after her. As it was, he had managed to remain on his dignity by the magisterial visitation to Gundagai and a stay at the new run at Nanda, where he was staking out his second son Richard. He was expansive to his son-in-law about the new grandson and all Mungee doings, but the subject of the Maneroo wedding was taboo. He reiterated his attitude towards the whole affair as he tied on his night cap and waited for his wife to extinguish the candle.

"I believe Philip has insisted upon cutting himself off by marrying the Pool hussy. Well, he can see how he likes getting on without me."

"Industrious young people with colonial experience like Philip and Charlotte need have no fears about getting on."

"So that is your argument! On that score it would be a good thing to marry our girls to any rowdy as long as he has colonial experience — and not to think of family at all!"

" 'Surely men of low degree are vanity, and men of high degree are a lie: to be laid in the balance, they are altogether lighter than vanity'," quoted Mrs Mazere, and blanketed further conversation on the plea of fatigue. Sleep soon came to her, but her husband lay wide awake and restless.

Though he was highly emotional in temperament, Mazere was veritably soft-hearted at the core. But his temper was so undisciplined that it befooled him. Indeed, it was owing to his high temper that he had found himself in the colonies. A chip off his father's block, it seemed that father and son were unable to co-exist harmoniously under the same roof. This, coupled with a spirit of adventure in the younger man, at length resulted in his being cut adrift from the parental home and flinging off to the colonies, when the century was still young.

Opportunity awaited a young man of his education, who had been brought up among the landed gentry of the south of England. His first post in the colony was official and, as part of his duties, he was required to see that the convicts to be flogged received the prescribed number of lashes, and of the requisite severity.

The ferocity of fellow creature to fellow creature sickened and horrifed the young man. After the first ordeal, he was violently sick at the stomach. Following the third, he flung himself moaning on his bed, completely unnerved. Never, never, he vowed, would he witness such barbarity again. For over a week, he suffered headaches and a cough and some fever. It was, in short, funk, and he threw up his post and decided to take up land.

To sum up, he had not that cold, ruthless brutality which is the basic ingredient — when stripped of its glamour — of the courage that involves the sacrifice of others; that courage which results in deeds of daring that crown their initiators as heroes about which sagas are handed down through the generations. He lacked the essential "nerve".

It was entirely beyond him to look on in cold blood while a fellow human was suffering the torment and pain of fifty or a hundred lashes. The wealth of the Indies, the pangs of starvation — neither could have bribed nor driven him to again witness the duty of the depraved monsters who wielded the rawhide thongs with pride in the fiendish artistry of their work. Had some cruel stroke of fate sentenced Mazere himself to the lash, he could never have bared his back and walked to the triangle with the spartan fortitude of some of those early unfortunates who, while taking up their positions, would call upon the floggers to do their worst; or those, their blood spattering the surroundings at each cut, their backs raw from nape to loin, who could turn with a grin upon their torturers and say, "If that's all you . . . . can do —"; or those who, after receiving fifty lashes, jibed at the officers till they were ordered back for a second dose. Then out into the chain gang again, into the heat and dust with their swollen, gangrened, flyblown backs to be bent again in the construction of the great roads — northern, western, and southern — that were to be the main arteries of the new nation and that have remained forever as monuments to the men who made them.

The automobiles purr softly along those roads today, up by old Emu Plains, where nary the shadow of an emu has fallen for many a long day; over the Blue Mountains to Bathurst; by Homebush, Moss Vale, Bowral and the high, clean, windswept Southern Tableland; by Goulburn and Yass; Cootamundra and Gundagai; Wagga Wagga and Albury; on, on to beautiful Melbourne. Do the shades of those manacled labourers ever come back to see the automobiles roll along the highways that they built — in such agony and humiliation that

23

some preferred and connived at the death penalty in preference to life in such hopeless and brutalising misery? Do they know that hearts swell and tears fall in remembrance of them a century later? Have they forgiven as fully as they expiated? And those who had authority over them, from a generation lacking gentler understanding of men's deviation from ordered paths — have they repented and been scourged and purified?

Thus young Mazere fled from officialdom, taking up land near Parramatta, and presently was captivated by the elfin figure of Rachel Freeborn. As soon as she was ready — when she was just seventeen — they were married and began a family. The first years went by and eventually Mazere was lured by stories of the deep, rich soil further up the country and the money to be made growing wool. When, by thrift and industry, they had acquired implements and the nucleus of flocks and herds, young Mazere and his friend and neighbour, Brennan, went on a tour of exploration. They nearly settled at Berrima, thought about Yass, and flirted with Goulburn and Bungendore, but something a little better just over the next blue spur of the ranges always beckoned them. They finally halted at Bool Bool, beautiful as paradise. Here the young men staked out their claims, applied for licences and were warmly welcomed by the families who had preceded them.

The two young men travelled their livestock up and lived in a humpy for the first summer. During the slacker winter months each assisted the other to erect dwellings of slabs and stringybark, with greenhide hinged shutters as windows, in readiness for their families' arrival. Mazere, being the better farmer, stayed up country with the houses and livestock while Brennan returned to Parramatta, took charge of the families and, with the aid of a couple of bullock drivers, began the pilgrimage. Their goods were piled on two-wheeled, springless, bullock drays to which the faithful Snaileys, Blossoms, Strawberries and Ballies of that decade were yoked — and it was trudge, trudge, bump, bump, day after day. It took three months to make the journey which motor cars do today between one dawning and the next.

When it rained they hove-to under the drays, and were well protected by splendid new tarpaulins supplemented by stringybark lean-tos; when a stream was high they camped on its bank till it was navigable. They had roast duck and kangaroo tail soup for dinner —

24

sometimes — and they had damper for breakfast and dinner, always; they heard the little koalas cry in the trees at night like lost babies, and at dawn the kookaburras waked them with wild, abandoned laughter.

Little Rachel Mazere cut her first tooth at Mutta Mutta crossing. Young Tim Brennan broke his collar bone at Bowral, and no one could do anything with him but Mrs Mazere. While they were waiting for the flooded Wollondilly River to go down, Tim's third sister, Bridgit, was born — for that's how it was, you know, for pioneer women up the country not so very long ago. It was there, on the banks of the river, that Mrs Mazere had her first unaided experience of midwifery, an art in which she was to become skilled.

Philip Mazere was happy up the country, out of reach of brutal officialdom and its demoralising effects. He was the right man in the right place and transplanted something of the imprint of the old country squire to his new estate. He introduced garden flowers to the district, as well as vegetables, fruit trees, vines, tobacco planting, grains, blood cattle, horse teams, steel ploughs, billiards, family prayers, daguerrotypes — the list grows too long. He was a progressive, peaceable, industrious and capable settler. He could ride well enough and shoot sufficiently for his needs, though he could never bring himself to slaughter the larger beasts.

9

Careless as to whether his father should set him up or down, Philip had determined to start driving a new line of coaches from Maneroo to one of the down-country townships. The Pools were to supply horses and have a share in the venture. Charlotte was to remain and conduct her father's house as before. Pool Senior was glad to retain her, for the next girl, Ada, had not her sister's capacity. She was accused of being lackadaisical. Certainly she was frail, but any woman in those days who had not given birth to a large family and fended for them without sparing herself was considered lackadaisical. Likewise, any man who could not fence, or plough, or build, or muster and draft and brand, and perform many other similar tasks from dawn till dark, six and frequently seven days a week, was a "poor crawler".

Both Charlotte and Bert were sensitive about their humble status and eager to imbibe self-improvement through every pore of their beings. They had no sooner returned from Mungee than they started their operations. The garden was enlarged, laid out properly and fenced; the few fruit trees planted from seeds by heroic old Mrs Pool were pruned and dug; the front room was ceiled, cracks in the walls were filled up and papered like those at Mungee, and the shortage of furniture made up by Bert's very creditable carpentering attempts. Old Pool let them alone as long as they did not worry him and continued to supply his meagre wants. He even contributed Bert to the household campaign for many days, and went out on the run accompanied only by Jim, aged eleven and a half, and Harry, a capable stockman of ten years.

A decision was made by Charlotte to procure a governess for the younger ones and was acted upon forthwith. But the first incumbent and her half-dozen successors fled in horror from the loneliness and primitiveness of the place, with its undisciplined children and the forbidding aspect of their father, with his one eye, his great size and his wild black beard and hair.

At last one came who remained. She was a woman in her forties, lacking in beauty but dowered with more durable qualities. She fitted into Charlotte and Bert's campaign miraculously. She was capable of imparting what she knew. She was experienced in teaching drawing, the piano and French as well as her own language, and she enjoyed bringing her pupils on. No passivity of temperament restrained her from reorganisation; she had to improve her charges or explode. This was providential in light of the challenge of the untamed Pool *ménage* and, with Bert and Charlotte on her every hand, things went with a swing.

The children were yarded under Miss Mayborn's dictatorship. The boys kept their boots on in her sight, and the girls adopted theirs permanently. They all washed their persons regularly, and the girls learned to rule their tresses, and to sew for themselves garments cut out by their capable instructress. Further, instead of taking to the woods at the sight of a stranger, trembling like pursued bandicoots and shyly examining the visitant from behind a gum tree or through the cracks of their habitation (now, thankfully, plugged up), they soon learned to offer hospitality unfearfully when rare callers appeared. With Charlotte and Bert, now quite intolerant of any waywardness, to police them, the poor youngsters never dared to be slack or fractious, no matter how exacting was Miss Mayborn.

Philip saw Charlotte only on Sundays and, to take advantage of the time that he was absent, Charlotte decided to ask Miss Mayborn if she would teach her and Bert in the winter evenings. Miss Mayborn was enthusiastic, and it was testimony to her quality that it never occurred to her to exact any tribute for the extra work involved.

Long days in the saddle chasing wild cattle or horses, branding them, breaking them for domestic use, splitting rails and slabs for home paddocks or additions to the homestead, and all the other arduous work that such a life involved, made Bert rather a sleepy pupil in the evenings. But he was game and persevering and eventually emerged from the ordeal with enough figuring to keep accounts, enough writing to manage his correspondence, enough reading to master the up-country press and to decipher — not without a struggle if they were handscript — the circulars and government notices which in due course were to devolve upon him.

This education was enough to put him on a level with, and above, some of the most successful and socially honoured of his contemporaries up the country. Charlotte made somewhat better progress, being in the house by day and not being above an hour with the younger scholars when her duties permitted.

Miss Mayborn continued at her post to the astonishment of the district. Just why was her secret.

Harriet Mayborn had been reared with all the refinements of the professional classes of the old country, her father being a canon of the Church of England and the nephew of a baronet. But then a criminal act of which her brother was convicted after a notorious court case broke up the home, killed her mother and ruined her father, of whom Harriet eventually became the sole support. When at last free and entering on her forties, she decided to cut old and painful associations and bury herself in Australia. But on her arrival she struck the financial panic of 1842-43 and, with many younger and more prepossessing candidates vying for positions, she found it hard to obtain a post in or around Sydney. Worse, when she finally did so, she was in danger of meeting someone who was acquainted with the details of the unsavoury Mayborn case. That is why she retreated up the country.

The illiterate Pools had never heard the name of Mayborn, and this commended them to her. She had found a refuge where no one seemed to realise that she had ever been possessed of parents or a brother, or to be curious as to how they had lived and died.

She liked Charlotte and Bert from the start. Their eagerness to improve themselves, and the reverence in which they held her was soothing to her unhappy soul. As time went by, it became evident that all that was wrong with the Pools was lack of opportunity, and that while they were totally uncultivated, they were neither irreverent nor indifferent towards matters of social refinement. She enjoyed her rapid progress in turning these young colonials into a semblance of respectable young people at Home. There was relief in the fact that there was no parental interference, and there was balm in the children's spontaneous friendliness. Their eagerness to give without reservation or any eye to profit revived her long dormant affections. They taught her to sit on a horse, and took her for bogeys in the swimming hole; they caught the pretty spotted native cats and tanned the skins to make a tippet and muff for her.

Thus she stayed and, staying, found peace and refuge and scope for her energies, while the lonely children expanded in her warm, constructive interest in their undertakings and exploits.

She was interested in all that she was told of the Mazeres and recognised in Philip Junior a gentleman according to colonial standards. But in no way did she recognise the social gradations of squattocracy. One colonial seemed as good as another to her, and so they mostly were. Superiority generally existed more in a particular family's perception of itself than in a consensus of the district's opinion. In Harriet Mayborn's opinion, the colonials were all below the salt, for she was a thorough-paced, narrow-minded snob only displaced from her natural element by disaster. It was fortunate that the Pools had experienced so little contact with their fellow human beings that they were quite oblivious to her view of them.

10

Nearly a year had passed and a child was expected both at Three Rivers and at Curradoobidgee, formerly Pool's Creek. Miss Mayborn was responsible for the retirement of the name Pool's Creek and the adoption of Curradoobidgee, the surveyed name of the run.

As Charlotte had no mother and as Mrs Mazere did not feel equal to the journey to Curradoobidgee, she decided that Charlotte should come to her at Three Rivers. Philip Senior was still implacable on the subject of Philip and Charlotte's marriage, but Mrs Mazere was fretful and ailing as she had never been before in such case, and in no condition to be worried. Her husband restrained himself and compromised, for he was, at heart, a kind man.

28

"You can have Charlotte here for the event, as long as it is not made an excuse to open the door to the whole brood. But I shan't have Philip here and that baggage can go packing back to Maneroo again as soon as she is able."

So Philip accompanied his wife on the journey, aware of the fact that he must turn back before Three Rivers. Her time was distant only a week or two. She rested the second day in bed at a stockman's rude hut on the Jenningningahma, and on the third went on again on horseback over those precipitous peaks.

At the edge of Stanton's Plains, Hugh and Rachel were waiting in their mother's gig to meet them and make Charlotte welcome in their mother's name. Philip turned back a few miles from Bool Bool and spent the night at Brennan's place. His heart ached to leave his young wife thus, but his own and Charlotte's loyalty and affection for his mother dictated it as the best policy.

"Sure ye've done right, Alannah!" said kind Mrs Brennan. "Yer dad will come round soon. The little stranger will open the door and we'll all take care of Charlotte and the baby and sure ye can come here to see it!"

Mrs Mazere was happy to have Charlotte and though Charlotte felt depressed by her separation from Philip, she bore herself bravely and with a minimum of self-consciousness. She had brought a packhorse laden both with her necessaries and gifts for all, including a splendid meerschaum pipe for His Nibs which he accepted a little awkwardly but secretly appreciated.

Charlotte conquered. Philip Senior dared not irritate Mamma, and his temperament was such that he could not be ungallant to a splendid young woman who had asked nothing from him and who bore herself with unconscious dignity and unfailing goodwill, while surrendering nothing of self-respect nor independence.

Baby Philip Mazere, the third of the Australian line, arrived punctually and he was not much more than sixty hours old before his affectionate father held him in his arms. A loaded blunderbuss would not have kept Philip away, but for political reasons his arrival was not announced to Papa.

It was understood that Charlotte was to stay at Three Rivers until after Mamma's confinement. Baby Philip's aunt arrived three months later and was called Rhoda. Mrs Mazere did not regain strength as speedily as usual and clung to Charlotte who was cordially pressed by all to remain. Even Papa quietly suggested to her that she stay until

29

Mamma should be quite well. This took her on towards autumn and, when an early fall of snow covered the hills over which she would have to pass in order to return to Curradoobidgee, Mamma suggested that she spend the winter at Three Rivers. Charlotte was eventually prevailed upon to do this, as Miss Mayborn was most capably managing the home at Curradoobidgee.

11

Before spring came again and melted the snow from the passes of the Bogongs, a change had taken place in the household of Curradoobidgee. The altered appearance of old Pool had been for some time the pabulum for wit-sharpening among the settlers of his district.

"He's dug out a Christian name. He's become James Pool," sniggered Timson of Wombat Hill to Squeaky Gilbert of Maryvale and Larry Healey of Little River.

"Yes, an' he's cut a yard off his beard an' half a yard off his hair an' got a new hat!"

"He was mighty flash in his young days maybe, an' he's breakin' out again in his dotage," said Larry Healey.

"It's the Mazere connection is going to his head," said Timson.

"Old Mazere, I hear, keeps as cool as a Greenland seal about that an' won't have Philip near the place." This from Gilbert.

The next time they met, old Healey began, "Did ye hear that all the fish is dead in the Yeuecumbeen? Pool's Creek runs into it an' he took a bogey after twenty years!" This raised loud guffaws. Larry Healey had a sharp tongue in his head.

Then, when Pool was seen in Cooma in a fine suit of Parramatta tweeds and a collar — in broad daylight, by the vast population that frequented the two stores and pubs, the smithy and carpenter's shop — they said he was either going to turn bushranger and outdo Jacky-Jacky as a swell, or get married. They were right on the last count. Miss Harriet Mayborn was to become the second Mrs Pool.

The fact that Pool should marry her was not as surprising as that she should marry him, in that society in which every girl who had four limbs and reasonable features lived in a state of siege from the age of fourteen until she capitulated.

"Pretty good for an old boko of forty-seven!" chuckled Timson.

"Sure she's no chicken herself, must be all of that!" said Healey.

30

"Aye, but a highly educated lady from England —" interposed McEachern of Gowandale.

"Och, ye don't know what's behind these ladies from England. I reckon she's never had another chance. Lots of them over there don't."

Miss Mayborn was herself the most surprised of all to realise that she was now Mrs Pool, an estate she could never have countenanced save for the fact that she had for ever cut the painter of her past. Coming to Pool's Creek with a mind unprejudiced by the rumours that had dogged its master, she found him shy but neither exclusive nor disagreeable. She saw him in a light that his fellow settlers would have incredulously derided. Some months after her arrival it had occurred to her, as she sat before the fourteen-foot hearth on winter nights enjoying one of the good novels of the day, that he had no similar outlet, and she suggested reading aloud.

"Oh, all right," he had said, not without suspicion. She began with the up-country papers to which he listened with avidity. Next she experimented with an adventurous romance of Bulwer Lytton and then went on to Scott. The effect was magical. It opened up a captivating world to that half-wild, restricted, lonely mind that had never known a lecture or a play. Since man began to keep home in a cave, he has been held captive by the story teller; this one listened greedily to any sort of a story with a naive though quick understanding and a memory as photographic as a child's. Robinson Crusoe caused him to walk up and down with excitement, his taciturnity vanished in a flood of discussion.

Then, one evening, after she had been with the children about eighteen months, Miss Mayborn remarked, "Dear me, the children are all getting on so well with their lessons that I'll have to leave you and find fresh pupils!"

Thoroughly alarmed by the prospect of losing the new world that had been opened up to his deprived understanding, Pool waited till the children were in bed and then plunged in desperately. "Supposin' you an' me should get spliced like them people you're readin' about?"

Miss Mayborn, scion of the English aristocracy, was dumbfounded but did not lose her head. Pool, fearing disapproval, hurried on, "You ain't got anyone belonging to you an' the youngsters won't be so long disappearing now. Besides, they are all set on you."

"Please say no more. I must think about this."

31

"How long will you take to think — a week?"

"Oh, no, two months at least."

"I'd rather you'd make it only one," said Pool.

Miss Mayborn retreated to a disturbed and sleepless night. She was in a cleft stick. She must accept his proposition or abandon this refuge where she was free from the tragedy of her past. To find another such refuge would be more difficult each year and all hope of a competency in old age had gone in the effort to save her brother twenty years before. This life was primitive and lonely when compared with what she had been brought up to expect, but it was sweet to be free from ostracism and among people who loved and had need of one.

To gauge the children's attitude, she hinted at leaving them. Their spontaneous response was to burst into wild howls of dismay. Her heart was warmed and reassured.

What better could she do with her life?

She was of that managing disposition which found greater satisfaction in reconstructing a tumbledown house along her own lines than in being presented with a palace unalterable. Women of her type revel in improving the most unlikely material. Pool was only about her own age and a splendid physical specimen. Clipped and dressed properly, she recognised he would be handsome. All her snobbery and sense of superiority left her. Someone really wanted her, found her companionship a source of delight. Her motherliness and generosity saw a man who only wanted a chance.

She capitulated.

12

When the news was conveyed to Charlotte she was dismayed for a moment. But, recovering her poise, she saw that it would be to the family advancement and would go a long way towards conquering the social inferiority under which the motherless Pools laboured.

Old Mrs Mazere, as she was unfailingly coming to be called, had found Charlotte a great support and suggested that, owing to the advent of a stepmother, it would be wisest for her to remain at Three Rivers. Undecided, Charlotte wrote to her husband explaining that though she was happy enough, nevertheless she feared becoming lazy amid the softness and luxury of Three Rivers. She was lonely for her own dear sweetheart and wanted little Philip to know his daddy. In fact, Charlotte fervently wished that Philip could start in a little place of his own, but loyally did not express it. Her strength lay in her self-containment. She was one of those able to thank God for the things she never did and those she never said.

In response to her letter, Philip thereupon employed what capital he had saved in buying a share in the main line where he would double his earnings, and said that he hoped to return to the land within a year. But a little later there was bad news. Philip had been robbed one week and had suffered a broken leg in a smash the next; now he was laid up at a wayside shanty near Yass. Charlotte hurried off to him without delay, her purse supplied with money from Mamma, a fact unknown but probably not unsuspected by Papa.

Remaining with Philip till he was able to return to work, Charlotte realised sadly that it would probably be better for her to return to Three Rivers for the present. Her return was heartily welcomed. Old Mazere had missed her more than he admitted and Mrs Mazere had felt her absence sorely. Though still hardy, the elder woman was beginning to feel the need of rest. She had always been public-spirited, as much as was compatible with her day and locality. She took a prominent part in advancing the church, and women for miles sought her attendance at their confinements, or brought ailing children to her. Her skill and resourcefulness had made her beloved of her richer neighbours as well as her poorer. They liked to have her as a consultant in addition to anyone else they might be able to retain. The poor preferred her to the doctor; they were sure of finding her sober, and they were probably not incorrect in believing that she knew more than him, and also did more. She supplied them with linen and food and medicine from the provident store chests of Three Rivers homestead. Her liniments and ointments had wide fame and, it may be noted, were the basis of commercial products in a later generation.

For all such activities Charlotte freed Mrs Mazere Senior by taking hold of the household, as naturally as breathing. Too inexperienced to know quite how to set about laying her own plans, she then found that another child was coming, and this held her hands again.

Thus she bore herself patiently till more than a year of separated married life had passed and the news of gold discoveries came to change the tenor of life in the colonies. Situated as he was, Philip Mazere was one of the first to hear the news and be away to the diggings at the Ophir, as it was then called. He arrived there in the first

33

big rush in the autumn of '51, without travelling up country to say goodbye to his wife and child.

The gold fever took the country by storm. Not only did the discovery of gold appeal to the gambling streak in man, ever ready to adventure all on chasing the rainbow or the snark, but the new way of life came as a welcome relief to those tired of the monotony and isolation which were the pioneers' greatest hardships. Without a backward glance, they left the plough and the herd behind in the lonely bush, running like children to a Punch and Judy show.

George Stanton was left with but one shepherd but, being knowledgeable and able enough to be his own head stockman, his situation was not as difficult as lots of others'. The blacks were welcome that year at Mungee, which now reaped the benefit of its early generous treatment of them. Old Mazere was fortunate that he could turn to manual work again himself, and felt the better for it. "It's taking a little of the pot off me," he explained. He was lucky too in still having Hugh at home; Grubb, his imported (and transported) gardener, also stuck. Grubb was a true lover of growing things. Astonished by the luxuriant growth of his beloved crops and plants in the rich soil and genial climate, enjoying independence in his own cottage with his wife and children — that was Ophir enough for him.

Charlie Slattery, one of the Three Rivers stockmen, was one who ran. Ellen, his wife, was glad to be reinstated with her boy in the comfort and sociability of the homestead, and the Mazeres were relieved to have a trained helper not likely to be carried off by some swain as soon as she began to be useful.

Philip had appeared to do well for a time. Glorious tales of his finds filtered through to Three Rivers and he sent his wife and mother brooches of queerly shaped nuggets of gold, almost like flowers or animals. For a time, he sent Charlotte a good deal of money, which she was careful to hoard, but then that dropped off; Philip said he was afraid of the bushrangers sticking-up the coaches and rifling his communications. Later he wrote that the diggings were played out at the Turon and Ophir, and that he was off to Mount Alexander in Victoria where there was a solid mountain of gold.

Charlotte was anxious to follow her husband to the diggings but the second child, James, hampered her and even old Mazere was against her going.

"Stay where you are. If a man can't make a place to settle down,

34

a woman and children won't help by dragging after him," he said with solid commonsense and a more straightforward appraisal of Philip than his wife and mother's loyalty permitted.

CHAPTER II

Both young Philip Mazere and Charlie Slattery had been absent at the diggings for about a year the day that Cornstalk Bill Prendergast came in from Gundagai talking of the rising flood. Charlotte had been more than three years married, much of which time she had spent as a leading member of the Three Rivers household.

She followed the children into the great kitchen. Her voice was rarely heard unless specially invited, but her hands were usually first and most capably employed in any practical need. When she appeared, undertakings generally received an impetus.

"Goodday, Bill! Any hope of it giving up?"

"Goodday, Mrs Philip! Not a ghost of a chance as far as the signs go — looks like we'll soon want the Ark. There won't be any weddin' for a few days, if it depends on a parson."

"That means that everyone will be staying longer, and we'll want more food," said Charlotte. "How's the oven, Ellen?"

"Just about ready."

Charlotte was a striking figure in her voluminous skirts. Her glossy black hair, satin smooth, was looped back over her ears and confined in a knob. Her clear dark skin bespoke health, her steady movements strength; she was a woman made to wear in soul and body. She turned back her sleeves, tied on a large apron and went to the fireplace where there still were hanging in the chimney some of the

36

smoked hams of bacon and mutton that had abounded there at the beginning of the winter. With a poker she swung the lid off the great camp oven of cast iron which, set upon its triangle, commanded a large subsidiary fire of coals in one corner of the mighty fireplace that occupied nearly the whole head of the big flagged room where most of the domestic operations took place. In the oven two monster turkeys and a couple of fat ducks were sizzling. After turning them with a fork — blacksmith made and of almost satanical appearance — she basted them with an iron spoon of similar origin and proportions and then turned to the boilers, her face reddening in the heat of the open fires in a temperature reduced by the rain from 112° in the shade to 100°. The boilers swung above the main fire of logs and contained families of plum puddings of various sizes.

Then Ellen removed the door of the brick oven which protruded from the side of the kitchen, and its cavernous mouth revealed an apartment big enough to shelter a robber. The floor was spread with a mass of glowing embers from the bark of the native apple tree, which was so well suited to this purpose that a forest of these trees now stood ringbarked and dying between Three Rivers and the township.

"Another twenty minutes and it'll be just right," said Ellen, distributing the fire to the furthest corners with an L-shaped implement on a six-foot handle.

"I'll have the pies ready by then," responded Charlotte, placing an enormous pastry board and roller on the table. Taking the fruit that was coming to the boil in an array of commodious saucepans, Ellen filled pie dishes big enough to bathe an infant, while Charlotte adjusted roofs, ornamented them around the eaves and cut roses for the centre. They were filled with plums, peaches, Kentish cherries and nectarines. Bill looked on, fascinated by the ease of the performance.

Ellen next scraped out the coals and ashes and in went the pies. With them, on a vast iron sheet beaten into a tray, went scores of tartlets, some spotted with currants, others to be later enriched with honey or jam. Last to go in were the juicy turnovers. With fifty guests invited and the possibility of anything up to a dozen casuals calling in, food had to be supplied as for an army.

Isabel Stanton now came to announce that the great work of icing the cake had just been completed by herself and Amelia. Everybody, Bill included, trooped off to the hall of the Big House, selected as the coolest spot for this operation, to see the masterpiece.

The Big House was a modest structure when all was said and done, but in those days it was the wonder of the district. When men were their own architects and builders, designs were of necessity simple; while a house with its various additions might stretch in sweet abandon over as much as an acre (each successive edifice being separated by some yards so that in case of fire, a man did not run such danger of being deprived of his entire homestead in one fell swoop), it never went upwards more than one storey, owing to technicalities that were beyond the capacity of the amateur builder. But Philip Mazere had announced, "I'm sick of these colonial beehives and rabbit hutches. I must have a house fit for a man to live in." The Big House had resulted. Of stone, with the usual bull-run narrow hall straight through, it was built on the skillion pattern with a large room on either side of the front door and two smaller ones at the back. It was dignified by a splendid verandah on three sides, which finished in a little box of a bedroom at each end. But the pride of the place, setting it apart as a veritable castle, were the narrow breakneck stairs (in fact, little better than a ladder) that ran up to the fabulous upper storey. Upstairs, there were four bedrooms and a large square landing for linen-cupboards and, though towards the outer edges of the rooms the ceiling was not above six feet from the floor, this fact did not detract from the superiority of the place. Young people — and old ones too — were thrilled to stay with the Mazere girls, just for the experience of going upstairs to bed.

So Mr and Mrs Mazere, their daughters and youngest son took possession of the Big House while the rambling Old House became the special domain of Hugh, male guests and the married members of the family when they were in residence. The Big House in time was also outgrown. Mr Mazere grew tired of being so crowded at his own hospitable board that he hadn't room to flap his elbows when attacking the mammoth joints. Carving in those days was no dilettante exercise. So he had recently built a dining room, facing the kitchen, upon his wife's insistence. It was a veritable squire's hall with ample space for most gatherings.

Mazere Senior, with his sons Richard and Hugh and son-in-law George Stanton, now returned, soaked and talking volubly of flood prospects, from the flats over the river.

"The punt won't be safe much longer," George was saying.

"And those poor devils over on the flats will be in for it," ventured Richard.

"It will most likely lift about sunset," said Mazere, "but unless Labosseer has the parson on this side of the Murrumbidgee by now, I shouldn't be surprised if the wedding doesn't come off tomorrow. How was it as you came along, Bill?"

"Must have been much heavier up the other side. The Bulgoa was a fair banker at two o'clock an' risin' fast."

"Another hour or two will decide."

The men went off to change and the kitchen was again invaded by the women and children, the visiting servants from Mungee and Nanda being set to work peeling a large tub of potatoes. The task of creating the floral decorations, which had been left till last, was now out of the question. "We can get up early in the morning," said Emily.

Mrs Mazere came in from the dairy which, with the fowl-run, was her domain, and announced that the thunder had soured all the cream. "The cows will have to be milked at daylight to get cream in time for the wedding breakfast," she said.

After he had changed into dry clothes, Mazere called for the mail bag, which no one else ever opened unless he was absent. He took out the few letters, insisting on knowing who they were from as each person addressed laid claim. Then he settled down with the newspaper, reading out aloud, as was his custom, interesting items to his wife. The colonial generation was not interested in politics or philosophy or public events, and Mazere frequently deplored their lack of conversation. Though he enjoyed dominating any discussion, he found the monosyllabic responses he was wont to receive from some victim anxious to escape to discuss horses and dogs with his bullet-headed cronies, somewhat discouraging. George Stanton and he hit it off all right while they went round the station and farms, but in the evening Mazere liked to throw aside his day-to-day concerns and talk on more challenging subjects.

Towards sundown the rain ceased. "It may run off in time to allow the parson and Labosseer to get through by hard riding and an occasional swim," said Mazere optimistically.

"I don't believe the rain has properly started yet," George Stanton demurred.

Bert Pool and his sister Louisa arrived in time for the evening meal, and Tim Brennan Junior came to discover if Labosseer had got through. Mazere had consented to the presence of the two Pools, on probation as it were. His wife gave Bert a cordial welcome, for he and she had become great "mates" on the jaunt from Pool's Creek to Mungee.

"Well Bert, it's good to see you again — what a great fellow you have grown," she exclaimed as she patted his shoulder. "And here's little Louisa, grown taller than myself. Charlotte has been looking out for you for days. Emily, you must take great care of Louisa."

This Emily was very ready to do. She looked with romantic interest at Bert who, after the years of Miss Mayborn's direction and with his exceptional physical endowment, had turned out quite a dandy. Louisa was an eager, gentle girl, slightly younger than Emily, and shyly enraptured with every turn of this great romantic adventure.

Emily took Louisa up the wonderful stairs to the upper storey where the bridal finery occupied a room to itself. Bert went off to the Old House with the men. What a splendid company presently appeared around the table that was laden with meats, fruits, vegetables, preserves, pickles, bread, butter cakes — all the good things of the earth in abundance. When the hearty appetites were all satisfied, the family set about a variety of tasks, guests lending a hand according to custom, more necessary now than ever since the rush to the diggings had depleted the number of "hands" available.

In case the rain came on again and the river rose any higher, Mazere gave instructions for all the gates and sliprails leading from the low banks along the river both on the Yarrabongo side and at the junction of the Bulgoa to be left open, so that the stock would have access to the high ground surrounding the house and stretching away for miles behind it. Even the pigs were let out of their sties. Then everyone settled down to pass a sociable evening. But no sooner had the children been sent off to bed than a terrific thunderstorm seemed to concentrate on the valley. The rain pelted down and the thunder and lightning were phenomenal.

"Surely this is the final shower," said Mrs Mazere. "It must have rained itself out by now."

But at the end of an hour the racket on the roof was so deafening that they had to shout at each other to be heard. It seemed as if the roofs must give way under the weight. Some of the men tried to go out to reconnoitre, but were driven back drenched, hardly able to stand in

40

the rain. They all remarked on the peculiar character of the lightning.

Little Joseph Mazere was wakened by the noise and lay in his bed, fascinated by the queer flashing light. As it entered over the door, he caught a glimpse of the big tarantulas huddled there, for the light lingered strangely about the lintel, like the blue flame on the Christmas pudding after the match is put to the rum.

"Something's struck," murmured Richard.

"It's a water spout," said Mazere. "It can't last long." But it went on unabated.

At about eleven o'clock, Grubb, the gardener, and his wife and family appeared at the kitchen, drenched like water-rats.

The flood waters had reached the bottom of the orchard where his cottage was situated. "With our young children, I'm afeard, sir, to wait till it comes any nearer," he said.

"That's right, Grubb, the mistress will tell you where to shake down," said Mazere. "God above," he added, "it must be the Flood itself. We'll all be drowned if it keeps on much longer." But it kept on and on.

"God have mercy on the poor people on the flats! I hope they have sense like Grubb to get away to some neighbour," said Mrs Mazere. Then, as no one could settle to anything, she called the household together for the usual evening service of Bible reading and prayer.

At about two o'clock in the morning the roaring downpour eased off, though steady rain continued. The Bulgoa could be heard roaring like Niagara, and there was a considerable torrent rushing past the back gate where hitherto no watercourse had been known. Bill Prendergast was not able to go to his lodging in the loft above the coaching stables and was given a shakedown in the billiard room adjoining the dining room, most other rooms being crowded with family and the verandahs being sopping wet, the water having broken the spouting in many places and cascaded inwards.

It was a moonless night, and through the windows they could see nothing in the howling blackness. The rushing waters sounded like the ocean itself.

"Well," said Mazere finally, "there's nothing to be done but go to bed and wait to see what the morning will bring us."

In the kitchen, with one last task to carry out before going to bed, Charlotte took a great batch of beautifully browned loaves from the oven. Louisa accompanied her for a sisterly talk. Mrs Mazere went to Rachel's room to comfort her lest the girl should be perturbed about the bridegroom's safety. Kissing her good night and blessing her, she said, "He'll come through as soon as he can, my child and, in any case, you'll begin married life quite soon enough."

Soon the whole household was asleep, with the easier rain as a lullaby.

CHAPTER III

Simon Labosseer, the bridegroom of the morrow, had found favour
with the master of Three Rivers long before the daughter did anything
besides ridicule him for his ability to intelligently discuss all kinds of
subjects, political and otherwise, with her father. There were other
bonds as well between the two men. The surname Labosseer, like
Mazere, was the corruption of an old Huguenot name, though the La
Bossière family had taken refuge in Holland while the de Mazières had
fled to England. The name of de Mazières had speedily been
anglicised, but La Bossière retained the original spelling till he became
domiciled in the colony.

On his mother's side he sprang from one of the great Dutch
seafaring families; a remote ancestor had served as one of Dirk
Hartog's lieutenants in the celebrated expedition of 1616 to the west
coast of Australia. Family tradition and legend had therefore early
turned his thoughts towards the continent called New Holland, but his
family had long since left the sea for professional and mercantile
pursuits, and it was as a surveyor that the young man had presented
himself for acceptance as a colonist about eight years before the night
of the great flood.

In those days, his English had been stiff and bookish, and the
impossibility of pronouncing his name intelligibly to the colonials,
many of them illiterate, speedily resulted in its simplification to

Labosseer. But that was an infinitesimal matter compared with the complete upheaval of existence he underwent in changing not only from one hemisphere to another but from one nation to another. Nevertheless, he was a brave and resourceful man, well-suited to his calling, and his education and personality made him popular with all his superiors, from the Surveyor-General downwards.

Yet he might never have come on this roving expedition had a certain young lady of high degree in Holland accepted his proposal of marriage. But she had preferred his elder brother and certain estates he was heir to, and that was why the young man had returned to his boyish dream of going to Australia. He could have held office in the colony had he so desired, but the wound to his self-esteem had been deep and he stuck to the bush where his foreignness confirmed him in his natural self-containment.

He had been four years in the bush and was nearing the age of twenty-six when he was sent up the country to make new surveys of the country west from Mungee. He came — as all emissaries from the Surveyor-General, the Commissioner of Lands or the Bishop — to Three Rivers and was there received by the Mazeres with all the hospitality for which the place was renowned, even in that age when hospitality was an obligation as binding as ever it was to the ancient Greeks.

Upon noting the exquisite profile, the blue eyes, the wealth of brown curls of the little beauty called Rachel, he was delighted to accept the Mazeres' cordial invitation to stay over a few days.

Young Labosseer was soon in high favour with his host, with whom he found himself in agreement on a number of topics, including the conversational and other shortcomings of the native-born. They discussed many things, the quiet but observant guest with an eye all the time upon Rachel, petite and lightsome of movement but well developed for her fourteen years. She was vivacious, impetuous and radiated superabundant health.

Meanwhile, Mazere found himself so pleased with his guest that he invited him to assist with the church service which he conducted every Sunday morning for his family, servants, and any visitor that might be staying at the homestead. And all the time the magnet for Labosseer was young Rachel's beauty, and her youth that was blossoming into womanhood. But Labosseer's good standing with the parents had placed him, in the girl's estimation, as merely an old fogy for whom the best napery must be used. The other young people

44

noticed him principally for the foreignness of his speech, which they found amusing.

On Monday morning Labosseer spied Rachel, armed with a carving knife as large as a scimitar to cut cabbages for the midday dinner, in the extensive enclosure of the vegetable garden. Alert for the opportunity, he stepped down the path after her.

She did not notice her follower and was startled by his voice as she stooped over a cabbage.

"Will you not let me do that for you?"

"Oh — no, thank you! You wouldn't know how, would you?" There was a spice of mischief in the question. It was then, without further prevarication, that he delivered himself of his determination.

"I am very sad that tomorrow I leave you."

"Are you? How funny!" replied Rachel, bursting into a peal of laughter. "Can't you come again?" Simon laughed too, infected by her youth and merriment. He was a young man come again to the country of love, after a lonely exile.

"Yes, I can come again, and while I am not here I want you to promise me something," he said seriously.

"What is it?"

"That you will think of me."

"What for?" demanded Rachel.

"Because I shall think always and only of you," said he, coming abruptly to the point. "I want that you shall regard me as more than a friend. I shall speak to your father and then one day..."

Rachel took a fleeting look at him and was alarmed by his strange agitation and the crimson which mantled his fair skin under his tan. An old man, a friend of her papa and mamma, to be talking like this! He was drunk! He was mad! He was a foreigner! Any of these strange states being equally objectionable, she flung the carving knife and corpulent cabbage towards him with all her might and with more energy than aim, and fled to her room from which she refused to appear or to give any reason for her seclusion.

Ducking out of the way of the knife as it flew past him to land in the neighbouring carrot rows, Simon picked up the great cabbage that rolled towards his feet. He was nonplussed for a moment but then gave himself up to enjoyment of the agility and beauty of the fleeing figure as it leaped over cauliflowers and rhubarb and finally disappeared behind the gooseberry bushes.

"I have startled her," he mused. "She is very young and

45

innocent. She has not before been spoken to by a lover."

Her apparent lack of sophistication gave him a thrill of satisfaction when he thought back upon the proud coquette who had merely practised upon his adolescent emotions.

"I shall speak to her father," he decided and, proceeding to the kitchen door, knocked ceremoniously and presented the cabbage and knife to the cook with a stately bow. "Miss Rachel has cut this cabbage."

The cook thanked him, whereupon he bowed again stiffly and departed.

"There's an old-country gentleman for you, even if he's only a foreigner," remarked the cook, who was a recent arrival through the offices of Caroline Chisholm, and uncomfortably homesick. "Different from these convicts and jumped-up colonials."

The next day, as Mazere was accompanying his guest an hour or two on his way, Labosseer astonished the older man by broaching the subject of Rachel.

"Rachel!" exclaimed her father, almost as surprised as the child herself had been. "She's a child!"

"Another year or two and she will be a full-grown woman."

"It was only yesterday I was dandling her on my knee."

"But it would not be distasteful to you, that in time —"

"Wait, man, wait. It will be years before she is old enough."

"So long as the suggestion does not merit your opposition, I shall wait," said Labosseer. "I am a patient man. I am accustomed to waiting. Time runs quickly."

Mazere rode back to Three Rivers anxious for the solace of his wife. It was disappointing that Labosseer, who promised so well as to companionship, had, like the mere colonials, primarily an eye to his daughters. In any case, the thing was preposterous.

He summoned Rachel to him in his office in the Big House where he kept his accounts, books, pipes, papers and telescope, and asked her if Mr Labosseer had said anything to her.

"He started to say something queer, Papa, but I thought he was mad — or drunk."

"Mad, drunk or in love — there's much of a muchness in any of the three states," said Papa, "But they are the way of human nature and it is good if a man can escape the drunkenness and madness and suffer only the love." Dismissed, a puzzled Rachel left her father musing in his office.

46

By a word here and there, it leaked out that Labosseer, the Dutch surveyor, was casting glances towards Rachel and that her older sister Isabel was threatened with being left on the shelf. Mrs Mazere refused to countenance such light talk. "No daughter of mine shall marry before she is eighteen if I can help it," she reiterated firmly. "She will have all she wants of married life — and too much of it, after that age. It would be even better to wait till twenty-one."

But time, as Labosseer had observed, ran quickly, and the quiet, patient man never swerved from his purpose. From time to time, some choice present would arrive for Miss Rachel Mazere or a member of her family. A wonderful shawl or scarf from the old country for Miss Rachel, a piece of china for Miss Isabel, a chair or mirror for Mrs Mazere, a book or atlas for Mr Mazere. A year or so later, and derision had ceased. His letters and presents now aroused pleasant expectations. Rachel began to find him younger than he had seemed at first and his old-world courtesy set him apart from the more casually mannered sons of the neighbouring settlers.

Mrs Mazere remained firm on the subject of early marriage for her girls, but when Rachel reached sixteen, it had become a definite understanding that at eighteen she should change one corrupted Huguenot surname for another. Labosseer at this time started to prepare a home, having decided to go in for wool-growing. He was tired of the camp life entailed by his profession, but to enter upon a sedentary life in officialdom was also irksome to him, after the free, open-air nights and days. A station homestead offered a compromise, and his knowledge of the country was useful to him in selecting a holding. The country farther south appealed to him more than did the hot, parched regions towards the Bogan or the Namoi. He chose the cool, well-watered, flower-strewn plateau adjoining Gowandale and at one end running near to Curradoobidgee. He had not only influence but also capital, accumulated both by his steadiness and the perquisites of his profession, and a legacy from his family. Two years before his marriage he began to prepare the homestead, erecting buildings, sheepfolds and sheds, orchard, gardens and agricultural plots.

The two years had passed and it was the eve of the wedding and the big flood.

CHAPTER IV

At the first streak of the grey dawn, the little bride was at her window, anxiously observing the sunless, humid sky. Though the rain held off for the moment, an occasional growl of thunder warned that the heavens were not yet appeased.

The customary song of the Yarrabongo as it flowed around an elbow bend at the southern end of Bool Bool was buried deep in a turgid surging sea of muddied water, stretching over a mile eastward. Only the veriest tips of the riverside foliage were visible above the sullen water flowing towards Stanton's Plains.

Grubb and his wife were already outside, gazing forlornly towards their bark-roofed abode. Built near the bank of the river, only the top of the chimney and the ridgepole showed that it was still standing. Mrs Grubb was weeping for the loss of her few goods and chattels, some of which had been brought all the toilsome way from the old country.

Soon the whole household was surveying the flood. The swollen and confined waters of the Bulgoa still roared like a cataract in a north-western direction from the back gate.

"Well, there's no hope of Labosseer getting here now," observed Mazere. "I just hope all the people on the flats had the sense to leave their homes, or they'll have been drowned, without a doubt."

"I wonder how they're getting on at the Plains," said Isabel.

"The water couldn't touch 'em there unless it was Noah's flood itself," said George. "Pa had enough of the water in the flood of '44. He took no second chance of a bath when he built the new house."

"The people in the bend must all have been washed out. I wonder if we could help them with clothes or food," said Mrs Mazere.

"Indeed, yes," said Mazere. "Bill, as soon as you have breakfasted, you go up to town and see how they are."

"All right, Mr Mazere. Crikey, I'll have to swim across the hollow though!"

In the hollow between the homestead and the township, there now swept a swift stream where hitherto there had been only a winter swampiness, or in wetter seasons, a trickle of a creek that could be stepped across.

"I pray that Labosseer and the parson are safe, and don't run any risks trying to get here in a hurry," said Mrs Mazere.

"If they don't turn up in a day or two, we'll have to appoint a clergyman — and there'll be a whole mob of us ready to step into the bridegroom's shoes," said young Tim Brennan gallantly to the bride. Bert's eyes, bent in the same direction, were full of dawning admiration.

"He'll be here soon enough," said Mrs Mazere imperturbably.

"Soon enough for her to have plenty of married life," said Mrs Richard Mazere, née Amelia Stanton, who was feeling irritable with her spouse.

Bert, who had been gazing across the floodwaters, suddenly pointed across the river. "I think there're some people on the roof of that place to the left."

"Brown's place! My oath there are," confirmed Bill.

"Run, Emily, and bring me my telescope," commanded Mr Mazere, and Emily scampered away with Louisa Pool to get it. Through the telescope, a family could be descried sitting on the sloping roof of a hut on the flats.

"Nothing can be done for them from this side of the river, that's a certainty," said Mazere.

"And nothing from the other side either, till the water goes down a little," said Tim Brennan.

"Terrible loss of property and stock," said George.

"And all the crops on the flats," added Richard.

"It might have been worse," said Mazere equably. "Think of the poor folks farther down who've lost all their goods and chattels.

Anyway, if there's not another water spout, this probably should have run off sufficiently by tomorrow for us to see where we really are."

"Let us have breakfast and then see what we can do to help our neighbours — and thank God for our own escape," said Mrs Mazere.

They turned to their duties. Some of the men went off to find and milk the cows and to see about the other stock. The women set the living rooms in order and laid the breakfast table for which, under Charlotte's supervision, great pans of chops had been fried and a cauldron of potatoes boiled. With so many people having already arrived for the wedding, and none of them having bird-like appetites, provisions had to be on a grand scale.

But the flood and the disturbance of the wedding plans filled the family with a restlessness detrimental to its normally ordered undertakings. After breakfast the telescope was set up in the little hall window upstairs, and from this point one or other watched the plight of the hapless family marooned on the roof out on the flats. Also reported were sightings of beasts going downstream, both dead and alive. Occasionally the under rind of a melon floated by, looking like a face on the tide. Logs and trees swept past, making such a pile of debris in the lower bend that only a fire would be able to eventually dislodge it.

After breakfast, despite the fact that the stream in the hollow was well above the girths, Bill, Richard and Hugh saddled up and rode off to the township. They were back in an hour with the news that the people at the lower end had been flooded out early the previous evening and now were quartered with their neighbours who lived on the higher levels of the township proper.

"We have cooked enough food for twice as many people as are here at present," announced Charlotte, officer in charge of the larder.

"Well, the senior Stantons and Brennans and Saunders won't get here for a week so we have plenty of space to put others up," said Mrs Mazere.

"I told them that," said Richard, "but they all seem to be pretty well dug in for the present."

The trying position of the family on the roof occupied everyone's attention. The telescope showed them at midday still without a rescuer and Bert announced that he would see what could be done. The Aborigines, he thought, might be of some help, and he asked for the latest news of the Mungee tribe, which usually reached Maneroo in the warm summer months but this season had not yet appeared.

"Too easy a life at Mungee," said George. "Isabel has them as fat as pigs and as lazy too."

"They moved on somewhere the day before we left," said Isabel.

"I saw a camp on the edge of Stanton's Plains as we came along," said Bert. "If Nanko or Yan Yan or Lac-ma-lac are over there, they might be able to help us organise a rescue."

The young men set off after the midday meal, relieved to escape from inactivity and armed with the wherewithal for smoke signals. Arriving at a point where the Yarrabongo was confined between steep, craggy banks, Bert sent up a long, straight signal of smoke, easy to do since there was no wind, and thus announced his presence. In a little while, a similar signal replied from high ground further up the gorge.

"There they are, all right!" exclaimed Bert triumphantly. Going a little higher up the river, the young men could see the camp across the gorge safe above water level. Speech would not carry across the noisy water, so by means of deft gestures and using pieces of bark, Bert suggested the shape of a hut. Then, making a doll out of his handkerchief to indicate a woman, he pointed in the direction of the marooned family. The blacks signalled that they understood and the Three Rivers contingent went home to await developments, speculating on the extent of the detour necessary for the blacks to make their way around the floodwaters, and whether they would be able to ford the Wamgambril River which ran between their camp and the flats.

It rained steadily during the afternoon, but there was no renewal of the terrific cloudburst of the previous evening. The telescope still showed the poor family, including an infant in arms and a couple of toddlers, sitting in the rain.

"Fortunately the corner posts are of red-gum, and well sunk, or the house would have caved in by now," said George Stanton.

At sunset a cheer went up from the watcher at the telescope, who announced that the blacks could be seen taking the woman and baby off in a canoe. Dusk hid the second canoe load from sight, but later a fire signal went up which Bert said was intended to convey that all was well.

"Oh, Mr Pool, could you send a signal back to thank them?" asked Rachel eagerly.

"I might if you call me by my right name," he said shyly, and that this request was acceded to was proven by Bert soon making wonderful signals which entertained the whole household. Joseph, who had elected Bert as a hero, was so impressed that a little later he was found on the verandah endangering the safety of the household by setting alight beacons of candle bark he had purloined from the kindling wood, for which misdemeanour he was promptly sent to bed.

Following the tension of the day and the unprecedentedly late hours of the previous night, the household assembled early in the big dining room for the family prayers that were always said before retiring. The usual order of procedure — a chapter from the Bible, read by Mrs Mazere (the Old Testament in the morning and the New Testament in the evening), followed by a prayer read by Mr Mazere from the big book which had been presented to him by the Bishop on one of his visits — was slightly altered that evening when Mr Mazere indulged in a little rare extempore communication with the Lord, thanking Him for His mercies to the household and supplicating Him to preserve all others in danger, neighbours, friends and dear ones.

The last reference everyone knew to allude to Simon Labosseer, and the little bride had tears in her eyes as she went to kiss her father goodnight. Holding her affectionately, he said, "Don't you worry now, child. There's no one alive knows more about this part of the country than that man of yours. He mightn't be as showy as some, but he has a headpiece with something in it." This remark was meant to serve the double purpose of reassurance for Rachel and rebuke to the Pool lad, but Bert was oblivious, intent only on the little quivering face.

A little later, Bert sought out Charlotte, who was in the kitchen with the servant women studying which of their viands would "keep" one day longer in the muggy atmosphere, and planning how to maintain the fort if the rain went on and on.

"I say, Charl," he began when they were alone, "that poor little Rachel is awfully cut-up about her intended. You tell her if the rain doesn't get any heavier, the big flood ought to come down in another day, and then I'll go poking around to see if I can't get him here."

The adventurous Bert was mixed in his emotions just then. He had a lurking wish that Labosseer should never arrive at all, and yet wanted to be the hero to lay the bridegroom before Rachel sound and well, for the sheer joy of seeing gladness and gratitude suffusing her pretty face.

And thus passed the first day of the great flood at Three Rivers.

CHAPTER V

The next dawn showed a considerable lowering of the floodwaters, though the main streams were still far from navigable. Bert, Richard, and George Stanton's brother Jack went out early on horseback, exploring in various directions. On their return, Richard reported that he had seen the punt caught in the debris at one of the elbow turns of the Yarrabongo, and that there was also a boat caught behind a log at the same place. Sadly, Jack Stanton told of finding Joseph's creamy pony drowned and jammed against an uprooted tree. At this news, Joseph raised such a howl of bereavement that Bert said, "Don't make such a noise, old buffer. I'll bring you a new pony next time I come. There are whole mobs of ponies at the Head of the Rivers. What would you like — a skewbald or a piebald or a —"

"He'll have none of those ponies, thank you," interrupted Joseph's father, rather more sharply than the occasion demanded. But the rebuff passed over Bert; Mazere was afraid that a wild pony would not be sufficiently gentled for the little boy, he surmised. Only Charlotte was hurt, for she knew from her father-in-law's tone that Bert was not finding favour as she had hoped.

He had been across the Bulgoa, Bert went on to say, and had seen the drowned body of a man which a shepherd had found in a creek near his hut. Mazere was incredulous — it did not seem possible that anyone could have crossed the Bulgoa. But Bert and his splendid black

53

mare, reclaimed from the wild horses of the Bulla Bulla Mountains, could perform feats beyond normal men. Black Belle was a good-tempered as well as a goodly beast, and by this sign, as well as her points, was supposed to be a descendant of the famous old runaway sire, Clifton.

The rain continued with hardly a break, and the soaked earth became a vast bog. Horses sank to their knees on the high ground around the homestead, and the family went in above their boot tops if they stepped off the awnings and flagged paths. Fannie and Rhoda, going to the garden to seek raspberries that the rain was ripening en masse, fell down several times in the mud. Their yowls as they struggled and rolled about brought Emily on to the back verandah, and her hoots of astonishment on beholding them brought some of the others.

"Regular piccaninnies," laughed Louisa.

"Goodness gracious me!" exclaimed Mrs Mazere, scarcely recognising the infants of her middle age. "Deary, deary me! Ellen, Ellen! Prepare a warm bath immediately and bring it here to save making a mess of the house."

The two little girls were coated with rich, clayey black mud, from their stout little lace-up boots with the pieces of metal around the toes to their flaxen curls. The mud had got into their eyes, their nostrils and their mouths, and they shrieked as if possessed. The spectators, shouting with merriment, did not help the situation. Their mother, keeping them at arm's length, slipped off their garments and, with towels about their little fat bodies, they were hustled into the tub. Before long they were reinstated in society, but were forbidden to leave the verandahs and areas covered by awnings.

Joseph, being the oldest of the small fry, was set to watch the little ones "play horsies", and was also warned to keep the visiting children away from the beehives which were accommodated among the pot plants on the back verandah. The "horsies" — dainty gum switches with the leaves left at the end for tails — were mounted and away went the riders, little boys astride and little girls running beside their steeds so as to represent the prescribed seat for women. This was an absorbing game, especially when a steed had a fall or when the ringmaster, unable to control a tendency to tease, trod on tails. But then, entirely forgetting his commission and considerably bored by such young companions, Joseph went poking about amongst the bees — Papa's stinging English bees. One of his small, uninitiated followers

54

put an inquisitive nose too near, a fat fist closed on a protesting insect and Georgie Stanton, the heir of Mungee, roared as if a branding-iron had touched him. The hand of the sorry little boy speedily swelled beyond recognition and his irate mother rendered him first aid with a blue-bag, after soundly cuffing his uncle.

Joseph's holiday from school, which had been declared both in honour of the wedding and also because of a domestic upheaval that his teacher, the doctor's wife, was undergoing, continued owing to the flood. But he was too old to play with the babies and not old enough to supervise them, and what with leading Mick Slattery into mischief he was such a nuisance that eventually, to their intense delight, he and Mick were permitted to go to the big barn, which at this time of the year was almost empty of hay and in the present crisis was being used as a theatre for certain masculine pursuits. Emily and Louisa longed to go too, but their approaching young-ladydom forbade it.

To comfort Joseph and as a compromise in the matter of ponies, Bert had managed to skin the deceased creamy, and his beautiful skin was to be tanned and used as a rug on the floor of Joseph's bedroom. By midday the hide had already been salted down, and then Bert showed Mr Mazere how to set up a handy little tan-pit by stretching a large size in greenhides over a frame mounted on stout posts set in the earth. This job finished, the men cleared out the last of the old hay from the barn and with the aid of Tiny, the house terrier, engaged in a massacre of mice. Mr Mazere, not caring for this primitive and nauseating sport, returned to the house, after which the young men practised shooting at various targets. Bert had a six-barrelled revolver from Baker's in Fleet Street which had found its way to Maneroo via the diggings, and which he had been itching to exhibit. They all acquitted themselves creditably, Jack Stanton and Tim Brennan tying for second place after Bert. Bert even let the wide-eyed Joseph have his first shot, holding the small podgy hand in his and encircling the thrilled little figure with his big strong arms.

Then said Bert, "I bet I can hit a blowfly on that wall." The wall was about thirty feet distant.

"Go on! You couldn't even see it!" said Richard.

"Put up a bit of charcoal the same size and let me have a go at that first, if you don't believe me." The challenge was accepted and Bert hit the mark three times out of four using his right hand, and twice out of four using his left.

Later, at the dinner table, the talk was all of Bert's feats, and

55

Joseph, allowed to sit up with his elders on this special occasion, was breathless with worship of his hero. He hung on Bert's arm asking when he was going to let him have another shot.

"We'll have to get up a shooting match, at a tenner a side, and challenge the district to put up someone against Bert — to shoot blowflies on the wing, left-and-right-handed with a revolver," said Tim Brennan, full of enthusiasm.

"I'm a bit out of practice," said Bert modestly.

There was a loud snort from Mr Mazere, and the family noted signs of displeasure in their chief. Bert's obliging disposition and his readiness to plunge in during the emergency had latterly been prepossessing his host in his favour — the construction of the tanning plant had particularly pleased him — but this shooting business reawakened his prejudice against the Pools.

Mrs Mazere, sensing the cause of her husband's annoyance, sought to change the subject. But that proved impossible with so many young men all enthusing about Bert's prowess, and at the end of the meal, their host rose abruptly and left the room, after rapping out, "What does a decent, *honest* man want to carry an arsenal around with him for? The blacks are not dangerous, and bushranging no longer exists in these parts. You come with me, Mamma!"

Mrs Mazere followed him to his office where, after slamming the door, Mazere thumped the table angrily. "Don't let that bushranger come here any more!" he shouted.

"I don't like all this talk about shooting either," said Mrs Mazere placatingly, "but you know what young fellows are."

"There's a mighty difference between young men, let me tell you. They're not all highwaymen."

"Oh, there's no harm in Bert really — the boy's never had a fair chance, that's all. And since we are now connected with the Pools, it would be better to give them a chance to make good connections than to try and shut them out."

"I don't want any ticket-of-leave men raising themselves by me!"

"Ticket-of-leave men are not uncommon in these parts — take your friend Saunders, for instance."

"Saunders is at least a man of good family and education. But old Pool doesn't know B from bull's foot, and was probably sent out for sheep stealing."

"Perhaps, but Charlotte and her brothers and sisters are freeborn

56

like myself, and the new stepmother has educated them wonderfully."

"Ha! I'd just like to see how she has trimmed up old Boko Pool!"

"I'd like to see her too — she must be a splendid woman.".

"It's a pity she can't reform Bert. Can't be civilised even at a wedding — comes armed with a double-barrelled gun and a revolver! What for, I ask you? You've only to look at that mare of his to know her sire was Oswald's stallion, Clifton, that got away from Goulburn Plains six or seven years ago and has never been yarded since. Though he used to be seen often enough up by the Head of the Rivers. Why was he never recaptured, tell me that?"

"No one fit for the task, I suppose."

"Old Pool could have done it. Why didn't he?"

"No one asked him politely, perhaps. Remember that he did not spare himself helping Philip recover your shorthorn bull."

"I'm tempted to throw that boy out tonight, flood or no flood."

"Bert was only a little boy when Oswald's horse got away."

"Bert's dad wasn't a little boy. Look here, don't interrupt me. I know without seeing and having my nose rubbed in it that old Pool — old convict Pool — planted that horse in the same way as he has planted blood cattle. And then he innocently runs the unbranded yearlings in, puts his mark on their hides and has the best stud farm in the colony, up there in his lair among the gorges, at the expense of decent people."

Mrs Mazere nearly said, "When I was up there at the wedding," but checked herself in time and said, "I've been told that Pool gets the credit for what Larry Healey of Little River often does, only Healey is a more artful dodger."

"God help Labosseer starting up there! You'll see — old Pool will start sheep next year, and then Labosseer's stud rams will escape — and it won't be the dingoes that will make away with them."

"Pool started sheep last year," protested Mrs Mazere.

"Of course he did, to be ready for Labosseer's rams. I must open his eyes. He'll be no match for that gang, up there in their own lair."

"Well, Papa, don't make a fuss till the wedding is past. We can see what's to be done then."

"I don't want him here again. If there is one thing I cannot abide, it is lack of principle in a man."

Mrs Mazere soothed him as best she could and Richard was given a hint about suppressing the shooting matches. Emily Mazere and

Louisa Pool meanwhile had reached the arms-entwined stage of infatuation peculiar to young girls of their age. Louisa's charm was enhanced for Emily through being the sister of such a prodigy as Bert, and Louisa found everything about Three Rivers enchanting.

CHAPTER VI

1

In spite of continuing rain, the floodwaters were rapidly running away into the Murrumbidgee. By Friday's dawn the gardener's cottage was visible as far as the window panes and, between the homestead and the river, tree tops were beginning to reappear.

The young men were kept out of mischief that morning by Charlotte's enlisting their aid in saving some of the fruit, which the rain and humid atmosphere was ripening abnormally fast. Encased in oilskins and top boots they gathered raspberries and gooseberries, figs and mulberries from the bushes and trees about the house. But in the new orchard on the slope the fruit was already beginning to spoil and housekeepers were alarmed lest their stores of jams and pickles and dried fruit be short next winter.

The men presently came in with buckets and tubs of fruit, and all the women were mobilised to top and tail the gooseberries and pick over the other fruits for jam. Then it was put into huge cauldrons, with sugar by the hundredweight. Armies of vessels were mustered in readiness. A number of rockmelons were used in the same way. The cavernous oven was heated and filled with numerous fruit pies, and everybody had so much to eat that it was a matter of wonder to see the indelicate appetites that were brought to the midday meal a little later.

Those were the days when skilled and capable women, zestfully occupied in indispensable household arts, were unacquainted with boredom or nerves, and when men had to develop courage and strength in keeping with manhood. Those were the days!

After diligent scrutiny through the telescope, Mr Mazere gave it as his opinion that a good deal of the maize crop might be none the worse for its immersion. But he looked in vain for most of the trees in the old orchard.

"Must have been washed out by the roots," said Grubb sadly and, upon a tour of inspection, he descried some of them caught on a split-rail fence beyond his cottage.

Made restless by the unaccustomed idleness, Bert decided to set out on a tour of exploration in the direction of Gundagai. Jack Stanton, Tim Brennan and Hugh Mazere were to accompany him as far as the Mungee crossing. But first they would have to cross the Bulgoa, about three miles from the back of the homestead. The midday meal was hurried forward, and the young men rose from it a little after noon.

The coach road crossed the Yarrabongo twice by punt in order to avoid miles of steep going, but by taking the hills the horsemen could avoid the big stream. The Bulgoa was a swifter, more turbulent stream than the Yarrabongo, but not nearly of such volume.

"I do hope you'll be able to find Simon," said Rachel at Bert's near-side stirrup, patting the glossy and affectionate Black Belle. Bert, already taken captive by her beauty and youth, felt in that moment something of the nobility of real love and was anxious only for her happiness.

"You be sure if I find him I'll bring him here as quick as I can," he said, genuinely eager to restore Labosseer to his bride unharmed.

At the Bulgoa, still dangerously swift, the riders had to put their legs on the beasts' withers, but they got across without swimming. They then visited the shepherd who had discovered the drowned man, and whom they found in great distress. Because of the weather, it was imperative that the burial should take place immediately. The young men took the responsibility of ordering this, and the shepherd proceeded to make a grave as well as he could in the sodden ground. The young men gave a hand and the deed being completed within half an hour, they rode on together to the Mungee, which, after a wide angle, joined the Yarrabongo about ten miles farther on. The Mungee was still a banker, foaming along in a dark, muddied flow and when Bert tried to drive Black Belle into it, she jibbed on the brink, rearing and wheeling.

"Better be sure than sorry, Bert," said Hugh.

"If Black Belle refuses something, it would be warning enough for me," cautioned Tim Brennan.

"For me too," agreed Jack Stanton. "You wouldn't catch me risking my life for that old foreigner. If he's drowned..." He shrugged. Jack's hopeless pursuit of Rachel was well known. Most of the unmarried men of the district would have been glad to plunge into Labosseer's shoes at a moment's notice, had they been vacated. Labosseer was not a popular winner. The native born resented everything about him; he was a foreigner, older than his rivals and in with officialdom. They considered he had been unjustly favoured due to old Mazere's snobbishness, and that the little beauty was being sacrificed.

Bert chuckled. "We mightn't be as fond of him as we ought to be," he said, "but if Rachel wants to marry a Dutchman, or Yan Yan, or any sort of a cove at all, that's the sort of cove she must have."

With the memory of Rachel's beauty in the back of his mind, and his peers to be outdone in the foreground, no advice would deter him from attempting to cross the river. Taking off his clothes, he rolled them up in his oilskin coat and hitched them to the top of his head. He put the bridle reins out of the way, loosened the girths and, springing onto Black Belle, rushed her into the water, choosing a long stretch above the crossing. When the snorting, protesting beast had been spurred so far into the current that she might as well keep on as turn, she struck out bravely. Then Bert, by way of the crupper, slipped over her rump and seized her tail. The others rode along the bank, watching and exclaiming apprehensively. The Mungee had an evil reputation and was not a stream to be trifled with; it was full of treacherous holes and undercurrents. There was also the danger of horse and man striking a snag. But at last youth, strength and daredevil courage prevailed and the man and his horse were seen on the opposite bank. Bert shook out his clothes to show they were none the worse for his swim, put them on, steadied his excited mare, waved his hat and went on.

Bert figured in two maidens' prayers that night, romantically in Emily's, with a blessing in Rachel's — because he had gone to find her husband-to-be and, perhaps, also a little for his own sake.

2

Bert returned next day in time for the midday meal but was unable to give news of Labosseer further than that he was supposed to be on the other side of the Murrumbidgee. A settler had told Bert that on the previous Tuesday it was known that Surveyor Labosseer was at the Royal Hotel in Gundagai awaiting the Bishop. As far as anyone knew, he was there still. The Murrumbidgee had been about two miles wide at Gundagai at its height and was still over a mile, too much for even Black Belle and her master, though she now had such confidence in him that she would have attempted to swim any water that he rode her into.

A discovery was made that afternoon. The rivers had filled with such suddenness that fish washed out of their haunts in the deep holes under the high banks could be picked by hand out of potholes scattered wide over the fields. They feasted on fish for two days in Bool Bool. Beautiful little golden and silver beauties previously unknown to the residents were washed up from recesses that had never been reached by hook and bait. Some of them, covered with flame-gold scales, had whiskers and ruffs as decorative as ever had the royal fish in Japanese and Chinese prints. Bert put some of them in a tub for the children, but Mrs Mazere objected to keeping creatures in captivity unless they were likely to become happy members of the family, like the great white cockatoo and the orphan lambs, pigs, calves and foals that had come in their season. So it was understood that the fish must be returned to their natural habitat as soon as it was safe for them.

Since the Stantons' station at Mungee could be reached without having to cross the Mungee River, George decided to take a ride there on Saturday afternoon to see that the homestead was safe and that the shepherds were continuing vigilant against dingoes. Only Richard accepted George's invitation to accompany him. The attraction of Emily was too much for Tim Brennan; Bert and Jack likewise had their magnets, and Louisa was secretly enraptured that Hugh too decided to remain at home. The men occupied themselves again in gathering the fruit and in making bullets from the lining of a tea chest in a little mould constructed for the purpose.

The women spent much of the day reprovisioning the larder with cooked foods. Three Rivers being a religious household, vegetables were the only hot dish permitted on Sundays, no matter what the weather or the company. Even the Bishop had to eat cold meals at Three Rivers on Sundays.

As work slackened off in the late afternoon, some of the young folk

62

suggested a little dancing to enliven proceedings. Though Mrs Mazere condemned both cards and dancing, she had given way a little regarding the latter, which could be enjoyed occasionally with strict limitations. But card playing could only go on in the barns or in the men's rooms after she had said her prayers and retired. Billiards she also considered a tool of the devil, but since there had been a billiard room in Mr Mazere's ancestral home, it was something he was determined to have at Three Rivers, devil or no. When it was finally built, the billiard room was much reverenced in those parts, setting the homestead apart in the minds of the settlers as a sort of baronial hall. It was difficult for Mr Mazere to find trained opponents, but the young men who came to call were apt pupils and found that by learning the game and deferring to him in it they became welcome visitors to the house where his daughters' bright eyes shone. And billiard-playing was much more congenial than trying to follow the thread of old Mazere's discourses on public affairs, and hazarding acceptable responses.

Mr Mazere, being in the habit of taking an afternoon snooze on Sundays and other days when work was impossible, retired for that purpose on the Saturday in question. Mrs Mazere accompanied him and, their presence withdrawn, dancing to music supplied by Bill Prendergast's Jew's harp began on a back verandah safely out of sight of the windows of the Big House.

As a ruse intended to further his association with the Mazere girls, Bert concealed the fact that he was a champion dancer and, with the connivance of Louisa, asked Rachel for tuition. All the assembled girls, married or single, were fair with youth, health and hearty zest in life, but it was Rachel with her blue eyes honest and fearless as her mother's and her bright brown curls who most attracted Bert. She was, too, only five feet, three and a half inches high, and this seemed wonderful to a young man six feet one in his socks and a member of a family all long of limb and lean of frame. Every word that issued from her exquisitely fashioned little mouth had for him an enthralling significance. Consenting to teach him, she was as nimble on her feet as a gazelle. Bert was entranced with his ruse.

He had however omitted to alert Charlotte to his scheme. Coming from the kitchen to the dining room seeking vessels for the fish and pumpkins, pies and jam which she and the servant women were handling, she was attracted by the hilarity on the south verandah and, on seeking its cause, was astonished to see her brother oafishly

63

clutching Rachel in a suffocating embrace that lifted her well off her feet.

"Not quite so tight," Rachel was saying. "And you will manage better if you stand farther away."

"Oh, I beg your pardon! Let's start again," said Bert.

"Dear me, Bert!" exclaimed Charlotte. "What's the matter with you? You were a splendid dancer long before I left home."

"Not these new dances," said Bert quickly.

"That old polka! You and I used to dance it till we were tired of it."

Louisa, now feeling free from her contract, exploded with laughter. "It's such a lark to see Bert pretending, my sides are aching," she giggled.

"All this rain has given me rheumatism," said Bert lamely, but this explanation was unacceptable to Rachel. There was no coquetry in her. Her dignity as the bride-to-be of a man of the standing of Simon Labosseer had been affronted. Bert was a stranger, one of the almost banned Pools, and he had presumed to make a laughing stock of her.

In the break, the voice of Joseph intruded. "You was going to measure us all, Bert, and the littlest child was to get a prize and the littlest grown-up was to pay a forfeit."

Indeed, Bert had appraised the heights of the lasses over fifteen and had seen that Rachel was the wee-est. The one to pay the forfeit — to wit, Rachel — was to have been banished with him to some spot to think up a new game for the company. But now Rachel, offended, departed, flashing him an annihilating, dark-lashed glance which was so bewitching that Bert wished that she could be quite alone in a situation of great danger from which he could save her — flood, blacks or fire. But the blacks were tame and his valued friends, and the only people needing to be saved from the flood had been the family on the roof, the matriarch of which was already far gone in the unshapeliness and drudgery of unrelieved child-bearing. Why couldn't a situation arise in which it was necessary for him to snatch up Rachel to the pommel and ride away, away, like young Lochinvar, on the unequalled Black Belle? But the good old days were only in the story books that his stepmother read to his father. Life nowadays was as flatly free from romance and danger as the palm of his hand.

The clamour of the children recalled him from his dreams and he said, "Bring me a carving knife to cut off your heads while I get a bit of raddle to make the marks."

The splendid blade with the deerhorn handle which Rachel had thrown at Simon Labosseer four years before was produced and the business of measuring began. Bert placed the tip of the carving knife on the broad whitewashed post of the dining-room doorway, and the heads came under. No one among the small fry was forgotten — Mazeres, Stantons, Grubbs and Slattery — every child able to stand up was given his chance. Next came the men, who made a cluster around the six-feet mark, and then it was the women's turn, Charlotte leading at five feet, eight and a half inches. Each time that the level of the knife was certified by the onlookers to be exact, Bert made a line with it and wrote the number of feet and inches at one side, while Emily, eagerly helping, wrote the initials on the other. Even Ellen reluctantly submitted to being measured.

Mrs Mazere, when she reappeared, also had to be measured, Bert substituting her for the other Rachel who refused to appear.

"Mamma is the littlest girl — she'll have to pay a forfeit!" cried Joseph.

"I'm beginning to grow downhill," she said.

"All the best things are done up in small parcels," said Bert.

"There're some fine things done up in big bundles too," she kindly responded. She was not letting her husband's displeasure with the exuberance of youth lessen her affection for Bert.

When everyone had been measured and the prize given, time was slack in the dripping, late afternoon as they awaited the evening meal. But with sharp knives and fingers skilled in their use, the men decided to cut their initials opposite their heights and those of their fancy in girls opposite theirs. Emily looked for Bert to carve hers, but it was Tim Brennan who officiated. Bert carved R.M. opposite Mrs Mazere's mark, Hugh delighted Louisa by cutting L.P. for her and the three fellows divided the work of carving the initials of the married ladies between them, Charlotte's falling to Bert, and Bill Prendergast cutting Ellen's initials the deepest of all.

There the record was.

Hoity, toity! when Mrs Mazere discovered the carving disfiguring her doorpost! "It looks like a sly-grog shanty," said she. "It must be planed away before Mr Mazere sees it!" To deface walls was not allowed by the Mazere curriculum of gentility.

Planing hard ironwood in the upright position would have tested the best plane and adzing it might make the post hollow-backed, this evil being worse than the first. The calves having to be penned, the ducks housed, the logs for the morning fire poled in, the kindling placed in the chimney corner to dry, these and other chores diverted the transgressors till it was dark and the evening meal was set.

Late that night Charlotte, concerned about Bert's delinquency, made some stiff whitewash mixed with rice water and obliterated the initials as best she could. The morrow was Sunday and no superfluous work was encouraged; and then, as the ensuing days slipped by, the carving was forgotten. A generation later when the family was scattered and some were dead, the initials on the old doorpost were discovered, dug out from the whitewash which, with the advance of commerce in the colony, had become paint, and they became a tender memorial to the zestful days of yore.

CHAPTER VII

1

Every evening, rain or shine for the last fortnight, Mrs Mazere had made her way to the ridge at the back of the homestead and gazed across the river. A little to the right of the cottage that had recently housed the family rescued by the blacks, there stood the hut of Piper, a shiftless settler whose wife who had given birth to seven children in about six years. The last two births had almost cost the unfortunate creature her life, and her situation was often discussed by the married women when husbands and maidens were out of hearing, with indignant threats of just what they would like to do with Piper.

A month or two back, Mrs Piper had pilgrimaged to Mrs Mazere and had implored her to assist her in her approaching travail. Mrs Mazere had readily given her promise to do so, and had instructed Piper that should his wife's time come without giving him a chance to get to Three Rivers, he was to signal, on any evening up until nine o'clock — at which hour the good lady and her daughters normally went to bed — from the point across the river, whereupon she would immediately set out.

Walking in the appointed place on the Sunday evening of the flood, when the rain had given up for an hour or two, she suddenly saw Piper's prearranged signal — the blaze of a fire and then a burning brand whirling round and round in the air. Mrs Mazere hastened back to the homestead and, after seizing a newspaper, hurried back to the ridge and sent up an answering flare.

It was nearing eight o'clock, a sullen, cloudy night without a moon, and already nearly dark. The Yarrabongo could be faintly discerned, like a white road, foaming around the bend above the township. Its unusual roar filled the heavy evening and told that it was still in wild flood, even though the waters of the cloudburst which had buried its voice on the first two days had somewhat run off. The punt and some boats were gone. No horse could yet breast that stream and be sure of coming out alive.

Nevertheless Piper's signal had been made as arranged, and Rachel Mazere responded according to her pledge.

She hurried back to the kitchen and announced, "Piper is signalling!" The supper table was being cleared by the many joyous young hands that made light of the work. Under Emily's direction, Tim Brennan was carrying the mighty dishes of beef and poultry towards the pantry, a great apartment next to the dairy, where they were placed in the big fly- and ant-proof safes. Hugh was helping Louisa lift back the long home-made benches that served as chairs, placing them in readiness for Sunday evening prayers which Mr Mazere would conduct at eight sharp. Rachel was stacking the plates and cutlery which Bert and Jack Stanton then carried to the kitchen, where they were being washed by Ellen and dried by Eliza and Susan, the two visiting servant girls, and where Bill Prendergast was in charge of the hot water supply. Isabel and Mrs Richard were busy with the younger children, and Charlotte was calmly directing operations so that all might be kept going in an orderly fashion in spite of the holiday spirit that rioted amid so goodly and youthful a company.

"Signalling now when he knows it's impossible — the fellow never was fit to be out of irons!" exclaimed Mr Mazere.

"These things always happen at the most inconvenient times," said Isabel.

"Poor soul, it will likely be the death of her," said Charlotte.

"Not if I can help it," said Rachel Mazere, *née* Freeborn.

They all crowded around and looked at her, silent, expectant. Mr Mazere found his voice first, and there was apprehension in it. "My dear Mamma, what can you possibly do, with the Yarrabongo in such a flood?"

68

"There's a boat, isn't there?"

"Not a boat left from here to Gundagai," said her husband.

"Oh yes, there is," she replied promptly. "Bert told me there were two saved at the other end of town, Dr James's and Isaacs'."

"Yes, but they've got holes in them," said Bert quickly.

"Now, my boy, don't you tell a fib before your Maker at a time like this. You told me both those boats were in working order." Bert saw that subterfuge would fail, and knew now what Mrs Mazere had in mind. If only he had realised before, he thought, he would have sneaked out and loosed the boats on the current.

"I think you said the doctor's boat was the best," continued Mrs Mazere.

"Yes, and the doctor's the one to use it, if anyone does," said her husband, catching at a straw. "This is his work!"

"Perhaps, but he's another one who ought to be kept in irons," said his wife. Everyone knew of the doctor's weakness for the grog and that his wife acted as his keeper when he had a particularly bad attack of delirium tremens. She was thus unable to carry on her school for the present, another reason why Joseph's vacation was being prolonged.

The doctor had been banished to Australia by his family, who could no longer endure the disgrace and the dissipation of his talents and patrimony. He had been accompanied by his wife, the daughter of a naval officer, who had sentimentally believed she could reform him, as girls will in the egotism of passion, oblivious of the evidence that if God and his mother cannot make a man, there is seldom much to be done with the spoiled material. Alice James, however, was like most of her sex, once caught in the toils — martyred but unaware of martyrdom. She started a school and the settlers were glad of it; governesses up the country tended to be married off so quickly that the children had become quite accustomed to hiatuses in their education.

When a birth was imminent among the well-to-do settlers, it was customary to secure the doctor well in advance, and to shepherd him away from grog till the event was safely past. When he was in his senses he was popular as "good company", and his weakness was too common to incur ostracism.

"Just because the doctor should be kept in irons is no reason you should lose your life in this piece of foolhardiness," argued Mazere.

"I looked at the river today in case Piper should signal, and I think two strong rowers could take a boat across at the other end of town. We could start at Isaacs' farm. We'd probably be swept down as far as..."

"You'd be swept to glory, and no probability about it," said Mazere.

"...as far as the punt crossing," she calmly finished.

"Let me go, Mamma," said Charlotte. "I'm a poor one beside you, but I'd do my best and I'm ever so strong. And I used to be a good swimmer."

"No, my dear, you are young. Your life is before you, whereas I have almost finished my work."

"In the name of God, woman, have you gone out of your senses?" exclaimed Mazere, thoroughly alarmed.

"I couldn't leave a sister woman in that plight without trying to help her. It would haunt me to my dying day. God will take care of me."

"Risk *your* life to save one of that wastrel Piper crew; the thing is madness!"

"The woman's life is in danger and she is suffering terribly." Rachel Mazere remembered the woman's hysterical pleading and thought of those things that the women talked of when men were not present.

"Your life will be in greater danger than hers if you try to cross the river tonight. Take it on a commonsense basis — one woman's life is as valuable as another's. If you lose yours and don't save hers, that's two gone instead of one."

"I believe I can get across all right, and I have made a promise."

"You will not leave this house tonight. I forbid it," said Mazere, his voice rising. Everyone stood tensely.

"Now, who is going to take me?" said Rachel Mazere. "I need strong arms."

"I cannot offer to take you, Mrs Mazere, much as I hate to refuse you anything," said Tim Brennan. "It'd be murder I'd be guilty of to let you get into a boat with the current of the Yarrabongo what it is tonight."

"I should think so," said Mazere.

"Let me go over alone first," suggested Bert. "I'll see how the current is and find out if the case is really serious, or if it can wait till morning."

"Yes, Mamma," agreed Isabel. "That's a most sensible plan.

70

And if the rain keeps off, the river will be a lot lower in the morning.''

"There's a mackerel sky," said Hugh. "I was looking just now and every hour will mean a difference in the fall of the river, if there's no more rain.''

"And every hour to a woman in her agony, my boy, is an eternity. *You* will come with me, Bert, I know. I'll get ready.''

Tim Brennan saw the look that Emily cast at Bert, while Charlotte noted Bert's eyes seeking Rachel's. Seeing that look of Emily's, Tim Brennan stepped forward. "I'll go too, then," he said. "I know the river better than you, Bert.''

"If one of you dare enter a boat with Mrs Mazere tonight, I'll stop you — even if it's with a gun," suddenly roared Mazere.

Tim Brennan looked irresolute, Bert Pool stood dauntless. Emily and Louisa wept in each other's arms.

"Who is the master of this house?" demanded Mazere, and guests and family quailed before the rising tempest. But his wife, seeing his trembling hands, knew that it was only fear. She was very dear to him, his other half in deed and spirit, and he was stricken with that failure of nerve to which he was prone, that failure of nerve which attacks certain dispositions when it comes to a showdown with sheer selfless intrepidity.

"Who is the master of this house?" he demanded again.

"You are," said his wife gently, "and it would ill become you, Mr Mazere, you a magistrate and a leader in this settlement, to hold back from any neighbour in distress, and that neighbour a weak, desperate woman.''

In the midst of the controversy, Charlotte saw Rachel the younger steal around to Bert. Looking up at him, her sweet beauty enhanced by her eager pleading, Charlotte heard her say, "You'll keep her safe, won't you? I wish she'd let me go too, only I'd be no use.''

Charlotte had not realised how singularly handsome her brother was until that moment when he bent towards Rachel, his brow and lips illumined by the kitchen candles, and she half sighed as she thought of Simon Labosseer coming to marry Rachel as soon as the flood went down.

"That I will," promised Bert. In the stress of the moment the compact was sealed by a clasping of hands, and Charlotte could see that her brother was lifted right out of himself. No deed of daring or ancient chivalry would have been beyond him that night. The

71

Yarrabongo was but a puling dragon, its teeth already drawn.

"The Piper woman is only struggling with natural causes, she'll pull through," said Mazere lamely.

"It's a pity you men couldn't have a little practical experience of those natural causes and then you mightn't be so easy about it," his wife said with a touch of asperity, and turned to get ready.

"You don't leave this house tonight!" bellowed Mazere as his fears for her safety took possession of him.

They all stood irresolute again except for Rachel the younger, who went off after whispering to Charlotte, "We'll get out those things she has had ready for Mrs Piper." Charlotte woke as if from a trance and went with the girl.

Husband and wife confronted each other, and family and guests went out and left them alone.

2

"Tim, are you a good swimmer?" asked Bert.

"I reckon there's none on the river can beat me, and if we *can* get across, I know where we can get a horse on the other side. But it's suicide! It's not only the current — the river's full of logs and trees that are sure to catch the bottom of the boat."

The young men went to their rooms to get oilskins and gumboots. The women stood around talking in hushed and anxious tones. But they knew that no matter how loudly Mazere raged, when left alone with his wife in any controversy, she always had her way. So they were not surprised when presently Mrs Mazere reappeared in a pair of Wellingtons with her voluminous skirts tucked above a shorter petticoat. Over these she had an old oilskin coat and her hair was caught in a tight cap. She looked a strange mite, but no one smiled.

Mr Mazere issued forth from the house with her. Charlotte and Rachel carried oilskin valises packed with simple medicaments and other necessaries. It was too boggy for Mrs Mazere's gig, but every saddle in the place had been put on some sort of horse, and a considerable cavalcade mounted and went off in the darkness.

Left behind were Mrs Grubb, Amelia, Isabel and the two visiting serving-maids. Emily and Louisa were also among those who obeyed a sharp command to stay at home. Ellen, however, had scrambled up behind the willing Bill Prendergast.

"Papa looked as if he had been crying," Emily whispered to her new friend.

The horses sank above the fetlocks and, in some places, to the hocks, as they progressed. There was practically no talking. But the dogs of the township sensed that there was something unusual afoot and gave tongue accordingly as Bert led the way through the town to the doctor's boat, moored in a backwater that in normal times was the storekeeper Isaacs' horse paddock. It was Bill Prendergast, doubtless, who spread the news of Mrs Mazere's intention as he went to Isaacs' loft for a rope and another lantern. Soon practically the whole township had turned out. Isaacs, McHaffety the butcher, Brown the blacksmith, O'Grady the publican, Browning the brickmaker, the carpenter and sundry others including a percentage of wives joined the procession, all agreeing that Mrs Mazere was stark mad; in weighing her life against that of the suffering Mrs Piper, the vote would have been unanimous for the sufferer to be left to her fate. There was no certainty that Mrs Piper would die or indeed that Mrs Mazere could save her, and the roar of the swollen river as it raged around the bend had a menacing note that boded ill for the men determined to pit their strength against it.

"Devil a bit would Mrs Piper or the Queen herself get me to risk me life in that boiling current this night for any cause whatsoever," said McHaffety, an honest Irishman expressing what others felt. "Don't ye be letting her attempt it, Mr Mazere! Exercise yer authority. I'm surprised at ye! Standin' by and permittin' murder, it is that ye are!"

"I'm surprised at you, Mr McHaffety, with so little pluck — wouldn't you help your neighbour then?" chided Mrs Mazere.

"Och! Murder alive, I'd stop the best neighbour ever a man had from throwin' her life away for nought!"

"Now that I see the river up close, I forbid you to get in the boat," said Mazere to his wife.

"Now that I see it, it's not nearly as fierce as I was expecting," she responded, drawing herself up to her full height of five feet one inch.

"We can't stand here and see you go to certain death, Mrs Mazere," came a veritable chorus from the men. Then, from the high point across the river, came Piper's signal again, frantically operated.

"It's like that blackguard of a Piper to be thinkin' a weak and tender woman could come across the river on a night the like of this. Sure the man is a black-hearted criminal," exclaimed McHaffety.

Piper's red brand twirled round and round wildly.

Rachel Mazere, forty-four years of age, the mother of twelve children, nine of them living, and five grandchildren, stepped into the boat.

Bert followed her and then Tim Brennan. Browning and Isaacs held the boat, up to their knees in water.

"Give me the things," said Mrs Mazere to her daughter and daughter-in-law. Charlotte and Rachel rushed into the water with the valises.

"Oh, Mamma, I do want to go too," cried Rachel.

Bert looked to his gear by the light of Cornstalk Bill's coach lantern, but it was the light of Rachel Mazere's pretty eyes that lifted him out of himself so that his body seemed infused with a strength that the river could not defeat.

"Oh, *dear* Bert, do keep her safe," the girl gasped.

"With my very life," he pledged. She wanted to say something more; eagerly he bent his ear to her rosebud lips. "I'm so sorry I was cross about the dancing. It was a lovely joke on me."

A large, rough hand — Terence McHaffety's — led the little form gently from the water. Mrs Mazere took the rudder, pointing the boat upstream with all her strength, and the two strong young men stood to their oars. The male watchers raised a cry, half cheer, half protest: the women were silent. Beside himself now, Mazere rushed forward. "Stop! Stop! In God's name I implore you once more, before it's too late. Rachel, Rachel, come back — I'll do anything you want."

"Hugh, take care of your father and see that he doesn't sit around in his wet clothes. God bless us and keep us safe," called Rachel Mazere. The oars ceased splashing in the smooth backwater. The boat had reached the stream.

The men were silent now; the courage of the little woman had shamed rather than exhilarated them.

The lantern still showed the boat's position, as the craft rushed rapidly into the black waters of the stream. Suddenly the lantern spun round like a top, bobbed for an instant, whirled around at incredible speed and went out.

"God Almighty! They are gone! This is the end!" groaned Mazere.

Bert and Tim, strong swimmers, might escape, but Mrs Mazere in her Wellingtons and heavy skirts, never. Her husband rushed into the floodwaters, beside himself. Bill Prendergast and Hugh pulled him back.

74

"Let's make flares along the bank. Get straw!" shouted Bill, and some of the men rushed off to the stables.

Mazere raised shout after shout. A thousand voices came back from the sullen night, but none of them human. The old Arab stallion sidelined in the orchard at Three Rivers could be heard whinnying to his harem; the homestead and township dogs barked and howled incessantly. Millions of frogs croaked in the pools created by the flood. "Craig, bunk! Craig, bunk! Bunk!" went the big bass fellows. "Cheetity, cheetity!" responded the little ones. Mazere coo-eed frantically, but no voice replied from the roaring river save its own.

"Come, Papa," said Rachel. "They can't possibly coo-ee. It'll be as much as they can do to hold the boat across the current. Come, we must bear up till we see what happens. Bert and Tim are very strong."

"Curse the one for a damned flash bushranger and cattle duffer, and the other for a wild terrier from the bogs! But for their showing off, your mother couldn't have got anyone to help murder her," he fairly screamed at her. But Rachel's heart had lifted with the courage to which she was heir. Bert and Tim must win. They were so brave and splendid. It was impossible that they should be defeated.

The flares served only to accentuate the blackness where the river roared. The laughing jackasses in the trees nearby, disturbed by the commotion and fires, laughed and laughed in incongruous glee.

"I'll take my gun tomorrow and shoot every one of those devils!" roared Mazere, clean out of himself. He stumbled along the water's edge, inflamed by fear, praying, cursing, as the years of his life with Rachel came up before him in the anguish of waiting. He was a poor swimmer, and that quality which had made it impossible for him in earlier years to superintend the laceration of men's backs also made it impossible for him to plunge into the racing Yarrabongo that night.

The townspeople huddled together, discussing his lack of nerve out of the hearing of the family.

3

"Sure he must be a white-livered feller when all's said and done," observed McHaffety, whose back in its day had more than once stuck to his shirt, and he undaunted thereby.

"He should have put his foot down and forbidden her to go," said Isaacs.

"She *wouldn't* be stopped," said Browning.

"That little thing?" snorted McHaffety. "Sure he could have plucked her out of the boat with one hand."

"The littlest ones are generally the worst for having their own way," observed Mrs Isaacs.

"I think she did dead right to go," said Mrs McHaffety, "and only that baby Dennis can't be left, I'd have gone with her."

"Och, ye would now, would ye, Mrs McHaffety, but maybe I'd have had something to say about that," said her husband.

"And I'd maybe have paid as much attention to it as Mrs Mazere did to her old man," retorted Norah McHaffety. It was commonly supposed that McHaffety had procured his wife from the "Female Factory" at Parramatta, but wherever he had got her, she reflected credit on his taste.

There was a guffaw at her words.

"Mrs Mazere is a splendid woman and Bool Bool should be proud of her," said the quiet cultivated voice of Mrs Dr James, knowing full well that her spouse should have been in the boat in place of Rachel Mazere. The townspeople murmured in agreement and, honouring in their generous heart two brave women dear to it, steered the talk back into anxious speculations as to the safety of the daring souls in the boat.

Yet there was a general feeling that they would get through. Tim Brennan came second in reputation for valour and strength only to Bert Pool, who had already laid the foundation of a reputation that became legendary.

But Philip Mazere would not be comforted. The devil of it for him was that lack of physical courage for which a man condemns himself and is condemned.

"God Almighty, if your mother is drowned, I'll never lift up my head again. Why didn't I get into the boat with her?" he moaned.

"That would have been silly," said practical little Rachel. "You are heavy, Papa, and can't swim or row like Tim and Bert."

"Oh God, if your mother could only be safe at home again, I'd give everything in the world I have."

"I think it would make Mamma very happy if you were to forgive Philip for marrying Charlotte, and have him home again and set him up."

"If Mamma is safe, I shall put Philip at the top of my will."

No one thought of going home, and presently they were heartened to see fire signals issuing from the point opposite from which Piper had operated.

"They're saved!" shouted Mazere. Bill Prendergast was not so sure. He thought the signals might be coming from the blacks in answer to the townspeoples' flares. Nevertheless, the thought that the blacks might be present brought comfort to those waiting.

4

When the three in the boat reached the current it took prodigious strength and level-headedness to avert sudden wreck. The impact with the current resulted in the shipping of a good deal of water and put the lantern out but, with determination and skill, they made a slight, oblique progress and presently had as good a chance of reaching the far bank as of returning to the near. But though the men pulled upstream for dear life, their strenuous efforts scarcely even acted as a brake on their rapid rush downstream. Bert soon got his night eyes and, in the gleam of the water, saw that they were below the punt crossing, about halfway between Bool Bool and Three Rivers homestead, by which time they had hoped to be across.

When Mrs Mazere knew how far downriver they had been carried and how swiftly they were being borne along, she felt for the first time the full danger and realised the extent of her impetuousness in risking the lives of her neighbours' sons.

"Hold on like blazes and make a big swerve at the bend," roared Bert.

"The river runs in under a high bank where the Bulgoa comes in," shouted Tim.

"The Bulgoa might help us to swerve out."

"It will pitch us to glory — that reach has never been bottomed!"

"We'll leave it this time for someone else to bottom — cheerily ho, my hearties!" said Bert.

"Mrs Mazere, hang on to us now — if we're tossed out, we'll know where you are," said Tim.

"If we're pitched out swim for your lives and never think of me," she shouted. "I command you in God's name — I got you into this."

"We'll argy-bargy about that later when we have more time," retorted Bert.

Rachel Mazere prayed from the bottom of her soul. "Spare the lives of these brave young men whom I have brought into danger, and may I too be spared for a life of usefulness in Thy service, for Christ our dear Saviour's sake. Amen."

Her prayer was answered. They were whirled by the inrushing Bulgoa right into calm water, the only effort necessary on their part being to maintain equilibrium. Nearby, a little pinch of high ground was above water; Tim jumped out and, up to his middle in the river, held the boat while Bert picked Mrs Mazere out and carried her to safety. Bert was to remain with Mrs Mazere while Tim, who was familiar with the flats, was to go off and find a horse, and dry vestas with which to light signals for those waiting across the river.

But almost immediately they saw the blacks' signals and by means of lusty coo-ees, Bert was not long in getting in touch with them and thereby procuring a horse. Seated on the horse with a wet coat as a saddle, Tim leading, Bert walking beside her and the blacks lighting the way across the inundated flats, Rachel Mazere was not long in reaching the Piper hovel.

Mrs Mazere's skirts were soaked but the night was warm and humid, and excitement made her oblivious of her physical condition. The patient's need was so urgent and terrifying that she started to the poor creature's aid without stopping to do more than doff her oilskins and cap and put on a big apron from one of her valises. Mrs Piper's situation inclined Mrs Mazere to reflect that, had God given birth to His Son Himself instead of imposing the task upon a woman, it might have resulted in fundamental reforms. But she suppressed this thought as blasphemy, instigated by the Devil.

Bert and Tim, finding that they could be of no assistance except to keep a fire and a supply of hot water at the ready, which Piper himself was quite capable of doing, and, in any case feeling exceedingly ill-at-ease in the face of the Piper woman's travail, got another horse and returned to the high ground near the river to signal that they were all safe. The folks on the other side were satisfied when, through the telescope, Bill Prendergast swore he could discern the back light of his coach lantern. Everyone returned to their homes. Mazere, before retiring, called his household together in fervent thanksgiving. Meanwhile, Bert and Tim went splashing along through the flood backwaters to The Gap to discover how the Brennan and other households had been faring.

5

Timothy and Maria Brennan had come out from Ireland as *free* immigrants, a fact of which he was boastfully proud. A few years later, Maria Brennan and Rachel Mazere had become greatly attached on the long pilgrimage from Parramatta to Bool Bool, and were ever after as dear as sisters to each other, each giving assistance to the other at the birth of their children. Brennan was only a few months younger than Mazere and, since his wife was the same age as himself, she was some years older than her friend Rachel. Barney, the youngest Brennan, was a year older than Joseph Mazere, and his inseparable at school. Mrs Brennan had had only eight children — six living — but they had told on her more than Mrs Mazere's dozen. She was a shapeless mass of a woman, an inch taller than Charlotte Mazere, but these days rather helpless owing to her bulk and the faulty knitting of an ankle that she had broken some years before. She walked with a stout stick and sat down a lot, but nevertheless carried out a large share of her home's work with competence and energy.

The Gap household, being quite frankly and happily devoted to card-playing, did not retire as early as that of Three Rivers, and they were all about when the dogs announced the arrival of Bert and Tim.

"By the holy St Peter! The Saints preserve us, Maria! See who's here!" exclaimed Timothy Senior leading the two young men in.

"God help us, is it ghosts ye are?" said Maria, "Holy Mary preserve us! Is it bad news that ye bring, or why would ye be breasting the river and it at such a flood as was never seen before?"

"No, Ma, let us get a dry skin and you give us a good feed — and then we'll tell you all about it," replied Tim, as he kissed her.

"Make yerself at home, Bert, ye're welcome," said Tim Senior, shaking hands heartily for, though it was the Pools' first stay at Three Rivers, Bert was well known at The Gap. It was through this channel that Charlotte maintained relations with her family at Curradoobidgee.

"We've had supper," began Bert politely, but Tim exclaimed, "Crikey, mine is all shaken down long ago, I want a real good feed to set me up."

"Well, when I come to think of it, I could do with a bite or two myself," admitted Bert. When they reappeared in dry clothes, an enormous spread awaited them.

"The like of such a flood has never been contemplated. Speech has completely left me to properly describe it," observed old Tim.

"Oh, but it's a flea bite here to what it was at Three Rivers!" exclaimed Tim. "Old Mazere's orchard is washed out by the roots, and a man was drowned across the Bulgoa, and Joseph's creamy pony was drowned and..."

Then ensued a chorus of excited voices relating the various

79

incidents of the flood. When a lull gave her the opportunity, Mrs Brennan inquired, "And what brings ye two gossoons over like wild men, riskin' yer lives for no necessity and to grieve yer families maybe — and ye not worth puttin' them to such sorrow?"

"Sure we came over for to bring Mrs Mazere," said Tim, winking at Bert in his anticipated relish of the effect of his announcement. The girls — Bridgit, Mary and Agnes Brennan, and Maud Saunders, who had been staying over since before the flood — stopped their chatter. Mrs Brennan reached for her stick and made an ineffectual effort to rise from her seat.

"Och, faith! Ye're drunk or dreaming or liars, the pair of ye!" exclaimed old Tim. "For what would ye be attemptin' the life of a fine woman like that for?"

"She wanted to come," said Bert nonchalantly. He was very much at home in the friendly atmosphere of The Gap.

"Yes, being the pair of gentlemen we are, we could only do what a lady asked us," said Tim Junior, with a glance at Maud Saunders. In consonance with the derring-do spirit, a sudden spasm of the lady-killer had awakened in him.

" 'Tis the Piper woman has sent for her!" said Mrs Brennan, lurching to her feet this time. "The saints preserve us! Babies always choose such times for their arrival."

"It's Mrs Charlotte you mean, isn't it?" asked Mary disbelievingly.

"No, the real and only authenticated Mrs Mazere Senior herself," replied Tim.

A great hubbub ensued, the young men giving a graphic account of their adventure and, now that danger was past, not taking trouble to minimise it.

"My oath, we had a near squeak! I wouldn't attempt it again for all the tea in paradise, would you, Bert?" remarked Tim.

"Oh, I don't know. I'd do it again this minute if it was necessary," Bert replied dreamily. He was wondering why on earth it couldn't become necessary to perform some valorous feat on behalf of the younger Rachel.

"Sure that unfortunate Mrs Piper must be in a very bad way to demand anyone to risk her life in such circumstances," observed Mrs Brennan. "Did ye get any idea of how things were going at all?" Tim took his mother aside to tell her how badly things were indeed going. Mrs Piper's degree of distress had proved far more unnerving to the young men than the swirling black currents of the Yarrabongo.

"Och, I knew it. Sure I knew it! Well, Tim, there's a good lad — go ye and harness up old Bally and take me over at once."

"Ma! You must be crazy!" Tim gasped, surveying his parent in alarm.

"Sure I'm no more crazy than Rachel Mazere herself is this blessed minute. Who would I be to leave her all alone in that trouble and me to be sittin' down easy the while?"

"But Ma, it's impossible! We had to put our feet up to get across Back Creek and —"

"Sure I'll have to leave mine down, but a little water won't do them any hurt."

"But Ma, the place is a sea all the way to Piper's. The wheels would sink into the mud and it'd take a team of bullocks to get them out."

"I mean to ride a-horseback," said Mrs Brennan, without blinking an eye.

"The horse will put his foot in a hole and roll on you."

"God help us then — Bert is the venturesome one I must go gallivanting with this night," retorted his mother with a laugh.

"Another brave girl, bless her!" observed Bert. "Well, I'm ready. Let 'em all go for a kangaroo hunt this minute if they like!"

Old Tim rose up with a snort like that of a terrified bunyip, swearing by all the saints that he'd tie up "any man, woman, child, dog or cat attemptin' to go out this night!" He was much noisier than Mazere had been, but the threat of disinheritance carried even less weight on the right bank of the Yarrabongo than it did on the left.

"Rachel Mazere an' me has been together in too many a crisis for me to desert her now. Has she not, ever since Tim broke his collar bone at Bowral and the young rapscallion carrying on like one possessed, and since Bridgie was born at the Wollondilly, been with me in all distresses? Would she leave me now to anyone else whatever, not even the blessed Pope himself if I'd be needin' her, an' sure I'm goin' to stan' by her this night, if it's the last night I ever stan' by anyone. An' it's yerself, Tim Brennan, would be the first to ask why I was not goin' to an' old friend and neighbour! Shame on ye for losin' yer senses!"

"By the good Lord above, me wits would indeed have forsook me if I'd be lettin' ye out this night."

"Sure I'm glad to have the ride a-horseback," continued Mrs

Brennan. "I'm gettin' too sedate entirely since I broke me ankle and it's the adventure of a jockey I love more than anything. I'll go get meself ready. Come ye, Mary, with me."

"She doesn't go out the door this night!" repeated Tim Senior like a parrot a little later, as Mrs Brennan came in ready for the fray.

"Now darlin', ye know I'm too big for to squeeze out the window at all, at all," she said, stooping to kiss him. "Be easy now, cushla ma chree, I'm wild for a little adventure!"

"The only danger is Bally going into a pothole, and I'll walk at his nose all the way," said Bert, trying to reassure Tim Senior.

"And I'll walk beside Ma, ready to grab her if Bally stumbles," said Tim. Bert chuckled inwardly, envisaging Tim being pushed out of sight in the mud.

Bally was saddled, girthed, surcingled, cruppered and haltered, and a great valise of necessaries was strapped on the off-side. Now the problem was how to get Ma aboard, in the absence of a steam winch. Mrs Brennan hadn't been on a horse since her accident, and her already ample person had noticeably increased as a result of her more sedentary existence. Her side-saddle was enormous, something like the platforms attached to the backs of fat draughthorses, from which ladies of the circus are wont to spring through hoops.

"Lead him to the meatblocks and bring me my footstool and chair!" This was done. Leaning on Bert while Tim held Bally, and Mary and Maud steadied the footstool and chair, she trod from these to the meatblocks. Then, with Bert still as leverage, she subsided on to her howdah with great gasping and more good humour. She was a real old brick, Bert thought, as jolly as they make 'em, but she was almost fifty and weighed a ton, more or less; why, oh, why, he wondered for the fiftieth time, couldn't the heroine of such adventures be Miss Rachel Mazere, right now probably sound asleep in the Big House at Three Rivers and dreaming of Simon Labosseer.

Tim Senior had refused to take any part in the proceedings, condemning them as "murder", but his wife rode safely to the Pipers', and if folks' efforts are rated according to their capacity, her effort was well nigh as heroic as Rachel Mazere's.

6

The story of how Mrs Mazere crossed the Yarrabongo in the great flood to help a neighbour was a favourite yarn with the old hands up the country while ever one of them remained to tell it. As related by the women, it was a story told proudly. "Your dear old Grandma! she was the bravest woman who ever lived," or "Our dear old Mrs Mazere, nothing could frighten her. She brought you into the world, young woman."

The men on the contrary generally related the tale to the accompaniment of tobacco and grog and guffaws.

"There was old Mazere running along the bank shouting that if God brought her back safely, he'd put Philip back in his will," one would say. And another, "Always changing his will he was," or "Gosh, I never saw a man as frightened as he was that night. Haw! Haw! It was the funniest thing I ever saw."

Since men suffer the delusion that courage is a male prerogative, they preferred this aspect of the epic; for when courage blazes forth conspicuously in a woman, they are shamed. Men have not yet learned, or if they have, possess not yet sufficient moral courage to admit that male courage is often nothing but a recklessness, induced when the temperature is high. But women's courage is conceived in cold blood, and thought upon, and that is why it is the more deadly. When men have the moral courage to realise that they are not the stronger, braver sex, and that in fact it is fear that drives them to amass their ghastly engines of destruction, with a maniacal lack of logic that by their amassing safety is promoted, the human race will be some thousands of years further on the way to the millennium than it is at present.

CHAPTER VIII

1

The next morning showed the river very little lower, but the sky was clearer and half promised that the rain might have passed for a spell. Daybreak found Rachel Mazere and her fellow nurse still with their battle to be won, and never had Mrs Mazere been so glad of the partnership of her friend.

Poor suffering Mrs Piper was not delivered until Monday evening, and then of a still-born child. Her two rescuers decided that the only way to care for her properly would be to remove her to a place of comfort and cleanliness, safely away from Piper and the children. Accordingly, Bert and Tim made a comfortable stretcher with stringybark poles and sacking, insisting on practising with Piper as the patient. The party set out early on Tuesday morning, Bert, Tim and the three blacks, Nanko, Lac-ma-lac and Yan Yan taking turns as bearers over the five miles that lay between Piper's place and Brennan's Gap. Mrs Mazere rode Bally this time and carried a Piper urchin in her arms while another child sat behind her and hung on by a strap around her waist. Bally was to be taken back later for Mrs Brennan and two more Piper infants, neither of them yet being able to walk. The two eldest children were to go to the Saunders' as soon as the roads were passable.

Piper ran beside the stretcher now bearing his wife, bellowing in

84

a fashion distressing to his hearers but relieving to himself.

"Sure a bellowin' cow the soonest forgets its calf," observed Mrs Brennan, and though it was rather free verse, its spirit seemed apposite.

Mrs Mazere would have taken the whole tribe across to Three Rivers had passage been possible, but Mrs Brennan objected. "A nice assurance to a bride this outfit would be entirely!" she said, and would not countenance the idea. As they set off with their burden, Bert wondered again why Rachel could not be the heroine of some romantic situation of distress that only he could alleviate.

Mrs Piper was presently laid in a soft, clean bed such as she had never known, while her children were safely disposed of between two neighbouring families who entered enthusiastically into the business of washing, feeding and comforting them, and of fashioning for them some new garments. In those days the large and generous households up the country could always accommodate unexpected visitors — from two to a dozen, regardless of age or sex — and take pleasure in the influx.

By evening, there having been no more rain, the river had dropped considerably; Tim and Bert decided to return to Three Rivers in order to find if there was any news of the bridegroom and to reassure Mr Mazere about his wife.

2

The crossing was comparatively easy this time, and the young men soon walked nonchalantly into the dining room of the Big House, making little of their exploit of Sunday. Mr Mazere was so happy to have confirmed the fact of his wife's safety, and that she would be returning soon, that he ordered a little dancing; Bill Prendergast performed on the accordion and the master himself made very good music on the flute. Bert had the opportunity of polkaing to his heart's content with Rachel, who now laughed merrily about the trick he had played on her on that other occasion when there was dancing. Emily also had the joyful experience of dancing with Bert, who was inspiring in her the passion of her life. Yet she entered Bert's consciousness merely as the younger sister of Rachel, whose wedding with his neighbour Labosseer was only postponed.

Tim Brennan, however, regarded Emily differently; for him she was a grown woman who would have to wait at least two years more

85

before her mother would consent to her taking on the responsibilities of a wife and mother.

The next day, Bert, Tim and Hugh rode away towards Gundagai, seeking news. They found the Murrumbidgee still nearly two miles wide, as there had been fresh rain on some of its other tributaries. The swiftly flowing expanse of water could not be hazarded by beast or boat. So they had to return as they had come.

But towards evening of the next day, the arrival of Labosseer surprised them all. On beholding him, Rachel uttered a cry of joy and unselfconsciously flew into his arms.

"Did you think I was drowned?" he asked them over the top of her head.

"The Murrumbidgee must have fallen a lot since last night for you to be here," said Bert a little stiffly. But he knew a good man when he saw one, and there was tribute in the heartiness of his handshake. Labosseer's manner was somewhat stiff also; he shared Mazere's prejudice against the Pools. However, he was polite. With his hand closed over that of the radiant Rachel as she clasped his arm, he could afford to be.

"I made a long detour to where the river was not so broad and swam my horse across, I holding the animal's tail."

"If you came by the head of the Nanda, that's seventy miles if it's an inch, and heavy going in the mud," exclaimed Tim. "Your horse must be pretty well tucked-up."

"He indeed needs attention," said Labosseer, who, though lean, was six feet two, heavy-boned and no jockey-weight in the saddle.

"Bill Prendergast is seeing to him," said Charlotte, who had just come from the kitchen.

"No better horsemaster in the colony," said Mazere expansively.

"Did you ride the Viking?" asked Rachel. On hearing that he had, she sped away, light-footed and laughing, to see him. Labosseer's eyes followed her indulgently and Bert's feet tingled to tread in her wake.

"And your clothes, how did you manage?" asked Mazere.

"I tied them on my head in an oilskin valise — for the rest, the day has been hot with a wind."

"Let me take you to your room," said Isabel leading him away. Well satisfied with his daughter's betrothed, Mazere turned to expatiate on Labosseer's feat, as a corrective to the popularity of Bert and Tim. But Bert had already slipped away to look at the Viking. Emily had followed him, and Tim had followed Emily. With a muttered imprecation on the degeneracy of the rising generation in everything that appertained to character or intelligence, Mazere composed himself to await Labosseer's return.

After resting his beast for thirty-six hours, Labosseer went back for the Bishop. The Bishop was not in his first youth and had been somewhat softened by town life, and hence progress was slow. Nevertheless he too swam the Murrumbidgee, hanging on to Viking's tail, while Labosseer utilised a slightly less valiant beast for the crossing, and an Aboriginal ferried his lordship's vestments across on the top of his head. Thus they came to Three Rivers on the eleventh day of the flood, which was Saturday. Though the Bishop was very tired, he didn't go to bed till he had conducted evening prayers. Even parsons, up the country long ago, had to be real men and ready for emergencies requiring physical strength and a little pluck.

On Sunday, the Bishop conducted a church service on the broad verandah of the dining room. On Monday, horsemen rode forth to apprise the wedding guests that the delayed ceremony would be held on Wednesday, just over a fortnight later than the original date.

A house party of nearly seventy could not be dull in days when social contact meant the apex of human enjoyment. At the wedding breakfast, Mrs Brennan was a leader of the fun amongst the older folk and hobbled a measure with the Bishop, the bridegroom, Mazere and many others. When there was particular commotion at the top end of the ballroom, which was made up of the dining hall, the billiard room and the wide verandahs, it was bound to be some gentleman contending for the pleasure of a dance with Mrs Brennan. Other dancers stopped to behold the elan of Terence McHaffety's performance with her.

Terence McHaffety and his wife, Norah, were present due only to an afterthought, and not without Mazere having strongly demurred. "It is not to be thought of, Mamma! The man is an ex-convict! Everyone knows that his back is like a ploughed field, and as for his wife..."

"It is more Christian to think of people as neighbours than to remember they were once convicts," said Mrs Mazere quietly.

"Really, Mamma, you have no self-respect. You need not be so friendly with ex-convicts — after all, all your own family are freeborn."

"Always have been freeborn," she replied proudly. "That is why I can afford to act decently to those not so fortunate."

Mazere glared and she hastened to avert his onslaught. "Philip, last Sunday night when we were crossing the river, there was a moment when I thought I should never see you or, indeed, McHaffety, again in this world. And later, when I was with that poor woman in her agony, it was brought home to me how unworthy is anything but loving kindness among men."

Her husband's anger subsided. He remembered his own agony of that night and, trumpeting loudly into his handkerchief to regain control, he remarked gently, "You are right Mamma. It shall be as you wish."

The McHaffetys graciously and without quibble accepted the eleventh-hour invitation, and added colour to the gathering by the efflorescence of their manners and goodwill. When McHaffety was an old man, and rich, he was heard to exclaim many a time, "Och, with all yer swells and their consequential airs today, there's none like the old Mazeres. Now, there were the real aristocrats for ye, without any of this exclusive pantomime to make themselves important."

The wedding, though the grandest ever seen up the country, was rather overshadowed by the excitement of the flood. Among the old hands, the wedding was ever a synonym for the flood, and vice versa.

The newly married pair had to remain at Three Rivers for two days following the wedding, until punt communication was restored. It was a great hour when Mrs Simon Labosseer finally appeared robed for departure — in dove-grey silk, so the ladies said, with a little bonnet with an exploded crown. This plus flounces and ribbons, and such dodges plain as the alphabet to the women but like Arabic to the men, were remarkably elegant. Enveloped in a voluminous surtout, she stepped into the gig her mother had lent the couple for the journey to Sydney, where they were to have their honeymoon. The gig was drawn by three horses in unicorn formation, which set a new standard for stylishness up the country. There were white ribbon rosettes at the horses' ears, white streamers on the whip and a snow-white rug for the knees. Simon took up the reins as Bill Prendergast pulled out ahead with a cheer: "Good health to the bride! Long life to Mr and Mrs Simon Labosseer!" before riding away to test the new punt and the roads.

A cavalcade of young men and women, well mounted and turned

out, acted as escort to the couple as far as Billings' Half Way House, where Labosseer had ordered a lunch to be in readiness. There they cheered the little bride, excited and half-frightened, and the groom on the first leg of their journey to Sydney. This destination also set a fashion, for not another girl from Bool Bool or its environs had ever yet been to the city.

3

Labosseer took an almost fatherly pride in his bride's delight in the gas-lit streets and fine shops of Sydney, and was liberal about the purchases she made for her family and friends. He was proud of the impression her beauty and spirited bearing made on his friends of the Sydney social elite, and numbers of them promised to visit Rachel as soon as she was settled at Eueurunda, her new home.

Her husband was taking her to no rude bark hut, but a home much like her girlhood one, and with even more amenities. The main dwelling was built of stone, with one or two architectural features of Labosseer's own country. Instead of the usual bull-run passage, a distinguishing feature of colonial dwellings even to this day, there was a decent-sized square hall, off which opened doors and passages, and there were cupboards and shelves to delight any housekeeper. Every room was papered with real wallpaper, there was a full drawing-room suite, and many imported pieces of furniture for the other rooms, including writing desks, bookcases and a sideboard. There were Brussels carpets, real lace curtains, silver candlesticks and, to Rachel's delight, three further surprises, acquisitions that had set the whole neighbourhood agog. The first was a piano, a sweet-toned Broadwood of solid rosewood. It had originally been the gift of a rich London merchant to his only child who, after marrying a wastrel, eventually ended up, husband, furniture and all, in the colonies. Later the wife had been glad to dispose of the piano in order to procure food and clothes. The second surprise was a vehicle, Rachel's very own and the first approach to a carriage in the district. The third was a companion, selected with great care, so that Rachel should not be lonely. Labosseer hoped Mrs Millburn, for that was her name, might also be something of a governess and teach his wife the piano, but in this he was rather failing to take into account the demands of the incessant child-bearing of that generation.

Hopes were high among those few Maneroo families who clung

to the ideals of refined society, despite their primaeval surroundings. A great deal was expected of Labosseer, the former surveyor; he was a man known for his high principles and for the fact that he always behaved like a gentleman, even in camp where he never let drop the class barrier between himself and his men. Much was likewise expected of a Miss Mazere. The fame of Three Rivers had spread far and the legend of the bride's beauty even farther.

4

Rachel always saw her new home, nestling under the brow of a hill crowned with brittle gums, all in bloom, as she came to it over the plains that March afternoon. A swift, clear stream circled the slope before it. Everywhere were flowers and blooming shrubs. The large flocks of sheep of later years had not yet eaten out by the roots the beautiful unnamed species, which now waved to the hub of the wheels among the tussocks and undulated like a glory of coloured waves when the wide-sweeping zephyrs caught them. They curved up to the front gate through the gum trees, their heavenly perfume filling the sunset hour and wreathing itself amongst a million moths, beautiful as butterflies, hovering in the air. The hills rang with the mellow, conversational calls of the magpies.

Rachel was delighted with the flower garden, where Mrs Millburn and a few others waited to welcome her. Among the older settlers, only four families had social standing approaching that of Labosseer. The others were ex-shepherds, ex-stockmen or worse, people with whom Labosseer desired no social intercourse. The four first families of the area were the Gilberts, the Timsons, the Healeys and the McEacherns: of these, in Labosseer's estimation, the nearest, the McEacherns, were also the dearest. Both Mr and Mrs McEachern were waiting to welcome the bride.

"The bonny body, I feared ye might be lonesome," exclaimed Mrs McEachern, folding the little bride to her motherly bosom. "Ah, the wee beauty!"

The McEacherns had brought household supplies in abundance, as the other families had done already, leaving messages that they would be over to see the bride next day. The McEacherns stayed the night, and by the time they left the next morning, Mrs McEachern and Mrs Labosseer were very good friends indeed. The former, as she departed, said, "Ye're to send to me if ye should need me, just as to yer own dear mother whose heart is wi' ye this morning, I'm thinkin'." Thus began a friendship between the families that goes on to this day.

Only a little further away than the McEacherns lived the Pools of Curradoobidgee. Among the gifts awaiting her, Rachel found a generous amount of blackcurrant jam, some eggs, and three hens and a cock, with a kind letter from Mrs Pool in which was the line, "If no one else has thought of chookies I know that these will be useful." The missive concluded: "Unfortunately I am not at all well at present or I should have been at Eueurunda to welcome you."

Rachel was delighted with the fowls, but her husband was not. "To that letter you will not reply, my dear," he said. "Mrs Pool's indisposition is opportune."

"Why? What's the matter with the letter?" asked Rachel.

"You will ignore it because I wish it," he said firmly.

Master in his own house, eh? His pronouncement was not, however, quite as masterful as it seemed, for in those days, as today, men often thought they were masters in their own houses, when all the time their wives were too kind, or too canny, to undeceive them.

CHAPTER IX

1

The wedding successfully past, communication with the outside world re-established and the floodwaters entirely gone, Three Rivers resumed its full and busy routine.

The devastation caused by the flood gave Mazere and his men a great deal of extra work. Since it turned out, in fact, that most of the maize crop had been washed out by the roots or had rotted, a late crop of potatoes and arrowroot was put in to compensate for the loss. Fortunately the new orchard on the higher slopes had not been badly affected, and the women speedily set to to peel and dry the fruit that could be saved, and tie it in bags of strong, unbleached calico in which it swung from the beams of the pantry. There was half a ton of fruit if there was a pound. Immense quantities of jam and pickles were set on great tables, the rough legs of which were set in vessels of water against marauding ants.

Mrs Dr James having taken up her duties again, a reluctant Joseph was bundled off to school. Dr James had been safely yarded up the country by a neighbour of the Mungee Stantons, where another young colonial was expected shortly.

2

Mrs Piper remained in a precarious condition for weeks. She was tenderly nursed and housed by the Brennans, and the children throve in their hospitable surroundings. But their reward to their saviours was to afflict both the Saunders and Brennans not only with a scourge of sandy blight, but also with the measles. Poor Mrs Brennan, in her fifty-first year, became so ill that Mrs Mazere had to go over to The Gap to pull her through.

The measles, even as the Piper baby, smote inopportunely. Mrs Brennan was a devout Catholic and had long looked forward to a district rally of those of her creed, to be conducted by Father O'Kennedy whose family and her own had been neighbours back in County Clare. Father O'Kennedy arrived just after Mrs Brennan's crisis had passed, and when Mary and Bridgit were sickening.

Brennan's Gap was thus closed to the visitor. But there was no other Catholic family of such social standing in the district, and Mrs Brennan refused to allow His Reverence to put up at ex-convict butcher McHaffety's, or at any of the abodes of the shepherds or stockmen. She asked Three Rivers to entertain him, and directed Tim Junior, who had so far escaped the maladies, to ride forth and round up every member of the Bishop's church for the rally. Three Rivers accepted the obligation, as became the hospitable nature of the place.

His Reverence arrived at Three Rivers on Friday night, and sat down to a banquet of fish taken from lines set in the river the evening before. Later, Mr Mazere invited him to assist at family prayers, which he did with *savoir-faire*. Ellen Slattery and Bill Prendergast both had a place of honour beside their priest. When Ellen had first come to Three Rivers, an uncouth shepherd lass, she could neither read nor write and did not even know how to say her prayers. But it had transpired that her father, as a boy, had been of the Catholic persuasion, and so Mrs Mazere procured a book from Mrs Brennan and asked her for some instructions. Every Sunday morning she taught her own children their catechism and read the Bible with them; every Sunday afternoon, after the dishes were washed, she taught Ellen her catechism. For one hour each day she taught her reading and writing and a little figuring.

She was careful to keep each creed separate. That was Mrs Mazere's idea of fair play to a lonely, motherless, ignorant girl. And, indeed, it matters little whether a person is a Gentile or a Jew, a Confucian, a Catholic or a Protestant, since St Peter will sort it all out in the end.

Sunday saw a big congregation at Three Rivers. The whole community was sorry about Maria Brennan's disappointment, which had resulted from her generous neighbourliness, and everyone who could ride or walk the distance turned up to worship, regardless of creed — even Mr and Mrs Isaacs, whose religion was as their name indicates — to do honour to His Reverence and Maria Brennan and Three Rivers and themselves and the cause of neighbourliness. Since not even half the visitors could have fitted into the big dining room, the altar was set up on the wide verandah and people spread all around. Afterwards, every soul was given a hearty meal, of the kind that was euphemistically referred to as "a little light refreshment", from the stores of Three Rivers supplemented by those of Brennan's Gap. Other neighbours had sent a turkey, or a loaf of bread, or a pound of butter, or a cake, or a boiled ham, or a crock of jam, saying "with such a crowd I thought this might come in handy".

His Reverence much enjoyed his stay at Three Rivers, and everyone who came within hearing of his cheery brogue was delighted as he went about his ministry over the next couple of weeks, christening, catechising, chastening, marrying and otherwise administering the sacraments to his flock.

When Tim described to his mother the triumphant proportions of the reception and service at Three Rivers, she sobbed aloud for joy and said as she wiped her eyes, "Musha, musha! There never was, nor could be again, such a woman as me dear Rachel Mazere. Now ye listen to me, Timmy, me boy — when next her heretic Bishop comes to the district, he spends a night, in all honour, at Brennan's Gap, and we'll give him a spread as will open his eyes. Mind now, 'tis yer old mother has set her heart on that same."

She had to wait more than a year, but the Bishop was deeply pleased by the invitation and was delighted to accept. It is part of the history of Bool Bool that he nearly smothered in the Brennans' goose-down bed, famed up the country for its succulent, flocculent proportions, and that he had suffered from dyspepsia for days owing to the surfeit of rich viands pressed upon him by the irresistible Maria. Thereafter it became customary for the chief of the Church of England to spend one night of his visit in great state at Brennan's Gap, and for his colleague to return the courtesy at Three Rivers. This tradition continued for as long as dear Maria and her good Timothy remained at The Gap; and when, of the four old neighbours, Rachel Mazere alone remained, the visiting Catholic clergy could not have omitted paying a stately call at Three Rivers without causing a break in established custom.

3

Emily was agitating for a visit to Mungee, ostensibly to keep her sister Isabel company. She hoped to get from there across the ranges to see Rachel in her grand new home. Before her departure from Three Rivers, Louisa Pool had rapturously invited her to Curradoobidgee and had made a plea to Mrs Mazere. But Mrs Mazere had said that it could not be thought of for the present. Charlotte afterwards warned Louisa that such a visit would not be acceptable to Mr Mazere, and the girls were dashed. It had not, however, prevented them from discussing possibilities in the big double bed upstairs at night.

"You see," Louisa had said, "Bert and I could just nick down to Mungee and bring you on from there, as easy as taking snuff."

Emily saw precisely. Her imagination was hazy as to the outlines of Maneroo but she could clearly visualise herself and Bert Pool riding across the ridges and plains. She could even see what she would be wearing on the journey, and would place a ribbon or flower to her cheek half a dozen times a day and enjoy the effect.

Each month saw her blossoming into fuller womanhood, a fact which Tim Brennan Senior remarked upon after the wedding. "Sure Emily will be the belle now. She knocks Rachel into a cocked hat already. Faith, I never could see what there was in Rachel to raise such a dust about. Sure, her hair was dark, and she never lookin' anythin' but a child!"

"Oh, but her lovely little nose and mouth..." said Mary.

"But it was all too little. Take Emily now, there's some proportions to her. Sure ye can see her without a microscope."

"Like yer old Maria," laughed his spouse.

"Sure! And all that yaller hair makes her look like an angel."

"That's what I think too," agreed Tim Junior fervently. "Emily is the prettiest girl in the district, bar none."

"It's not for ye to be thinkin' on that, me boy; ye should be castin' yer peepers where religion will be no obstacle to consummation," said his father. Young Tim's long, freckled face flamed at having inadvertently revealed what all the other young people had seen for months.

Emily was taller and more voluptuous of form than Rachel, and her big blue eyes, profuse golden curls and bright cheeks were so arresting that observers tended to overlook the irregularity of her features — the rather *retroussé* nose, the heavy chin with the dimple in it. This last feature she had inherited from her father, but where it lent obstinacy to his face, in hers it suggested good nature. She had a wide mouth and splendidly even, white teeth that looked well when she laughed, which was frequently, for she was an easygoing, generous-spirited girl, popular with old and young alike.

Baulked for the time being in her determination to get to Maneroo by way of Mungee or some other route, she set her hopes on Bert reappearing at Three Rivers through the auspices of Charlotte. Little did Emily realise that Rachel's presence in his own neighbourhood had disinclined the boy to roam. Emily had to content herself for the present with a high-pressure correspondence with Louisa, which could be carried on under cover of Charlotte. That Charlotte never commented on the missives enclosed in her own was instinctive rather than premeditated. Hard at work and absorbed in her own worries, she gave little thought to the gush of the girls, though even had she done so, she would have seen nothing to upbraid in either of the girls' dreams.

4

Rachel's first letter from Eueurunda was awaited impatiently by her family. When it arrived, it was quite a budget. She described her trip to Sydney to Emily and her home to her mother. She even sent separate little letters to Charlotte, Joseph, Fannie, Philip and Rhoda. At the end of her letter to Charlotte was a postscript:

> Would you please tell your stepmother when you write that I thank her heartily for the eggs and lovely blackcurrant jam, and more than all for the cock and hens, which are a blessing.

If Rachel had to send all around the world to her in order to thank her stepmother, then, thought Charlotte, it was clear that Labosseer was going to have none of the Pools at Eueurunda. The realisation wounded her gentle heart, but she made no sign.

Mazere was delighted with Rachel's letter to him. She had always been his favourite child, owing to her resemblance to her mother.

My dear Papa,

I am very happy in my new home with my dear husband who gives me everything I wish, but I miss you, dear Papa, and everyone at dear old Three Rivers terribly. I do wish that you would come and stay with me soon...

Clearly feeling brave at a distance, and now, as a soundly established matron, her postscript ran thus:

I hope, dearest Papa, as you promised to me that dreadful night when dear Mamma was in such terrible danger, that you have not forgotten to write to Philip and ask him to come back to us all soon.

In fact, Mazere was glad to receive this little jog to his memory. He had long felt that Philip's banishment was ridiculous, particularly since the cause of it had been a treasured member of his household for several years. And despite his prejudice against the male Pools, he had long ago recognised that Charlotte had the worst of the matrimonial bargain. To reinstate his firstborn as an act of thanksgiving for the safe return of his wife was a graceful way out of an untenable situation, but he had for some time been thinking it was not quite an honest bargain; now he meant to bestow upon Charlotte a dress length or two of the best silk to be had, and some article of jewellery as well.

He took his wife to his office in the Big House and gave her Rachel's letter to peruse. When she looked up, he said, "Mamma, the upheavals of the flood and the wedding have combined to delay me, but I should very much like to have Philip back again. I should be obliged if you would write to him of my decision."

Mrs Mazere gave thanks and went to tell Charlotte. Charlotte, never effusive, was too moved for speech.

"Write a letter at once, my dear daughter, and tell him to come as soon as he can," urged Mrs Mazere.

"Tell him," said Mazere to Charlotte a little later, "that his mother and I shall go with you to Gundagai to meet him. Then we'll come back with Bill Prendergast and you can have the gig to yourselves — it will be a honeymoon for you." Nothing if not impulsive, he suddenly blurted out, "You've been a good daughter to us, Charlotte my girl, and I shall make everything happy and comfortable for you and Philip now."

Charlotte withdrew, overcome, and Mazere, well pleased with himself, mixed himself a nobbler of toddy, of which he was growing very fond. Mrs Mazere, knowing how it would be with Charlotte, slipped out to her quarters and, clasping the girl to her, wept in company.

"I have prayed for this day — and it has come at last! You write and I'll write too, and we shall have the dear boy home before we know it."

But a shadow had fallen across the girl's face. "He mightn't come," she said slowly. There had been a different note in Philip's letters of the last year. It had filled Charlotte with an uneasiness that she had not passed on to his family.

"We must forgive his father for his short temper — for your sake, tell him, and his old mother's. Children must honour their parents, or they can never hope to prosper."

"I have been thinking for some time now of going to him," said Charlotte. "I think that would be the best plan, now that Papa has forgiven him."

"One step at a time — write to him first. Then we shall see what happens," said Mrs Mazere, her face radiant.

Apprehensive about Philip's reaction to his father's change of heart, Charlotte found the writing of the letter a formidable task. However, she expressed herself with a brevity that lacked neither clarity nor affection, which in one sense made her an aristocrat of letter writers.

The eagerly awaited reply was of such character that Charlotte did not show it to either of Philip's parents. He said they could go to blazes. He also said he had been very ill and had not yet been able to return to work. He asked Charlotte to come and live on the diggings with him.

Charlotte dwelt only on the fact that he had been ill, and that she must go to him.

"By all means — go and fetch him home," said Mazere expansively. "That is reasonable and becoming in a wife."

Charlotte prepared for her departure with so distinct a feeling of liberation that she suddenly realised that she had been something of a bond-maiden in the house of her husband's people, rather than enjoying the dignity of a married woman. All the comfort and kindliness she was leaving seemed nothing when weighed against the adventure and freedom which was beckoning her, and she was glad at the prospect of finding out how Philip really was.

She decided to take baby James with her and to leave young Philip with his grandparents and aunts, with whom he was a great favourite.

"You won't want to be burdened with a child on such a terrible journey. You can surely trust the baby to me, too," said Mrs Mazere.

"I'd like to take baby, Mamma," she said quietly. "I'm very strong. I can tuck him in my shawl like the black gins do their piccaninnies if I'm pushed. Philip has never even seen him," she added.

"Dear me, neither he has!" exclaimed Mr Mazere, getting up and taking the child, who liked to ride-a-cock-horse on his grandfather's knee. "Never seen your daddy. Hi diddle, diddle! Of course, my girl, you must take him to meet his daddy and bring him home. I'll give you an extra ten pound note to buy him a jacket. Hi diddle diddle! Now don't pull Gran'daddy's nose — listen to the tick-tick!"

Mrs Mazere said Charlotte was not to travel alone with a child, and that Ellen Slattery, who had long wanted to discover if her husband were dead or merely deserting, should accompany her. But when Charlotte was alone with her mother-in-law, she opened up her heart a little.

"Supposing that Philip is stubborn about his father, or has the gold fever so badly that he won't come home for a year or two — then it would just fit that Ellen could bring little Philip to me later."

"But, my girl, you must do everything in your power to bring him home and make his peace with his father."

"Of course, Mamma, but it's best to be prepared. I shan't say anything to anyone but you."

"Very well, we shall leave it like that and not upset Papa when he has come round so generously."

Charlotte did not expect to return at an early date. Philip had a streak of his father's pig-headedness. Charlotte knew what she feared and feared what she knew. Ellen was disappointed not to be going as well, but was buoyed up by the expectation of a possible summons later.

Charlotte was not to attempt the overland route to Mount Alexander. She was to go to Sydney by coach, and there be met and taken to Petty's Hotel by Matthew Freeborn, a brother of Mrs

Mazere, who had not forsaken his native district of Parramatta. She did not set out till April, when the cooler weather promised safer travel for the baby.

5

The drays carrying winter supplies for Three Rivers reached the Yarrabongo punt the evening before her departure. The camp fires of the teamsters gleamed in the bend of the river on the flats, and the bullock bells combined with the orchestra of frogs and crickets with which the earth seemed to pulsate.

On reaching the homestead, the teamsters began to unload early next morning. The arrival of the winter supplies was always a time of bustle for the household. Delightful it was to stow away the cases of currants and raisins, and the bags of white sugar and rice in the big ant- and mice-proof bins in the store room. Then there were great chests of tea with queer Chinese characters on the strange paper wrapping, with splendid linings of lead which later, after being melted down in a crucible and poured into a mould, would be made into bullets. There were sugar mats by the dozen, full of rich brown treacly sugar, delicious to taste and smell, which would be rationed out weekly to the station hands.

The tons of flour and rock salt were stored in the broad, sound lofts of the awnings that joined the various edifices of the homestead. Everything had to be carried up ladders, and the men engaged in a Herculean journey. Their clothes and persons were soon white with flour, these the only white beards in all the countryside. They laughed and boasted and challenged and bet and let out oaths, and even Mr Mazere took up one or two sacks to show he was still in his prime, for by such tokens was a man appraised in those days up the country. He could not be great by delegation alone.

But big Bullocky Bill from Mungee could toss a sack of flour as easily as other men could one of rice or sugar, smoking his malodorous cutty all the while with showy indifference, and he was honoured as the man of the hour. Bullocky, with the tailend of his glance, wished to discover if he was making the right impression on Ellen, a matter of some mystery considering the obliquity of her eyes. Cornstalk Bill Prendergast was only too sure and, as a corrective, strutted out with two sacks and suffered from the twist he gave his loins for many a day. He cursed duty which called him abroad that afternoon. Even so, the coach was nearly an hour late in starting.

There was a pungent smell of healthy sweat from bullocks and men alike, and of spices and foul tobacco, and of bread that was baking in the cavernous oven, and of delicious quince jam that was boiling in a veritable witches' cauldron of a three-legged pot, and of hops that were brewing for the bottles of yeast that sat in a row above the fireplace in company with the smoothing irons and various canisters. The several dray wheels were cutting up the well-swept back yards, and Blossom, Strawberry, Bally, Poley, Boko, Spot, Snowball, Beauty, Blue, Speckle, Darling, *et al*, chewed their cud and switched the vicious March and other flies from their broad, long-suffering backs and dreamed of a winter's peace beyond Mungee, but dreamed in vain; for the fashion of fencing on a grand scale was just looming over the ranges, and the bullocks were, in the dry frosty spells of the winter, henceforth to be dedicated to the business of transporting sawn and split timber about the primaeval forests of the new world.

The women waited eagerly for the unloading of the cases of crockery, the men's slop clothing, the bolts of material and the medicines and seeds, Mrs Mazere being particularly vigilant that small things like camphor, castor oil, pepper, cloves and spices in general should not go astray. Mr Mazere was eager for his negro head and his books. Even grey calico, needles, thread and buttons — more beautiful and varied than the buttons of today — had a grand charm in such circumstances. The little ones crowed with glee when the tins of barley sugar candy appeared. Joseph had prevailed upon his parents for a holiday from school and found the unloading of the stores a more thrilling occasion than the opening of the first Federal Parliament by the Duke and Duchess of York, which he would witness in his fifties.

Charlotte had not been away from Three Rivers since her arrival. She had not even been to Mungee or Nanda. She had settled deeply into the homestead routine, and her heart was wrung to be suddenly uprooted and facing the prospect of a long journey into unknown territory. But she did not give way to her feelings even when, just before she climbed into the gig, she finally kissed little Philip, all sticky with his share of the barley sugar. She was one of those strong, calm people who move through life like the seasons.

Mr Mazere was driving her as far as Gundagai. As they rattled away, she looked back at the dear group standing at the back gate till the gig dipped into the hollow where grew the tall, waxen-petalled, purple violets. Then down the slope to the punt and on again, along the long natural road where the waters had lain a few weeks back and where now the rich soil rose in a suffocating cloud of dust, till they disappeared, a speck upon the distant ridge.

Emily watched till the last, with sobs and a sense of desolation. How was she now to write so fully to Louisa? Because she had complained about the prospect of being lonely after Rachel's departure, Papa had promised to bring back with him Martha Spires, the daughter of the Land Commissioner from Gundagai, for a visit. But Emily's complaints had been intended to take her to Maneroo, not to bring the companionship of Martha, which would not increase the chances of seeing Bert.

6

Philip scorned the loving letters that Charlotte bore from his parents. ''Tell him to go to hell and keep his old corn patch. It's only a few acres shut in by a barren kangaroo run,'' he said roughly. The glamour of the renowned John Bull nugget, weight forty-five pounds, was bemusing his vision. He instructed Charlotte to inform his parents of his sentiments, but Charlotte's natural diplomacy and kindliness kept her from obeying him. Her letter ran thus:

Dear Papa and Mamma,

The baby and I have got here at last. It was hard to find Philip but people here are very kind. Philip has been more ill than I can say in a letter and is a shadow of himself. You would not know him. He had to send his mate to meet me as he is not well yet after inflammation of the lungs. The diggings are quieter in the winter so I must take care of the dear boy and get him strong and then he may be ready to go home. At present he says no. He is disappointed that I did not bring Philip too. It is very rough here, all the trees cut down and nothing anywhere but shafts like wells, and tents. There are plenty of things in the stores, which are big tents or humpys of bark with flags on top to show if they are English or Russian or some other nation. Some things are very scarce and nearly everything terribly dear. Honey is 3/6 a pound. How I wish I had some of the honey from dear old Three Rivers. I think the storekeepers strike it more lucky than the diggers because their job is steady. I wish I had some of

102

Mamma's fowls and eggs and butter here. I could make a fortune then. Cheese is 4/6 a pound; sugar 1/6; rice 1/-; coffee and tea 3/-; tobacco 8/-; salt 1/6; candles 1/6. It is light come, light go, with the diggers as far as I can see.

Philip has not struck it very lucky yet, but he was doing fairly well till he got sick. He has lost all his hair with the fever, but I hope it will grow again soon. I have to do my washing in a bucket and have only one pot for cooking and a pan. I sent you one letter about Sydney and another about the trip in the ship and Melbourne.

I'll write more as soon as I am settled. I have begun to ask about Ellen's husband and will let her know the minute I hear anything.

Charlotte could have said a great deal more but least said, soonest mended was her governing principle. Yet even her brave heart had quailed when she first beheld Philip. It was not just the dilapidated tent and the filthy blanket laid on a sheet of bark that served as a bed which dismayed her. In days gone by, the Curradoobidgee dwelling had been painfully primitive, and many a gently reared settler even two generations later was still familiar with a bark bed. It was Philip himself.

His eyes were bloodshot and red-rimmed following the fly blight which had smitten the diggers that summer, and he was as bald as an ostrich egg. Of the wealth of yellow curls once just like Emily's, there remained only the veriest rim around his nape, dried and dull as corn-stubble. Some of his front teeth were missing, knocked out in a drunken brawl, and he had grown rough in his language and careless in his person. There was little resemblance to the gentle young man who had issued forth from Three Rivers with toothbrush and night clothes, and who had regularly said his prayers before bed.

Charlotte put the tent to rights and set up a second. With her splendid strength and energy, she soon organised her life and felt pleased that Philip was not returning to Three Rivers for the present. She sang as she made herself a little garden of wild flowers, and sent back to Three Rivers for seeds for a vegetable garden. Her tents became a social centre for the better-educated diggers who liked to talk politics with Philip. She added two or three more tents, took boarders and did mending, and when a successful digger who was the proud possessor of a hut went away and "blew" his pile in Melbourne, she took over that abode and soon had curtains on its little window.

The diggings charmed Charlotte, as they did the majority of the stockmen, shepherds, sailors and other settlers who spent time there. In those days, before the advent of self-analysis, the diggers bothered little to explain the attraction of the goldfields, but, in fact, the isolation of the pioneer's life had a great deal to do with it. The countryman has always been mesmerised by town lights and the entertainment of the fair. In this respect he has ever been a child, seeking fairyland. If the countryman is thus attracted to the tinsel of town, the metropolitan denizen can rarely be weaned from it, for man is a gregarious animal.

And so, though it was the gambling instinct that lured men to the diggings on the chance of "striking it rich" and by one magic stroke raising themselves to affluence and positions of respect, it was their starved instincts of sociability that kept them there, shrinking from the return to isolation.

Charlotte had none of the gold fever. She saw far more clearly the ninety-nine chances against the possibility of striking it rich than the one in favour. She thought it unlikely that Philip would find a John Bull nugget or otherwise make his pile, but she had chosen him for himself, when he had been disinherited of all save a charming person, and she was not going to go back on him now that he was bald and ugly. Some creative instinct in women enables them to be forever hopeful of finding a grain of genius in the chaff of men's lunacy, so Charlotte let Philip go ahead in his own way. She went ahead too.

She saw at once that fortunes were to be made out of the community of diggers much more surely than out of the shafts. If she had had the capital, she would have started a store. Even so, she began in a small way and, being scrupulously honest, was a general favourite, but therefore not making such wild profits as some others. She made and sold soft drinks and green fly veils, the latter which the diggers used for the purpose of trying to keep the flies out their mouths and nostrils. She was paid in gold and, when she had a certain amount, she would deliver it to the Commissioner, who weighed it in her presence and gave her a receipt. At first Philip objected to her activities; in the tradition of Three Rivers, he hated his wife to be the servant of other men. But it seemed that the diggings were breaking down the class snobbery that had been transplanted so successfully from the Old World. To mollify her husband, Charlotte explained that she was only doing a little to help pay the expenses of bringing little Philip to the diggings with Ellen, as soon as they heard anything of Slattery. After a while Philip was reconciled to her work, and did not even inquire about how much she was accumulating.

She soon found herself preferring the diggings to Three Rivers; at least, the hardship of her new life prevented monotony. In fact, the whole experience was a wonderful adventure to her, and had been from the hour she had left the drays unloading at Three Rivers. She had been well looked after in Sydney by kindly, middle-class Uncle Matthew and Aunt Jane Freeborn, themselves finding Petty's Hotel a little overawing, and the duty of seeing Charlotte aboard the ship for Port Phillip a great adventure. Then followed the voyage, the equivalent for Charlotte of travelling to another planet, and her arrival in due time at Frank Liardet's pub where she awaited Askew, her husband's mate. The harbour, crowded with shipping, the bustle of city life, the splendour of Liardet's sitting room with its mahogany dining table and chairs, its blaze of mirrors and beautiful barmaid, quite dazzled the bush-bred Charlotte.

Then there was Askew, her husband's mate, who overwhelmed her with gallantry. He instantly became enamoured of Charlotte and would willingly have led her astray, but Charlotte was too inexperienced to come to any harm. She thought his overtures effusive and embarrassing, but accepted them as town manners, and Askew, unable to make headway, was further intrigued. Charlotte had been anxious to reach a husband so unwell that he could only send a deputy, but Askew was not to be done out of a day or two in Melbourne — and as much of Charlotte's company as possible. To delay their departure, he pretended urgent business during the day and took her to a circus in the evening. Charlotte was unbelievably thrilled by the gaiety, the beauty and the exploits, and also by the presence of certain "ladies" smoking cutties like the men, and flaunting themselves like — like — she knew not what. So these unbelievable creatures, of whom she had only heard faint echoes, really did exist, and their materialisation was terrifyingly thrilling.

The journey from Melbourne to the diggings presented no difficulties to one of her experience, and the gallantries of Askew lent it unusual excitement, in spite of her innocence.

It was the country-fair element of the great encampment that held her attention as she picked her way among the roisterous, card-playing, yarn-spinning, drinking men. The drunkenness was startling to Charlotte. The Pool family was unacquainted with alcohol, and though Mazere had his glass of toddy in the evenings or when he had a cold or feared he might take a chill from a wetting, it had not prepared her for such sights as she witnessed here. But the roughness did not distress her, and the constant, senseless firing off of every sort of gun when the men came above ground and lit a thousand fires at dusk, reminded her of home. Bert's blowfly proficiency had not been attained without constant practice, and, it might be said, the testing of her nerves by his many dangerous feats of marksmanship.

Philip was happy to have her with him and was soon considerably recovered from the fly-blight and the effects of the fever. He worked steadily, turning out gold at a rate equivalent to very good wages. With the companionship of his wife, his Three Rivers habits were somewhat restored. He rejoiced in the presence of his little boy and was anxious to have the other child brought to join them. Charlotte, in this first married home of her own, experienced a satisfaction which all the usefulness and order of her career at Three Rivers had not afforded. She was very busy with her domestic and commercial pursuits and she had an unabating interest in the canvas stores. Lovely to her were the flags flying above each magazine, denoting the nationality of the merchant — English, German, French, even Russian. She liked the riotous wealth of their contents, where sugar candy jostled Bass's Pale Ale, where anchovies dripped on to flour, and where tinned salmon and East India pickles, ankle jackboots, ladies' stays, babies' caps, tin plates shining like mirrors, raisins, tallow candles and herrings were often intermixed. Everything was procurable from a pick to a compass, and Charlotte saw lump sugar for the first time.

She wrote that Slattery had been on the Turon with Philip, but had left before him for Bendigo and Mount Alexander. She was making inquiries and would let Ellen know the minute they had any news.

So Mrs Mazere, away back at Three Rivers, read between the lines that the young people were quite contented where they were. But Philip's tardiness in accepting reinstatement fretted his impulsive and impatient father.

CHAPTER X

1

When Major-General Sir Oswald Raymond Mazere-Poole, K.C.B., M.P., the grandson of old "Boko" Pool, became desirous of a genealogical tree, he laid stress on the Mazere part of his cognomen. It was, by rights, one of his Christian names, but after the war, gaining his title and being elected to Parliament on the strength of his uniform, some conservative platitudes and the reverence in which the diggers' exploits on the battlefields were held, a hyphen, which no one dared dispute, crept into his name.

In accentuating the Mazere relationship and minimising the Pool, he was clearly a snob. Further, he was ignorant, but that was not his fault. The real founder of his fortunes was his grandmother, old Boko Pool's second wife, *née* Harriet Mayborn, and it was her name which should have held highest honour in the Major-General's family chart and which should have been repeated in family christenings. But, since one of the reasons for Harriet Mayborn's amazing marriage with old Boko Pool had been to consign that dishonoured name to oblivion, he was never to know of that branch of his lineage. His very existence, ultimately to climb to a position of importance in public life, originated in a miracle of which Harriet Pool was the author.

When the nine-days wonder of the Labosseers' arrival at Eueurunda had subsided, Mrs Pool provided the next sensation. The indisposition which had prevented her from welcoming the Labosseers to Eueurunda and which Simon Labosseer had considered opportune, was occasioned by nothing less than the approach of a half-brother or sister for Charlotte, Bert and the other Pools.

That the old maid swell English governess should so commit herself to the common humanities with old Boko Pool — that was news indeed!

"Begor' she's every minute of sixty!" said Larry Healey of Little River, which was exaggeration. She was barely fifty. Even so, seasoned matrons with ten or a dozen offspring usually went out of practice about forty-five, thankful that God's malignity to women did not often run north of that age. From Cooma to Goulburn and back to Michelago and Yass, the men exchanged ribald titbits about the approaching event, for men take an illogical pleasure in the exchange of obscenities about the basic facts of birth, and usually accuse women of a deficient sense of humour if they fail to be similarly amused.

So while the men guffawed, Mrs McEachern of Gowandale, the doyenne of women in her orbit even as Rachel Mazere was in hers, said to her circle, "It might go hard with the poor body, the first time at such an age," and, without waiting to be asked, she went to her neighbour and promised to do all she could when the time came. The time came in due course and was monstrous cruel, and Mrs McEachern had to send for her friend, Mrs Timson of Wombat Hill, for assistance. It looked for a week or so as though a funeral would be the next important happening on Maneroo, but with Mrs Timson, Mrs McEachern and Mrs Pool all setting their wills against such an outcome, not only little Raymond but also his mother were saved to adorn this tale.

The infant wrought a miracle in the lives of his parents. Before she was out of bed, Mrs Pool had planned that child's career. He was to receive his early training from her, thence to King's College, Parramatta, and on to the newly instituted university at Sydney. One might have thought that she would prefer to send him to Oxford, but this would have involved the opening of the sarcophagus of her past. In this blessed new country, she could safely give her child the best that it afforded.

It was at that date that the Pools began to write their name with an "e", so Sir Oswald may be said to have honestly inherited his pretensions in that regard.

2

The general suspicion that old Pool must have been sent out was well founded. His only crime, however, had been that of ignorance. Son of an English farm labourer wretchedly poor, he and some lads from his village had sallied forth on foot one night to see the lights of Liverpool. They had chanced to reach there at the time of a disturbance and, running to see what the crowd was about, they had been rounded up and sentenced to transportation to the colonies. What chance had the bewildered boy — penniless, friendless, rooted up? Illiterate, how could he know in what letter his name ended? He gave it as Jim Pool. Poor writing on the part of some clerk made it Jim Peel and, as such, he was assigned to a Scottish settler beyond the Cole River. Here, with nothing and no one to tie to, he lived in a kind of hard loneliness which confirmed his natural tendency towards silence. For lack of the most elementary medical attention, he even lost an eye. But he learned a great deal about sheep and cattle, and about trades useful to a settler, and he became as well acquainted with the bush as an Aboriginal. Shy, untutored, but industrious and dependable, he worked his sentence out without mishap, and, when free, became a stockman for a settler near Berrima. Here, in time, he married and was allowed to run his stock with that of his master. As soon as he had the means, he went up the country to Maneroo and began to find his feet a little as a stockman and bushman.

He never volunteered the story of his youth to his family, nor did they ask for it. His wife taught her children all she knew herself — that is, the Lord's Prayer and the alphabet. Much later, he raised no objection to Bert's and Charlotte's cultural campaign, and their introduction of Miss Mayborn, who took possession in a way as unexpected and unbelievable to herself as to Pool.

Thus he progressed. His first wife, poor soul, had been heroic but unavailing; his children had come like facts of nature. But now in his later years, when parents go soft about their offspring, he had a wonderful little doll smelling of scented soap and done up in clothes about three feet longer than they needed to be.

Inspired by the marvel of his new life, he suggested at this time that he should be taught to write his name. Though he had little conceit, he was endowed with a workable vein of vanity, which quality can be manipulated as a powerful force for development, for good or bad. When his fellow squatters signed their names to petitions or other documents, he had to make excuses or be humiliated by making only a mark (though there he was in the company of his much more pretentious neighbour, Healey of Little River).

His wife readily entered upon this adventure. He learned the alphabet, to spell short words and to sign his name as Jas. Poole, tractably accepting the "e". Of the many mysteries of his life, the matter of being called Peel during his convict days had been a small one. When he was free, he went back to Pool. Now he was Poole — with an "e". Thus there is no connection between Jim Peel, assigned labourer on the Cole River, and James Poole, eventually to be a highly respected squatter on Maneroo. And that is as it should be, and what unjust Fate owed him.

The fuss about Mrs Labosseer's carriage — the first four-wheeled vehicle to be seen up the country beyond Goulburn — led Mrs Poole to suggest to her husband that they should perhaps progress beyond the packhorse stage. Her stepchildren would never have described her as a rider, but they had taught her to get about on a horse, which she found very tiring. Poole was inspired to secure the first buckboard, or light wagonette, ever seen off a coach line in those parts. And whereas Mrs Labosseer's trap had but two horses, Bert, his father and young Jimmy had fine sport in breaking some of the three-parts brumbies from the head of Little River and eventually appearing with a dashing four-in-hand. It was a cheerful sight to see old Poole swinging his fiery leaders — better still it was to see their swift heels tearing up tufts as they rattled the vehicle at a hand gallop across the flower-strewn plains where they had been foaled.

Before the advent of baby Raymond, Mrs Poole had been content to find her outlet in books, on which Poole was ever ready to spend money. And money there was to spend now that the discovery of gold had put the colony on its feet following the stricken years at the beginning of the previous decade. She had found more pleasure in reading than in associating with people who lacked the social refinements she had been accustomed to. Now, suddenly, everything was different and she embarked upon a social campaign which she meant to win. No colonial clique was to be barred from her son, without his mother knowing the reason why. In fact, her neighbours unaffectedly acknowledged her as more than their equal. Her illness had brought her in close contact with the McEacherns and Timsons, and with her stepdaughter married to Philip Mazere, and with Louisa and Bert guests at the famous Labosseer-Mazere wedding at Three Rivers, the principals of which were now ensconced at Eueurunda, the most aristocratic establishment in that part of the country, there would have seemed to be no question about the matter.

But Simon Labosseer was still against any connection with Curradoobidgee. Some years before he had been a good deal in the Maneroo district as a surveyor, and at that date the Pooles had not been reclaimed by Miss Mayborn nor were yet connected with the Mazeres. The place had been alive with tales of old Poole, some of them exaggerated out of admiration of his feats as a bushman, some developing simply because, in his ignorance and distrust of his fellows, he kept to himself.

3

In those days, and for a couple of generations afterwards, there were a number of herds of clean-skinned horses and cattle at the head of the Muniong watershed. These had sprung from beasts, some of them blood stock, that had escaped from settlers in the early days and had made their way to the fastnesses of the wild and well-watered country. Here they throve and multiplied, with no enemy but the dingoes who would sometimes attack the newborn, and occasional severe winters. The blacks had early retreated from that locality, so there was no threat from them. There were fine beasts to be had by anyone up to the undertaking, though practically none were, save Jim Poole and Larry Healey of Little River. A man had to be familiar with the inaccessible gullies and gorges of the region to which the stock retreated when pursued, and he had to be able to ride like thunder on a locally bred horse. No horse from down the country was safe on those hills, the haunt of wombats and lyrebirds, or in the boggy lick-hole country with its myriad springheads.

Poole devised a way of baiting the lick-holes with salt. And in severe winters, when the wild horses stood knee-deep in the snow, he snared them in winged stockyards baited with hay. The Curradoobidgee stockyards were famous as the best and most extensive up the country. The outer fence, of four well-pegged, broad rails and a cap, was seven feet high, a veritable jail from which few beasts escaped. Poole Senior was the King Billy of the stock-riders on Maneroo, and tales of the hell-for-leather mustering, branding and drafting feats that took place there in his prime have been handed

111

down by the old hands to the present day.

Gossip was concerned with the constant replenishing of Poole's herds with blood strains which tempered the long-horned, raw-boned frames of the early bovine settlers that had come from South Africa. The brumbies owed a similar debt to more than one racing stallion or mare escaped from stud, and which had never been recaptured. Rumour had it that these escapes were assisted by Poole who, if he saw a bull or stallion heading for the wild runs, would speed them on their way. Though he was never seen with beasts with any but his own brand, he was certainly the possessor of their progeny. And he had a strange quirk of thriftiness that led him to take home the hobbles or sidelines of the escapees, though he never needed a fortieth of them. They accumulated behind his stables as a further damning indictment. The children never questioned their origin, any more than they did the presence of the wart on their father's neck. Philip Mazere had seen them and did not like their presence, but the charm and worth of Charlotte had made him overlook them. Larry Healey knew of them and was wide of mouth about it, so the rumour was well established on Maneroo in the pre-Mayborn days.

Larry Healey was of very different character to Poole. In fact, people trusted him even less, but Healey was a sociable being, as was his wife, while Poole had a poor sickly wife and lived in a primitive hut from which his unkempt children fled like frightened turkeys on the rare occasions that visitors called. Larry was a much more complex person. He might have come from anywhere, people admitted, and there were strange rumours connected with him, but he endeavoured to keep up his end in the public eye. His wife was a dashing sort of woman and, though she never introduced any new refinement into the area, no neighbour became the possessor of an amenity but that she didn't quickly follow suit, whether it was a piano or a crinoline. Healey's herds increased at a rate never contemplated by the soberer Poole, and his brands were frequently questionable, but he was dead careful never to bring home more hobble chains than he could actually use.

Let it be frankly admitted that when Poole found blood beasts making for the Head of the Rivers, he wasn't above releasing them from sidelines or hobbles. Dishonesty is not to be excused, but this equivocation was understandable in one so hard done by as Poole. It is also a fact that most great trading companies and businesses arise by "doing" or diddling someone, whether they be Aboriginals or new chums. New ways are not cut by those who stand too nicely on ceremony, and Poole was a real pioneer. Perhaps he was like the maize or potatoes put in to scourge unfriable virgin land, while Mazere represented the more domesticated species, such as fruits and flowers, which follow on after the track is blazed.

However, there it was. Poole remained silent and in the background, while Healey industriously circulated stories against him, which Labosseer, during his time as a surveyor, came to hear. Healey warned Labosseer that his horses would not be safe on Maneroo unless they were picketed to his own feet. Then Labosseer lost a favourite blood mare and Larry Healey rode with him for two days, pretending to seek her while he himself had "planted" her. He was like to suffocate from the joke, with no one but Mrs Healey in whom to confide.

"By me troth, ye'll never catch her this season," he had said to Labosseer, "without Boko Poole is set on her tracks — and devil a morsel of use that would be to anyone but himself."

When surveyor Labosseer left the district, Healey rode the mare openly, explaining that he had bought her from the surveyor. Much later, it was Healey's idea of a joke that led him to offer the old mare's filly as a hack for Mrs Labosseer. Healey played that trick on many people who considered him a friend. Poole never behaved in such a manner. As in the case of Mazere's shorthorn bull, he gave his aid generously, if it was required, and generally successfully. By the time Harriet Mayborn became Mrs Poole, he and Bert had long since retired from anything questionable in relation to their stock, in the same way as men who become savants or prime ministers are commonly on record as having retired from robbing apple orchards. Poole had been cleaned up and tamed domestically, and the Pooles were well liked by their neighbours. Labosseer could not have continued to hold out if certain other events had not come to pass.

CHAPTER XI

1

The squattocracy of Maneroo was disturbed at that time by the appearance of several families who took up runs on the outward fringes of Healey's Little River station and Poole's Curradoobidgee, which met in rough and inaccessible country, known as Eagle Hawk Gullies, to the south. It was whispered that these people were not only escaped convicts but also practising bushrangers, and it quickly became clear, in fact, that at the very least they were out-and-out horse and cattle duffers. They had no visible means of support save a few horses and cattle, the numbers of which fluctuated too rapidly to be legitimate. Barney Logan and Sandy Burn, who appeared to be the leaders, purported to do a little stock dealing, but it was believed that this was merely a cover for their criminal activities, for they rode about the country without ever applying themselves to a potato or wheat patch, or to the planting of orchards and vegetable gardens, usually the first concern of genuine settlers. When they set up a house of accommodation in the most unlikely, out-of-the-way place, their neighbours had more than a suspicion that it was a sly-grog shanty and a fly-trap for the unwary.

Logan had a very pretty daughter who was the bait here. He also had a wife about whom many strange things were said — amongst which were that he had won her in a bet, and that she was not married to him because he had a legal wife whom he had sold to a former mate for a brace of revolvers and a five-gallon keg of rum. His ex-wife and his former mate, it was said, were now wealthy squatters out towards Goulburn.

Later events will prove whether this was a fanciful story or no, but there was no fancy about the vigilance that became necessary to keep flocks and herds intact. For Bert Poole, Malcolm McEachern and Dennis Healey, who were inseparable cronies and who knew every corner of Eagle Hawk Gullies — it having been their playground since ever each could bestride a horse — one glance at a cow, colt or beast was sufficient for them to make an affidavit as to its dam or sire. For them, brands were usually a superfluous means of identification. They were not to be deceived by any beast or bird that ran, flew, swam, crawled or burrowed in those environs.

A confrontation was inevitable following their discovery of a sheepskin with the McEachern brand on it on a log near Logan's shanty. They proceeded directly to Logan's with the pelt and, as the place was empty and unguarded, they spread it before the door and wrote thereupon in charcoal:

SHEEP   STEALERS
AND   CATTLE   DUFFERS
WILL   BE   LAGGED   AGAIN

Then they rode home very pleased with their work, arriving at Healey's for supper. After they recounted their tale, Dennis taking the lead, his father broke out in a veritable sweat. "For the good of yer souls, boys, leave the Eagle Hawk Gullies crowd alone."

"We were only giving them a bit of a hint," said Dennis.

"Sure, and they'll take that as a hint to burn ye out, maybe. Sure a bad neighbour is worse than a mad dog. Shootin' him's the only cure, and ye'll swing for that — meself, I'd like to swing for something prettier than old Logan or Sandy Burn. And to return to the mad dog example — he's safe enough when he isn't stirred up. So now ye leave them sleepin' dogs to lie as quiet as ye can — do ye understand, boys?"

"Blinded lot of lags! We ought to prosecute and clear them out," said young McEachern.

"Sure now, we must beware of makin' trouble, an' we'll leave the lag business out of it. Many of the old lags are better men than the new

115

settlers will ever know how to be. The less said about that, the better."

The older men were all for peace.

"Leave 'em dead alone," was old Poole's advice to Bert. "If you get a pack like that down on you, you'll never know peace or safety again."

"The loss of a sheep or two, or even a cow, is nothing compared with what it will be like if ye incur the enmity of that gang," said McEachern to Malcolm.

And thus the young fellows, unable to stir their elders to action, felt just a little dashed.

2

Malcolm and Dennis felt worse when they heard Bert's news next day. The Poole dogs had barked a lot during the night but, since a possum just out of reach was enough to excite them indefinitely, no one had gone to investigate. Bert was out early in the morning, to be met by the first tragedy of his life. There comes to all young people sooner or later (and those who meet it later rather than sooner have been granted a reprieve), some grief, some mistake, some horror which seems to defeat understanding and be but a delusion of the senses. Such a shock greeted Bert Poole on that gusty morning, as the far winds from the south swept across tussock and shrub and rippled the miles of late summer flowers, putting an icy reminder of the month into the champagne sunlight that banished drowsiness from the youth's eyes. As he went to let Black Belle out of the stable, he saw nailed to the stable door certain objects that had not been there in the white moonlight streaming upon its hard oak surface the night before.

The exhibits included a pair of ears, a horse's tail and copious blood stains. The ears were black and soft as velvet, the tail black and curly. With a ghastly sensation of unreality, Bert tore open the door that was fastened by a hasp over a staple and a horseshoe. There was a gap at the back, which also had not been there the night before. Two broad slabs had been removed, and the beast had been led out the back of the mangerless stall by someone who did not want to risk being seen in the moonlight.

Following the tracks, Bert was not long in finding his beloved. She was standing in a little patch of ti-tree on the high bank of the creek which came singing down from the direction of Eagle Hawk Gullies. She whinnied fretfully to him to know what it all meant.

One look from startled, horrified eyes, and with every sense repudiating what he beheld, Bert tore back to the house for Jimmy, Ada and Louisa. Mrs Poole, hearing the extraordinary commotion, called him to her. He was glad of the refuge. "It's Black Belle! They've done for her! Poor little devil..." and Bert broke down and sobbed like a child.

His father, seizing his garments and putting them on as he raced out, followed the other members of the family to Black Belle. Mrs Poole comforted Bert with one hand and her baby, Raymond, with the other.

Soon the grief-stricken children were back, crowding around their stepmother. Black Belle, with her sweet temper, her beauty and her unequalled speed and strength, had been the pet of them all.

"My oath," said Old Poole on his return to the house, "the hand that done that was no new chum's!" He signalled Jim to withdraw with him, leaving the others with his wife, and presently a shot was heard. Soon the smoke of noble Black Belle's cremation pyre was blowing this way and that in the Maneroo winds. Poole had quickly done the best thing, and with fine feeling he and Jim piled the logs and branches high and wide so that only the glowing coals could be seen.

On closer examination of the stable door, Poole found tacked there a message scrawled on a blood-stained scrap of paper.

Bastards of lags will be safe if they mine there on bisnes.

Poole brought this in to show his wife. "I knew it!" he exclaimed. "Never stir up a hornets' nest."

"Wait till I get my gun!" said Bert, but his father had already hidden it along with all the other firearms. Bert was inclined to dispute his father's right to do this, but his stepmother urged restraint.

"If the old man thinks I'm goin' to take this lyin' down, he's barkin' up the wrong stump!"

"No, we shan't take it lying down," said Mrs Poole calmly. "But we'll just keep our heads and see what is going to happen."

After breakfast, Bert had a colloquy with his father, during which the older man told his son that he could have the Waterfall stallion in place of Black Belle, on condition that he promise to leave the talent of Eagle Hawk Gullies strictly alone.

"Would you take it lyin' down?" gasped Bert, believing that his parent must be in the last stages of senility.

117

"No — but the best way of doin' the thing is to wait your time, as if you was lyin' down. Never let the other fellow know your hand. Just wait your time — do you savvy that?" Poole Senior spoke in a low tone and his destroyed eye lent a sly, avenging expression to his face. "Mum's the word. Wait your time if it's ten years, put 'em off the track by sayin' nothin'. An' then some day their chickens will go home to roost."

The tracks of most of his neighbours' saddle horses made up a familiar alphabet to Bert. Mounted on Polka, Louisa's mare, so named for her sprightly, prancing gait and which Louisa had sympathetically placed at Bert's disposal, the boy spent the forenoon examining all the fresh tracks about the Curradoobidgee homestead. After a long and thorough search, he found something interesting about the tracks of two ridden horses on a bridle track about a mile south of Pool's Creek. Bottle-hoofed, locally bred beasts, only one was shod while the other spraddled the off hind foot when moving faster than a walk. Registering this in the Scotland Yard of his memory, Bert rode home to midday duff.

To cheer Louisa up a little, Mrs Poole persuaded Bert to take her stepdaughter to stay the night with Jessie McEachern. She further suggested that Jessie McEachern might come back with them, to stay for a day or two. The girls were to keep the young men from any rash reprisals, Louisa being so instructed privately.

3

The McEacherns were as horrified as the Pooles at the tragic fate of poor Black Belle.

"Didn't I tell ye?" said McEachern. "Now, what is a sheep compared with yon poor beastie? Ye go any further, and we'll no have a roof over our heads. It's no for the likes of yerselves to get into a fight wi' the likes o' yon. Yer hands would be held by respectability, an' they to have no limits on theirs."

That evening Denny Healey came over from Little River. He and Malcolm were for immediately taking a pot shot or two at the best steeds of their new neighbours at Eagle Hawk Gullies. The next morning, when the elder Healey heard of their intention, he was panic-stricken. The notice about bastards of lags had seemed far more sinister to him than the mutilation of poor Black Belle. Ashen-faced and trembling, he said to Denny: "For the love of all that's holy, let

118

them keep to themselves, and ye do the same! It'll not stop short of murder with a crew like that — every son of a gun of them a lifer, if I know the symptoms. The beast is but a gentle warnin'; a man or a house would come better to them.''

Thus the young men were enjoined to bide their time, but they found an irresistible fascination in prowling about the forbidden territory and seeing what they could see. They saw many another hide or pelt that they recognised as off a Gowandale, Curradoobidgee, Eueurunda or Wombat Hill beast — and they also saw pretty Nellie Logan. Malcolm got off his horse to talk to her, and her stepmother — or whatever she was — invited him and Denny to a cup of tea, and was most genial. Another day, when it was raining and Malcolm and Denny were soaked through, she gave them a taste of rum. Their threats of what they were going to do dried up after a while.

Bert remained aloof. The cruel fate of Black Belle had cut deep. She had to be avenged before his system could be purged. It was his first great grief, for he had never been conscious of deprivations in the pre-Mayborn days. He had never been hungry and his father had never been harsh to the children. The great trial had been the loneliness, though that had long since ceased to exist. His father's advice was easy to follow. The older Poole was a patient man, and Bert was like him...

He would quietly wait his time.

4

Thus life up the country unravelled, with few momentous incidents. Bert had his adolescent dreams, some of them patterned on the tales read aloud by his stepmother. The elders talked of the new land laws, the recently instituted councils of self-government, the best way to construct a wool-washing plant and the latest evidence of progress up the country, whether it was a bridge or a coach line. Political upheavals in Europe were not as interesting as another outbreak of the fearsome Cumberland disease, and even Sydney was a remote country.

The elders were beginning to find the fireside and, later, a feather bed, seductive after unrelenting activity from daybreak till the starry night came down. One or two of them had an occasional touch of lumbago or rheumatism and a few grey hairs were to be seen.

The young men, after equally strenuous days, saddled up at dusk and, wherever there were to be found other young people, and especially girls, the jingle of their silver-plated bits and stirrup irons could be heard with the thunder of their horses' hoofs. By ridge and gully, riverside and plain — those were the days of "Hey for boot and horse, lad, and round the world away".

5

The routine of Three Rivers went on with the regularity of a military establishment. The last of the apples had been picked and stored in fragrant hay in the loft above the jam pantry, in company with the pumpkins. In the dairy, cheese and vats of butter kept company with the crocks of eggs pickled by a method of Mrs Mazere's devising, much esteemed around Bool Bool.

After the first frost, to enhance their flavour, the Swede turnips and parsnips were buried in pits that produced hillocks like burial mounds near the stables. The potatoes had for some time been abed.

The crops gathered and sown again, the men were freed for winter tasks, as the women were for theirs. The orchard had to be replenished and pruned. Mrs Mazere was looking forward to planting loquat trees near the Big House, and brother Matthew had supplied her with orange and lemon slips which she believed would do well in the sheltered chimney recesses on the north side of the house. Grubb, the gardener, was busy building for himself a new abode above flood level; the loss of his goods and chattels had been more than made up from the resources of the Big House and those of its neighbours.

It was the time of pig killing, the lard being hung in bladders in the dairy and the hams being smoked in the kitchen chimney. Not a few improvident or inexperienced settlers would have a cut from the hams before the season of harvest came again. Candle-making followed, Joseph being delighted to help twist and thread the wicks, and the kitchen rapidly becoming a splendid, greasy mess. Soon there were abundant supplies of firm, fat candles to feed the gleaming brass candlesticks, beside which the women sewed the miles of seams and hems of table and bed linen, as well as the numerous voluminous inner and outer garments of those days. As they sewed, the men talked politics or cards before the mighty fire of boxwood turning to coals on the wide, white hearth.

The working-men were so called in order to distinguish them from their employers, though in those days and environs the only men who didn't work were either loony or incapacitated. Well, the cattle and horses all being branded, the calves and foals weaned and the grain threshed, the working-men — in the barn on wet days, or sometimes by lantern at night — cut chaff by the hand machine, shelled corn, prepared greenhide for its limitless uses, mended harness and fashioned bullock yokes. Some of this work found its way to the warmth and comfort of the great kitchen, where Bill Prendergast had so many rivals for Ellen's favour that Mrs Mazere took Ellen to the more demure atmosphere of the dining room to sew with her, Emily, Mrs Grubb and perhaps two or three of the stockmen's wives, whose services could be called on if necessary.

There was so much absorbing activity going on that Joseph had to be fairly dragooned into going to school. Sharp white frosts began early in May and, on his way to school on his new Timor pony, Joseph broke off and ate the little feathery spikes of hoar frost standing up on the rails. When he got off to let down the sliprails on the ridge beyond the hollow, he used to splodge about in the icicles that he believed sprang out of the ground like mushrooms, just to hear them crisping.

6

Emily was not finding life so thrilling. She had now given up hope of seeing Bert Poole till next summer and, to youth and ardent first love, that was a long way off. The letters between herself and Louisa were now short and formal since Papa did not encourage the correspondence, and the winter was already severe, with snowdrifts making the ranges between Gowandale and Maneroo well-nigh impassable. But love never knows its luck.

"There's a letter here from Labosseer," said Mazere one evening upon opening the mail bag, which he had left till the evening meal had been cleared away.

"Is Rachel quite well?" inquired her mother, as Mazere scanned the pages.

"Quite. Oh, here's a letter from her for Emily," he replied, handing it over, "but listen to what Labosseer says."

"Yes, Papa, I'm listening," Emily said dutifully, putting her letter in her pocket.

It is a very severe winter here. . . etc. Having in mind what you said in your last letter about the growth of the grass in your district following on the floods, McEachern and a few more of us would like to know if you could accommodate the cattle from this region. I should be obliged for your reply on this point at your very earliest convenience. Please tell me as far as possible how many cattle, if any, you and your neighbours could take for agistment, and what would be the charge per head.

"They'd never get them through in all the snow," said Mrs Mazere.

"They'll find a way," replied her husband.

Emily listened with consuming interest. If skilled stockmanship was needed in that region, it would certainly mean Bert Poole taking a leading part! Emily pricked her finger with sudden elation. She wanted to whoop for joy, as she bent her head over her seam.

"I'll see about this, first thing tomorrow," continued Mazere. "We should be able to stow away eight hundred head — or perhaps double that."

He came home at dusk the next day well pleased with his mission, and bringing his old friend Tim Brennan with him for supper and a game of cards. Tim Junior appeared shortly after. The three of them, having canvassed the district pretty thoroughly, were prepared to receive all of Maneroo's surplus stock upon the grass which had grown up lush and strong after the inundation of January.

It was the subject of conversation all through the meal.

Later, while the table was being cleared, Brennan Senior played a jig on the Three Rivers fiddle and joked with Mrs Mazere about the old days when they first came up the country. Before he was claimed for cards, Tim Junior found an opportunity to remark to Emily:

"You haven't followed Rachel yet — you'll be an old maid before you know it."

"If no one rescues me, I'll just have to put up with it," laughed Emily, thinking of Bert Poole.

"There's plenty would rescue you and carry you away on their pommel this night, if you'd say the word."

"Who on earth would be as silly as that?" she returned, a dangerous rejoinder in the light of the development of Tim's calf love since the wedding. Tim reddened but, too inexperienced to take the opportunity, saved himself by muttering, "Ned Stanton, maybe."

"Oh, that gawky creature! He'd probably let me fall off," she remarked, with contempt for Ned's youth. Bert was a real man, already in his twenties.

"Well, there's others," began Tim, but he was interrupted as Mr Mazere called upon Emily to get a cribbage board from the Big House. Tim was for following her, but Mrs Mazere waylaid him to know if he would carry some fresh eggs, laid by a famous Three Rivers hen, to his mother.

7

Mazere wrote to Labosseer the next day. Emily, knowing how long it took for a letter to reach Eueurunda, even barring delays like breakdowns or sprees on the part of the drivers, and having listened attentively to her elders as a modest young girl was enjoined to do, calculated how many days would pass before the cattle got through. Every evening, when the stars began to blaze their crystal glory in the frosty sky, she would steal up to the ridge behind the house where Mrs Mazere had awaited Piper's signal. There she'd strain her ears and eyes in the direction presided over by the constellation which the old hands called the Waggon Star, by reason of its pattern. For a number of nights there were only the familiar sounds which carried a mile in the miraculous air — Terence McHaffety admonishing his dogs, the bullock bells in the bend, or the curlews wailing in the hollow down from the back gate.

Then one night they were suddenly upon her. The dogs barked, there was the jingle of bitrings and stirrup irons, the clatter of swift hoofs on the stony ridge, the bang of sliprails thrown down and the shapes of horsemen pulling up at the Mazere gate. One of the horsemen flung off his horse and, with clicking spurs, went in. It was Bert! Though Emily had gone out night after night to watch for him, now that he was actually here she fled in a wild tumult of agitation from the ordeal of meeting him. Down past the stables and cow-yards and in by the vegetable gardens, past the Old House and the Big House, she took cover amongst the lauristinus shrubs, and listened.

Mr Mazere had come out and was speaking. "Well, Poole, have you the cattle here?"

"No, Mr Mazere, we left them camped in the bend beyond the new crossing."

"They'll be safe enough there. Grubb will take your horse. Come in! Come in!"

"No thanks. I must push on to the Brennans', they're expecting us. I just called to let you know that we've got here. I have Malcolm McEachern and Dennis Healey with me."

"Bring them in too. We're glad to see you all — there's plenty of room."

"It's this way, Mr Mazere. I've left my own stock up at Neangen with Dad and Jim — we are taking them that way to pasture at Mungee — and I've got to set off early tomorrow, after Tim Brennan and the Stanton boys have shown us where the cattle are to run."

Cruel, cruel! All this time Emily had lived only for his coming, and now there was to be nothing but this — the sound of his voice and the clink of his gear in the darkness. She felt desperate enough to rush out crying, "Bert, Bert! Don't you care? Won't you stay? Would you actually ride away again without ever seeing me at all?"

But help was at hand, for Mrs Mazere had come out to add her welcome.

"There can't be as much need for haste as that. I'll be bound the cattle won't budge," she said.

"It's not these cattle, Mrs Mazere, that are the problem. It was like getting into a feather bed for them. It's my own mob at Neangen."

"Can't you stay one night? I must hear the Eueurunda and Curradoobidgee news."

"Malcolm and Dennis know as much of that as I do, and they'll be staying down here with the cattle for the winter."

Cruel! Cruel! But Mazere hospitality could not countenance the prospect of neighbours from afar, friends of friends, on a frosty night on horses tucked by wheeling and driving wild cattle, passing on even half a mile further without having food, and Brennan's Gap was seven miles as the crow flies.

"It's early yet. You can have supper here and go on to Brennan's after. I'll go myself in the morning to help turn the cattle in," offered Mazere.

Bert was still undecided. "Mrs Brennan will be expecting us," he said and turned back to his companions to explain. Cheery voices replied. Both Dennis Healey and Malcolm McEachern were ladies' men and eager to gain admittance to the fabled Three Rivers, whence had come Mrs Labosseer.

"I'd be delighted," said Malcolm. "I'm hungry and cold."

"And I. We'd be thankful," confirmed Dennis.

"Very well then," said Bert. "Thank you, Mrs Mazere."

Emily regarded Malcolm and Dennis as deliverers and sped away to await her mother's instructions to lay the supper. The best napery

124

came out; the McEachern and Healey households were of high repute.

Mazere attended to his visitors, while Bill Prendergast lent Grubb a hand with the horses. The Waterfall stallion was put in a stall apart, even though winter had damped his blood and weeks of hard labour had taken some of the bounce out of him. The young men's personal valises, strapped to their pommels, had been packed with an eye to hospitality at Brennan's Gap, and presently they appeared, immaculate as to linen, with firmly disciplined locks, and cocky as English guardsmen in their smart boots, breeches and clanking spurs.

Healey and McEachern were a popular pair of curly-pated chatterboxes and regaled Mrs Mazere not only with the news of Maneroo but also with the epic of getting the cattle through.

"They kept breaking back as far as Billy-go-Billy," said Dennis.

"Cattle are more difficult than any other beasts to get away from their own beat," said Malcolm.

"Sounds like a pretty stiff job," said Mazere.

"You bet," said Denny. "Only for the Pooles we could never have attempted it, with the snow what it is. But I reckon Mr Poole knows more than all the rest of us put together, and Bert takes after him."

"How many did you lose on the way?" asked Mrs Mazere.

"Not more than twenty all told, I should think. They got away at the head of the Jenningningahma."

"Food for dingoes," suggested Mazere.

"More likely they'll be nabbed by the Eagle Hawk Gullies crowd. They're worse than a whole pack of dingoes."

The conversation turning to the depredations of these gentry, the subject of the attack on Black Belle came up. Dennis Healey was the principal narrator, being volubly supported by Malcolm McEachern. Bert Poole was the silent one, speaking only when called upon. He had changed perceptibly since the wedding, having gained pose and assurance and with all his boyish gawkiness left him. His silence made his beauty the more striking. He was six feet, one inch, in his socks, and straight and well formed from his well-shaped head to his long, sunburned fingers with the exquisite filbert nails like Charlotte's, nails which all the hard work of those days could not entirely disfigure. His black hair was straight and showed very white at the crisp parting. His brows were level and delicate, his nose straight, well formed and of dignified size, his lips firm and sweet and at present smudged by a

125

small, silky but flourishing moustache (just to show what he could do, for clean upper lips and chins were the order of the day among society leaders, the only hirsute garnish left below the eyebrows being a little patch of lawn beside the ears). And he was lithe and sure in every movement.

After the meal, when chairs were drawn around the great fire, he sat with his head against the wall, his seat tilted back. While Malcolm and Denny chattered to their hosts, their eyes all the time sought Emily, finding her brilliant complexion and yellow hair even more ravishing than the beauty of Mrs Labosseer. But Emily could not reef her glances from Bert. No god had ever been more alluring to an Attic maiden and, in sooth, his double would have taken some finding.

The demise of Black Belle gave Emily her opening. She expressed starry-eyed sympathy with Bert in his loss, having a struggle to keep back the tears. From this they went on to Charlotte and Rachel. Here was a topic where Bert had the pull over his companions, and so they left it to him and talked to their elders.

"Louisa and Mrs Labosseer have both sent parcels," said Bert, "but as I didn't think we'd be stopping here, I've left everything in the packs."

Cruel, unconsciously cruel Bert! Her heart fell to hear him so coolly express his intention of passing by without calling. Had he forgotten so completely the pleasant times at the wedding? But then she had been handmaiden to the rose. Now the rose was blooming near his own run over the hills, but she was not to know that. However, his next utterance restored her.

"When are you coming up to stay with your sister? And Louisa wants to know when you are coming to Curradoobidgee."

Emily was reassured. Bert was her first, her last, her onliest love, and she not yet sixteen. Was she in danger of being englamoured by the reflection of her own emotions? Skilled, hardened coquettes and adulteresses cannot be sure after a lifetime of experimenting, and Emily was but a novice.

"When did you last see Rachel?"

"About a week ago at Gowandale. I had a dance with her." His face lit up, making it irresistible. Emily giggled.

"She has forgiven you, then, for pretending not to know how?"

"She forgave me that same night. It is becoming a rule that we must always have that old polka now." It was characteristic of him that he did not mention that his family were not invited to Eueurunda, and that all their friendly overtures were ignored. In fact, Labosseer had not even invited him to join in with the cattle, and it was rare for men to be unneighbourly about droving or a cattle muster. However, the other neighbours had invited the Pooles, and the slight was not obvious except to the Pooles themselves. It had put Bert on his mettle though. He had straightway gone over the ranges to Mungee to see what grass George Stanton had. George had always been friendly. He admired Bert and had not the rigid Mazere principles about a brand here or there. Bert had found all the grass he needed and a welcome, so the matter resolved itself without loss of temper or face. Poole Senior and Jim Junior, now rising fifteen, were keeping the Poole mob up at Neangen, an open valley about twenty-five miles distant, preparatory to taking them on to Mungee, while Bert, who was more familiar with the route to Bool Bool, chaperoned the big herd to its destination.

It was Labosseer's slight that had made Bert decide to keep away from Three Rivers but now, since he was here, he could not visit his affront on nice, friendly little Emily, glowing like a rose, nor on kind Mrs Mazere who had been on the Poole side from the start.

"When you do come, there's a great time awaiting you," he continued.

"I'd love to go," said Emily longingly.

"Then why don't you? Maneroo is waiting to show you what it can do."

Mrs Mazere interrupted. "I'll give my husband a letter and packet tomorrow morning for you to take to Isabel, if you'll be so kind," she said.

"I'll be glad to take anything you wish, Mrs Mazere."

"Thank you, Bert. If you were going straight home, there are things I'd like to send your stepmother. Is she better now, I hope, and how is the new brother?"

"There's not much of him except clothes so far, but we all set great store by him."

Raymond was a whingeing little thing. The whole household had practically lived in the kitchen during his first year, creeping to bed barefooted for fear of disturbing his slumbers, a service which they cheerfully rendered to the joss that this miraculous creature was swiftly becoming.

As Mrs Mazere chatted with Bert, Malcolm deserted Mr Mazere

and took his chance with Emily. It was Bert who rose first from the fireside, with no backward glances or words, except to Mrs Mazere.

"When are *you* coming to have a little stay with us again, Mrs Mazere? That would be a great day!"

"Oh, I don't know, Bert. I'm getting too old and stiff now." But she laughed, well pleased with him.

"You're younger than the best of us," he replied, "and if you'll come to Goulburn by coach, I'll drive all the way to meet you there with Mrs Poole's four-in-hand."

They all went out to see them off from the back gate. To Bert it was "Goodbye", to Malcolm and Denny it was "We'll see more of you." Then the clink of bits and stirrups, men swinging on to restless horses in the dark, hoofs on the flint of the ridge, the clatter of the rails let down again, the wail of the disturbed plovers, the barking of the dogs at the township and the coo-ees for the punt.

Cruel, cruel, that Bert should be gone, and only that! All the dreams of his coming, and what had he said?

"I wonder old Labosseer ever looked at her sister while Emily was around," remarked Malcolm.

"Got impatient waitin' for her to grow up, maybe," responded Dennis. "Aren't you head over heels in love with her, Bert? If you're not, I've a presentiment I'm going to be."

"You ride on the curb till you've seen Mary and Agnes Brennan, and Maud Saunders, and one or two more."

"Have you got whips of them? No wonder you never let us break in before," said Malcolm.

Bert chuckled, well pleased to be able to introduce two such creditable friends as Malcolm and Dennis and to exhibit to them his familiarity with the delectable households of Bool Bool.

Soon it was other sliprails flung down, another pack of heelers and watchdogs vociferously doing their duty, and lights and welcome bursting from another home where the elders were as eager as the youngsters for company.

"So ye've had dinner," said Tim Senior.

"Thought you wouldn't get past Three Rivers," laughed Maria.

"Well, the girls are here," said Tim Junior. "Come on in and we'll have supper a little later."

"The night's only a pup yet," added Jack Stanton. Also staying at the Brennans' were Jack's brother Ned, Maud Saunders, and

Martha Spires, the last of whom had been enjoying a long stay around Bool Bool.

"There was a sound of revelry by night," is all that need be said.

8

"They're taking young fellows, those two," observed Mazere as he turned back to his fire. "Labosseer thinks very highly of the McEacherns."

"Yes, they are all nice boys," said Mrs Mazere, while Emily longed to hear special mention of Bert. It came from her mother. "Dear me, what a fine looking fellow Bert Poole has become since he was last here. He puts the others completely in the shade. I think he's the finest looking young man I have ever seen." Emily could have hugged her mother for joy.

"Too much of the flash bushranger about him for my liking," growled Mazere. "It might be all right while he's young, but wait till he gets another twenty years under his collar — he'll be just like the old gorilla." Mazere had only ever seen Poole in the *déshabillé* of a cattle muster, in the years before Miss Mayborn had groomed him.

"Bert gets his good looks from his father," persisted Mrs Mazere. "All *he* needed was trimming up."

"A glass eye would help, too."

"The loss of his eye was a misfortune and should not be made light of."

Nothing more was said on the entrancing subject, so Emily brought in the Bible and prayer book in order to speedily despatch the ritual of evening prayers and be able to go to her room where she would be alone with her thoughts.

Presently, upstairs, she threw open her window and, looking out on the stars blazing like jewels in the frost, relived the precious moments. They were so few and so barely furnished — but the lovers' mill can make a lot of very little grist.

He had ridden up, at last. He had come in. He had shaken hands with her. His presence had been real. Then the horse's hoofs — a strange horse, not darling Black Belle — had rung on the ridge and carried him away again. They would be at Brennan's Gap by now, and tomorrow — why couldn't Bert stay about Bool Bool with the cattle, and one of the others hurry away to Neangen and Mungee?

There was nothing now to be seen but the Waggon Star, wheeling around the half rim made by the ranges beyond which Bert would disappear, and nothing to be heard but the curlews. She said her prayers on the soft black and white calfskin beside the bed and crept in beside little Fannie, who whimpered at being pushed over to her own side in the cold bedding.

9

But next morning, Dan Cupid was kind; at any rate, he granted a reprieve. As Emily was getting her father his breakfast by candlelight, they were surprised by the arrival of Malcolm McEachern.

"Had your breakfast? Nothing up, I hope," said Mazere.

"No, I've been sent to ask if Miss Mazere can get ready by the time the girls come to go and meet the cattle."

"What girls?" asked Mazere rather shortly. Maria Brennan was much more modern than he approved, letting girls leather up and down the country like blackboys.

"The Brennan girls and Miss Saunders — and Miss Spires — she particularly wants to see such a large mob."

If the Commissioner's daughter was to be one of the party, that put a rather different complexion on the matter. Mazere went to confer with his wife, who was just getting up. "Do you approve of Emily tearing about the country with a lot of young men — like a drover or a blackboy?" he demanded.

Emily was already at her mother's side, pleading. "Oh Mamma, please say yes. I'd simply love to see so many cattle in a mob."

"I don't see any harm in it, Papa, since you will be there to take care of her. Young people need little outings now and then." Mrs Mazere spoke appeasingly.

"Oh well, if you don't mind if she gets her neck broken."

Emily sped away to slip on her habit. Soon her horse, Queenie, was saddled and oh, was it really true that she would presently be riding beside Bert and seeing his wonderful new horse!

It wasn't. When Dennis arrived with the girls, he announced that Bert had gone on earlier with Tim Senior and Junior, and that they were to follow.

"Is there any danger of the cattle having broken camp?" asked Mazere.

"No, Mr Mazere," said Malcolm, "but when Bert's on a job, you can never get him off it until all is ship-shape."

With the party went Barney Brennan, Joseph's indestructible companion. There was a clamouring from Joseph to go too, and he ran out with his boots and breakfast while the young men laughingly saddled his Timor pony.

On frosty mornings, the valley of Bool Bool was blanketed with thick white veils of mist which were torn away from her face when the sun wanted to look at her. She was just about this process as the young people rode away from the back gate of Three Rivers, the sun turning the veils to rosy pink and revealing the thousands of dew-laden cobwebs glistening on the thick grass. The horses galloped along till their flanks smoked and the bush rang.

The stockmen had broken camp, the packhorses were laden and the fires burned to coals by the time the party arrived. Emily could not immediately discern the form she sought. Bert was away in the timber on the far side, ready for any emergency. A night's rest and good grass had put new life into the beasts, and the sons of milking cows dedicated to tailing were not adequate to leaven such a mass of wild creatures. Some of the long-horned outlaws from the Head of the Rivers were inspired to make one last break towards their hereditary fastnesses. Bert's stockwhip could be heard like a rifle-shot in the clear air and after a glance, away went Dennis, Malcolm, Ned and Jack Stanton to reinforce him.

To the trained ear, there was a sinister, muttering note in the bellowing. It was more than the complaining, flustered lowing of bewildered cows and working bullocks — there was rebellion here which might become uncontrollable if not checked early in the day.

Mr Mazere and the girls rode safely in the rear, Mazere making himself useful with his stockwhip and heelers. The little boys sat on their ponies, as happy as pirates. It was all deliciously thrilling to the girls. To the men it was splendid, dangerous work, and the knowledge that their every move was being followed by admiring feminine glances spurred them on to even greater feats.

And how they raced and wheeled and propped on those desperate courses, bristling with obstacles and pitfalls! But horses and riders were native born, and the recalcitrant beasts were unfailingly foiled, with no mishap save the normal number of "busters" from which horses and stockmen rose up and tore off again, unsubdued. All eyes were on the Waterfall stallion, a showy beast so named for his tail and mane, which were silver against his coat of dark brown dappled with cream. It was evident he had been sired by a certain thoroughbred Arab, and his short temper suggested that he was of escaped "Traveller" stock.

"Safe as a lot of old milkin' cows!" announced Malcolm, riding up to talk to the girls when the day was won, his horse, second only to the Waterfall, with dilating nostrils and heaving, smoking flanks.

"Crikey, we was nearly done there once," said Dennis. "If it hadn't been for Bert on his Waterfall..."

And now Bert himself rode up and said a general "Good morning!" Alighting, he unbuckled his sweating friend, straightened the saddle-cloth, and then said casually, "I must be pushing on."

A clamour of protest, in which even Mazere joined, arose.

"What's your hurry?" he said, his hospitality getting the better of his hostility. "Won't you give your horse a night's spell?"

"He doesn't need it, thank you all the same," said Bert.

"He's a strange looking beast — where did you get him?" asked Mazere.

"That's Bert's second wife, so to speak," said Denny in an aside to Mary Brennan. "We were glad to see him reconciled — the girls were giving the widower too much sympathy for our taste."

"I'll never get over the loss of Black Belle," said Mary passionately, her ears, like Emily's, alert for Bert's voice.

"We got him as a foal three years ago. He was running with a black mare, the Traveller one that got away, and it's plain the sire was that old creamy that some say came from a circus in Melbourne."

"Humph!" said Mazere. "It always surprises me that those horses are never recaptured...Well, are you going to stay?"

"Can't, thank you. Our mob was ringing a bit when I left and they've had a long spell now. They might be scattered to glory by the time I get back."

He raised his hat to the girls, took the packet for Isabel Stanton and mounted his beast, now pawing the ground to show his temper. "Goodbye, nippers!" he said, slashing affectionately at Barney and Joseph. Infatuated, they piped, "Come again soon, Bert!" and "When can I have another shot? Oh Bert, why don't you come and live with us!"

Dennis and Malcolm drew aside for Bert's parting injunctions, and then he was really gone, raising his hat again and again, with a smile for all the young ladies, and not so much as half a glance in particular for Emily or anyone else.

It was now found that one of the stockmen had been injured. He had fallen on his shoulder and could not use his arm. It was decided that the shoulder must be out of joint or his collar bone broken. The matter of pain was overlooked.

"Emily, you take him to Dr James, and then on to your mother. She'll take charge of this," commanded Mazere. "I'll take your place," he added to the stockman.

"Thank you, sir," said he, who was not native-born, touching his forelock.

"You've had enough of this now anyway," Mazere said to Emily, who did not dispute it. It was a flat, dull day that now hung upon her. The little boys were likewise ordered to proceed back with Emily.

Emily was kind to the injured man as they rode along, chatting about the variation between Bool Bool and Maneroo country. To the shy senses of the bushman, Emily was an angel whose presence gave him palpitations; he would gladly have given his life to save hers had the need arisen. Fortunately he was unaware of her thoughts. Why, oh why, Emily was wondering, couldn't it have been the Waterfall that had put his foot in a hole? Why couldn't it have been Bert riding there beside her, instead of this poor fellow with his jungle beard, and his boots and home-made leggings that had known tallow but never polish? Why couldn't it be Bert needing care, instead of this poor fellow?

Bert, however, went on his way with all his limbs sound to complete his job at Neangen, and then stayed on at Mungee for the next eight weeks or so, with only a fleeting visit to Curradoobidgee.

CHAPTER XII

1

During this period, the young men from Maneroo — Malcolm, Dennis, and Charlie Timson as well — were variously domiciled with the Brennans, Mazeres, Stantons and Saunders. Their stockmen were tented or humpied around the adjacent gullies and ridges, as the pasturing of the cattle dictated.

The vivacious, comely young women of the Bool Bool stations had that quality of unfamiliarity which is always paraffin on the fire of romance, and the young men from Maneroo had that same allure for the girls. It was a merry winter for the young people. Mazere became heartily irritated by the gigglings and whisperings that went on between them.

"Goodness, Mamma — if the next generation deteriorates as much as this one has, our grandchildren will be idiots. I never saw such a crew! All they're fit for is to grin in corners and skit at their elders. If you make a sensible remark to them on any subject at all, they simply look foolish."

Mamma was on the side of the angels.

"Did you ever see such a collection?" he demanded.

"Not since you and I were their age," said Mamma, tying her nightcap under her chin. Suspecting irony, her husband grunted.

"You cast your mind back to what your father said about you," pursued Mrs Mazere.

134

"My mind goes back more often to what I said about him, poor old man, but I was too young to know any better."

"And that's exactly what our children will be saying presently — when life settles down on them a bit more."

"Ah, perhaps you're right. What would you think of us taking that trip to see the old folks in Somerset this year?"

"If Charlotte would come back and take charge, we might manage it. When are you going to write to your father about it?"

"I'll write next mail."

2

The marvel of the jolly intercourse was that it did not that year result in any marriages. Cupid seemed in a perverse mood and mixed the partners. Charlie Timson immediately laid siege to Maud Saunders but she awaited Ned Stanton, who was in turn singeing his wings at the Three Rivers candle. Tim Brennan and Dennis Healey also hovered there, as did Malcolm McEachern. It often seems that men select one girl of a circle as the belle and, sheep-like, all concentrate on her until she has been removed by marriage. So it was that now that Rachel Mazere had gone from the field, even as Charlotte had gone before her, Emily reigned in their stead.

"Are you waiting for Fannie and Rhoda to go off first?" Malcolm asked Emily on one of those occasions of "skitting" in corners, so deplored by Mr Mazere.

"Not quite," replied Emily earnestly, though love was lending her some wiliness. "Mamma will not let any of us marry before we are eighteen."

"But that will not be long now," said Malcolm. So would Emily have said, had Bert stood in Malcolm's shoes.

"Mamma would rather we wait till we were twenty-one, and I'd rather do that too, if you don't mind."

"That means that I'm not the right man," observed the perspicacious Malcolm. "Do you know who the right man is?"

This was too pressing. Emily took refuge in shaking her head, her furious blushes confusing her and making her lovely enough to eat.

"Is it that unlicked gomeril of a Dennis Healey? If so, I'll tar and feather him."

Emily laughed with happy relief. "No."

Malcolm became serious, his face paling under the tan, "Is it good old Bert? Because if it is, I'd have to leave the field clear." This was an unexpected consideration — he'd thought Bert to be fancy free. Emily saw her father approaching and saved herself. "Here's Papa looking for someone to play billiards with him."

Jack Stanton, upon the removal of Rachel Mazere, had turned his eye upon Mary Brennan, who had inherited her mother's size and charm. But her heart, like Emily's, was Bert's without the asking, and she was prepared to wait patiently about that portal for as long as her way was not barred by a bride elect.

The winter following the flood ran its course, and on the cattle Emily fixed her hopes of seeing Bert again.

3

That year the gold fever at the Victorian diggings was at its height. Charlotte wrote that Philip wanted to try his luck for just a little longer, and that then perhaps they would make tracks for home. Between them, Charlotte and Mrs Mazere had not allowed Mazere Senior to realise that Philip's tardiness in accepting reinstatement was more than tardiness, so the door was still open and Philip impatiently awaited.

Nothing had been heard of Ellen's husband, and Charlotte did not recommend Ellen making the journey to the goldfields. It would be like looking for a needle in a haystack, she said. In fact, Philip feared that Slattery had met with foul play. It was so easy to obliterate all trace of a man by throwing him down a deserted shaft, of which there were thousands. Charlotte begged dear Mamma and Auntie Emily to keep Philip a little longer till they sent for him or came to him.

She also wrote to Bert, telling him of some new-chum English squatters who had cleaned up a small fortune by droving a mob of bullocks from the Upper Murray to the diggings. They had averaged one ounce of gold, or about £4.0.0 per head, for about three hundred beasts — and they could have sold twice as many.

When Bert rode back on a visit to Curradoobidgee from Mungee, he and his father talked long into the night about Charlotte's idea. "The cattle are in prime condition," said Bert. "It's so warm down in those sheltered flats and gullies at Mungee — it's been almost as good as a stable for them."

The elder Poole's proposal was to take the cattle by easy stages, feeding them on the wide, virgin grasslands to be found in the overlanders' tracks. Poole and Bert, as the two most expert bushmen of the region, would conduct the overlanding and the McEacherns, Timsons, Healeys and Gilberts would be invited to participate.

"What about Labosseer?" asked Bert. "Are we going to ask him?"

"He hasn't got many cattle. Leave him alone. The McEacherns can ask him if they want to." If someone considered himself socially superior to Boko Poole, he neither resented nor disputed it. He was not a social climber. His wife, however, had other ideas.

"If you leave it to the McEacherns to invite Labosseer, you'll miss all the credit," she warned.

"I don't want no credit from him nor no one else. If they'll only leave me to mind me own business—" he replied.

"Yes, but the initiative in organising the drive is yours and you should have the credit."

This notion appealed to Bert. "How would you go about it?" he asked his stepmother.

"You could ride over and ask the McEacherns and Healeys tomorrow. Your father could ask the other two next week while he's out on the run, and we could send a polite note to Labosseer."

Poole did not veto this. He didn't know what "initiative" meant but, if it was something the Missus was set on, he reckoned it might come in handy. Bert and his stepmother consulted further, each having their own purpose in opening the doors of Eueurunda. Mrs Labosseer, they felt certain, was not against them; it was Labosseer himself. Now was the chance to give a lesson in neighbourliness. Mrs Poole wrote the letter:

Dear Mr Labosseer,

We hear there is good prospect of selling bullocks on the diggings and as soon as the weather is suitable think of setting out with the cattle we have on agistment at Mungee. We are inviting the McEacherns and other neighbours to join us and have pleasure in extending the same invitation to you. I shall be obliged if you will let me hear from you at your early convenience.

Yours truly
Jas. Poole

Next day being Sunday, Bert, Ada and Louisa rode over to the McEacherns at Gowandale to unfold the project. Since young Larry

137

Healey was there already, they did not have to make the detour to Little River. Alick Gilbert was also there, and Louisa had been for some time dear in his calf-love sight. But Louisa's dreams were of the grandeur of Three Rivers, and the things that an English guest from Brennan's Gap had said but couldn't mean, and those others which it would be heaven to hear from Hugh Mazere — and thus Alick found her a provokingly aloof maiden.

Ada's and Jessie McEachern's eyes were very bright, and none of the guests had to be persuaded to stay all night. Many things were talked of by the young people besides the overlanding project, and old McEachern was hard put to recall why trivialities should be so interesting to young people when there were weightier matters to discuss. Nevertheless he found a receptive ear in Bert. Jessie was disappointed that Bert allowed himself to be monopolised by her father to talk about the silly old cattle, and that he could not be weaned from this business by any stratagem that her maidenly modesty would permit her to employ.

Alick Gilbert was entrusted with the note to Eueurunda, which he delivered on his way home next day. Labosseer looked down his nose when he read it, though, as a just man and a gentleman, he felt the Pooles had won on points. Yet he did not show the note to Rachel. He suspected her of a lenient attitude towards the Pooles. The colonials lacked standards, and not only was Rachel native-born, but her mother before her. One could not expect...

But while Labosseer was stiff-necked and a foreigner, he was no fool and all for peace between neighbours. He couldn't decline to participate without causing comment and, besides, he wanted a good market for his steers. He thanked Poole for his invitation and said he would be glad to fall in with the neighbours. When McEachern put the matter before him, he did not mention the letter from Poole. Thus was prestige maintained.

4

Thus also was Emily justified in her faith in the cattle. It was not many days after old Poole's note to Eueurunda that there was no other subject discussed about Bool Bool. Emily sang and clattered about so merrily that her father remarked upon her elation to his wife. "What has come over the girl?"

"Ah, youth and springtime and love — the old, old story."

"Why, bless me, Mamma, you don't mean she's in love already? I've noticed young Brennan shining around her rather brightly. Nothing in that, I hope, though he's as fine a young fellow as you'll find among the native-born. But the difference in religion — it's better not."

"I don't think it will be Tim — unless he becomes such a nuisance that in the end she takes him just to get rid of him."

"What nonsense you women talk! Marry a man just to get rid of him — whoever heard of such foolishness!"

When it came down to it, Poole Senior felt he was the right man to lead the overlanding. None of the others could touch him in his own line. And the feel of bit and bridle together with the rhythm of a good horse, the promise of adventure about the diggings, the nights around the camp fires listening to the old yarns, the stars above — all these called him.

"Fine!" said Bert, when his father told him he would lead the overlanding. "I'd rather you did it than me. I'll go with you for a few days till the cattle settle down."

"Plenty of room for us both."

"We wouldn't have a beast left by the time we got back, not with that Eagle Hawk crowd about. Young Jim and the others would be no match for them."

"Just as you like," said the elder.

Great days followed for little Bool Bool with one of the biggest-ever cattle musters right in its own back yard. Deliciously thrilling was life to men and maids and little boys and horses and dogs.

It was that season of the year when there was a freshet in the Yarrabongo, and flowers everywhere. Soldier buttons bobbed their yellow heads in the orchards and cow paddock of Three Rivers, the loveliest native violets blued the ridges, and cowslips and sweetly scented cream mayflowers filled the hollows. English violets grew in thick mats in the garden and foretold heaven with their perfume, and Grubb had the felicity of planting English hedge-roses about the farms on the flat. That was the year that Mrs Dr James tenderly nursed five little plants of the English sweet briar, one of which she sent to Mrs Mazere who set it in a flower bed near the Old House. The colonial-born crushed its sweet leaves and smelled them and heard old Mazere tell how gloriously the sweet briar bloomed along the old lanes at Home.

The plovers and the magpies in the hollow behind the house fiercely attacked anyone coming near their nests, and the cry of young lambs mingled with the muttering of bulls. The valley echoed with a sound like thunder as the bulls tore up the earth and challenged their rivals with murderous intent, the procreative instinct being a madness in all male creatures — from men to grasshoppers.

The cattle had been capably tailed since their arrival in the valleys, and were in good order. "Tame as a lot of old milking cows," announced Denny Healey. But the cutting-out on the plains drenched many a horse with sweat and the fancy riding resulted in "busters" galore for skilled and unskilled alike. Tom Stapleton, one of the Pooles' stockmen, suffered a broken collar bone. In all the neck-and-neck contests wherein the danger and the glory lay and the best men took their places unquestioned, the big bay mare of the elder Poole and the silver tail of the Waterfall, like a pennant, were ever to be seen. Poole Senior had come into his own. His neighbours dropped the "Boko" and called him Mr Poole, or just plain Poole, asked politely after his wife and family, and recounted to each other admiring tales of his daring.

Mazere was taken aback by the physical appearance of James Poole, and to find that it was from his sire that Bert had inherited his striking looks. Standing shoulder to shoulder, the elder face in profile was Bert's, tanned and toughened. Wearing smart boots and breeches, father and son rode side by side the long day through. In those days, such men never thought of saying, or even thinking, that they were tired. Theirs was all the splendour, the hardship, the loneliness, the wonder of pathfinders in a noble, unspoiled continent.

The time of the cattle sortie was richly freighted with the social evenings so dear to the pioneer. When nightfall put an end to the men's activities in the saddle, and the cattle, having settled down to chew their cud, were left to the stockmen camped on the ridges, their employers rode to one or other of the stations, cleaned up, had a splendid dinner and afterwards joined in the joy of human companionship until a late hour.

They were eagerly pressed to turn in at any of the four homesteads, but, since Saunders' and Stanton's were rather out of the way, it was resolved that the Stanton and Saunders girls should come to help at Three Rivers and Brennan's Gap, with the young men dividing themselves between the two places to sleep. The Pooles, by right of connection, belonged to Three Rivers, as did the McEacherns by right of the friendship established between Gowandale and Eueurunda. Bert, however, preferred to stay at Brennans' and he often occupied Tim's bed there while Tim turned in at Three Rivers where, in Tim's view, Malcolm was poaching on his preserve.

James Poole Senior refused a roof. It might have been the call of the nights under the stars, or his way of avoiding the risk of a social slight, or just sheer shyness, but he stuck to the stockmen and to his tent. To bag him therefore became a social ambition. But even Maria Brennan with all her endearing blandishments couldn't get the tall, aloof man inside her door, and neither could Emily, the belle of the muster, who had them all collared, from old Tim Brennan to his son. Bool Bool began to wonder what sort of a siren the second Mrs Poole could be.

Mazere, who had given over muttering about bushrangers and who was riding with Poole when it came time to ease up on the sixth day of the carnival, said, "Well, let's call it a day, Poole. You had better come with me for a game of cards while the young people dance."

"No thanks! I'll keep an eye on the steers. There's a few gaffers there from Eagle Hawk are looking for trouble." And Mazere failed to move him from this position.

"Where's Mr Poole?" Mrs Mazere asked her husband as the men clanked and whistled along the verandahs, laughing at each other's tales of the day.

"I asked him, but he wouldn't come," said Mazere.

"You can't say he wants to push himself upon us." Later at dinner she announced, "I'll take a ride with you tomorrow and see the cattle."

"Why, Mamma, that would hardly be safe," said her husband.

"Safe as a church, Mrs Mazere. You come with me," said Malcolm, whose seat beside Emily had been usurped by the vigilant Tim.

"Very well. You shall be my knight," she laughed.

Mrs Mazere and Emily rode out next day, and saw the musterers bringing in a fresh herd from a gully beyond the plains. The flats where the backwaters had lain in January were now a depot, surging with cattle. Wild-eyed, long-horned, yellow beasts jostled other beasts that were heavy in the brisket and short in the horn, and old Tim Brennan called out to Mazere, "Sure that old gentleman of yours must have sowed a power of wild oats that time he escaped."

"A few of them bear his mark all right," said Mazere.

Tim Junior managed to ride in beside Emily, while Malcolm dashed off to do a little fancy riding.

"Dear me, can't those Maneroo men ride! My heart is in my mouth as I watch them," observed Emily, her eyes on Bert.

"They ride well enough," said Tim. "But it's a big price to pay for being so bandy."

"They're not all bandy," she protested. Both the Pooles were as straight of limb as Tim himself.

"Malcolm and Denny are, and so is Charlie Timson." But what did it matter what their legs were like — it would not help poor Tim. Emily wished he would cease chattering in her ear so that she could hear what Bert was saying to her mother. He had ridden up to that good lady, having said to his father just a few moments before, "There's Mrs Mazere, Dad. You'll have to come over and speak to her."

Presently he returned to his father's side. "Mrs Mazere says she has come out specially to see you," he said.

"To see me!"

"Yes. Wants to ask if you've had late news from Charlotte."

"You can tell her that as well as me." But Bert had capered away and Mrs Mazere, a sprightly and well turned-out horsewoman, was approaching on Wellington.

"You are very distant to old friends, Mr Poole," she cried gaily as he rode to meet her. "You've been a long time returning my visit to Curradoobidgee." She had him cornered there. He was aware of the crazy passes over which she had ridden at that time — against her husband's will, if gossip knew anything. Poole, of whom cruel circumstances had made something of a recluse, was really softer towards women than anyone suspected. He surrendered.

"Business has never brought me this way, Mrs Mazere."

"You've been here over a week."

"The cattle haven't been safe," he murmured apologetically, "and since the young fellers can't be trusted to stick to their posts with all the pretty girls about, dad's had to stick to it." A long speech for Poole.

"But they're safe now, aren't they?"

142

"For a bit, unless something starts 'em off."

"Well then, I expect you over this afternoon. Bert and the others can take your place on watch tonight and give the elders a chance. You must see your grandson, Philip. He's a bit like you, I think."

Later that day Mrs Mazere rode off with her prize in tow, and that's how Boko Poole at last came to Three Rivers. Harriet Mayborn's acumen was proven. Poole strode among the men that evening, the finest specimen of all save Bert, and Bert his own son to do him honour. Among the young chanticleers flapping their wings and crowing on the fence, thinking that they waked the morn, there may have been some with shriller pipe, but when it came to the final challenge, it was seen that though time had taken a little of the sheen from his plumage, it had also added sharpness and strength to his spurs. He strode among his contemporaries, the doughtiest rooster of all.

Little Philip had been brought to see his new grandaddy, but he was shy of the big, dark man whose dulled eye gave him a queer appearance. He clung to his familiar grandaddy of the rubicund face, which, in fact, was as well, for it made Mazere amiable and promoted good fellowship.

"Perhaps I'll find him a nugget at the diggings to remember me by," said Poole.

"It's his daddy he wants."

"I'll see what can be done," said Poole. Baby Philip stolidly maintained his silence as his grandfathers compared their experiences during the early days of Maneroo and Bool Bool, though Poole would not be led into going further back in his reminiscences.

Bert very readily went back to take his father's place on watch that night, while Poole Senior sampled a Three Rivers bed. And it was Bert who went with his father next day to bring the Curradoobidgee mob on from Mungee instead of delegating the job to the stockmen, as Mrs Mazere heard Brennan Senior urging him to do.

Mrs Mazere pondered upon the pieces in the puzzle of the young people's affairs. Bert evidently did not reciprocate the feeling she could see awakening in Emily, for he unfailingly chose to stay at Brennan's Gap in preference to Three Rivers. She would have thought this augured well for Mary or Agnes, but here he was, off again, in spite of being urged to stay. And though she recognised that Bert was a very responsible lad, he would not be quite such a slave to duty, she felt sure, had there been a girl in his fancy.

One person whose presence was largely overlooked at this time was Tom Stapleton, the Pooles' stockman who had broken his collar bone during the mustering. He had been well nursed at Three Rivers, well slept in a comfortable bed in a room adjoining the old school-house, and well fed in the cheery kitchen. It was the great adventure of Tom Stapleton's manhood. Inarticulate and painfully shy, his gentle, industrious person went unnoticed by everyone. But Tom noticed everyone, and one person in particular. He spruced himself up every evening during his stay in a suit of slops, bought years before, that the sun had faded into stripes where it fell on it through the cracks of his humpy. The cheap material was crumpled almost into accordion pleats. Yet the donning of the suit was Tom's offering. Ellen had thought it just one more offering at her shrine and had laughed, but when he continued to keep his shy distance, she had become puzzled.

The effects of a life of solitude and ignorance so possessed the boy that it was all he could do to keep from bolting each time one of the young ladies approached, and yet he would have stood all day without moving or eating, just to see Emily pass by. It was his joy at the end of the day — when Ellen's water cask was filled, the kindling placed and the calves penned — to sit on a case, or merely on his hunkers, bushman-fashion, in the dark corner of some verandah where he could feast his eyes without being seen — the nearest he had yet come to the feast of life. One day as Emily tripped past, a hairpin fell from her golden curls into the dust and, marking where it fell and making sure that no one was looking, he picked it up, fingering it like a talisman, and placed it in his waistcoat pocket.

The children discovered him, though. He could cut rakes, combs, ladders, spoons, hens and all manner of things from chips of wood and he was soon constantly being assailed by eager enquiries: "Tom, will you bring me something nice from the diggings? Tom, will you make me a horse? Tom, will you . . ."

But poor Tom was not to go on the big parade. After the cattle were settled down on the road, he was to take the family herds back to Maneroo and thence to his lonely humpy on the boundary of Curradoobidgee, out by the Head of the Rivers where he was the guardian of rock salt in the great solitude, and lucky if he saw another human being once a month.

144

One of the biggest mobs of cattle that had ever been seen up the country presently took the overland route. Upwards of a thousand head were driven forward from the flats to take the edge of the Great Plains on their southward way. It took some plucky riding to get the herd over the bush-lined bank and into the stream that was swollen with spring rains. As a protesting bellowing rent the heavens, the fierce cattle-dogs scarified the heels of the beasts, the cruel whips cut their hides. Those beasts at the rear drove the leaders forward, and in they went; the bellowing ceased, and then there was the magnificent sight of the expanse of water alive with heads crowned with horns as the cattle contested the swift current. Subdued by the immersion, they set off tractably through the township. They went right past Three Rivers homestead and the family climbed on to the roof of the cowsheds to get a good view. Away towards the red eye of the setting sun they went, the rattle of their horns and the crackling of their fetlocks making a stirring music as they swept past.

The stockmen hung on to the mob while their employers' sons had a last few lingering words with the beauty at Three Rivers back gate.

"What shall I bring you back from Melbourne?" asked Malcolm, dismounting to whisper in Emily's ear. Denny Healey galloped up and cut in with, "Whatever he's talking of bringing you, I'll bring two of 'em and better. He's just one of these havering Scotsmen."

"I shan't trust anyone but Ned Stanton," she said laughingly, but all the while with a sideways glance at the snowy tail of Waterfall as it flashed on the ridge like the oriflamme of Henry of Navarre. Wasn't he even going to come and say goodbye?

Presently Waterfall was champing his bit beside the back gate, but the rider was addressing himself to Mrs Mazere about the messages his father was to take to Charlotte and Philip.

Nearly every man in the place, including Mazere, Brennan Senior, and the elder Stanton and Saunders, rode out to help start the mob on its way. As for Terence McHaffety, he took a vacation from butchering and went on the route, drovers' fever having caught him well and truly. In those days, young boys and sons of well-to-do settlers were as struck to go a-droving as they are to go on the stage today.

Poole Senior was commander-in-chief and under him were Dennis and Malcolm, Tim Brennan, Charlie Timson, Alick Gilbert and Jack Stanton, as well as the stockmen apportioned by each of those sending stock. Labosseer sent two reliable men, good camp equipment and plenty of horses. Racing along as well, free and wide, was a mob of extra riding horses. Those horses bearing packs and camp gear had preceded the exodus to be ready for the first night.

As the noise and movement melted over the ridges, there fell on Bool Bool society a flatness like that following the end of a carnival. Mazere, Isaacs and the doctor returned late that night, after having had dinner in camp. The visiting girls returned to their homes next morning, after parting with kisses and promises to meet again soon.

A week later, the men who had gone to assist at the start of the expedition returned. Emily's heart was sore that Bert did not return via Bool Bool, as he surely would have done had his desire lain in that way. It was Tom Stapleton, looking for an excuse to make that detour, who brought the children a toy cart and doll he had found unexpectedly by the way.

Evidently Bert thought no more of the Brennan girls than of Emily, concluded Mrs Mazere. He was either fancy free, or the rumour that attributed his heart to Jessie McEachern had some truth in it. In her next letter to Rachel was the passage,

What a good-looking young fellow Bert Poole has grown to be.
Someone spoke of Jessie McEachern and him, is there any truth in that?

In due time came a reply:

I think Jessie thinks a great deal of Bert, but it is all on her side as far as I can see. Who did he show most attention to at Bool Bool?

CHAPTER XIII

1

The details of the cattle expedition do not vitally concern this story. Under Poole's leadership, the droving was a notable success; Tim Brennan, Malcolm McEachern and Denny Healey proved cool and unbluffable salesmen, and those beasts not disposed of at the diggings were bought as "stores" by squatters farther south. The partners cleaned up a satisfactory sum. A number of stockmen deserted to the diggings, but an equal number of disappointed diggers, seeing in cattle a fresh El Dorado, seized the chance to leave. Thus as many young men eventually returned to Bool Bool and Maneroo as had set out. No one fell ill or met with an accident or left his heart behind him. Poole saw Charlotte and Philip and brought back parcels and letters for both Curradoobidgee and Three Rivers.

The details of the undertaking were talked over for a long time, the particulars of Melbourne incidents being circulated for male delectation only. Meanwhile, the affairs for which Bert, to the astonishment of his companions, had forgone so great an adventure, began to ripen, to the great concern of the first families of Maneroo and Bool Bool.

It was now more than two years since the rush to the Turon. In the meantime there had been many people fossicking in other parts of the country in the hope of falling upon gold. Now the droving contingent returned determined to uncover a Mount Alexander on their own runs. James Poole's powers of observation stood by him. "The ridges beyond Mungee look most likely to me," he said.

He was shortly proved right by a prospector making a rich find on the edge of George Stanton's run. Immediately a rush set in, and the township of Coolooluk arose.

Thereupon Bool Bool swelled visibly. The square mile that began at the sliprails on the ridge near Three Rivers and extended to the town to include the butcher, the blacksmith, the public houses and Isaacs' store, was pegged out in streets. Mazere fenced in his property and planted ornamental trees along the fence running from the back gate to the sliprails. Part of the hollow where the curlews and plovers wailed, between the township and Three Rivers homestead, was set apart as a cemetery. Before the original inhabitants could blink, there was another pub, a post office, two more stores and a police station.

A flourishing trade ensued between Bool Bool and the hawkers who went over the hills to Coolooluk with their packhorses. These merchants bought anything that the Mazeres would sell, and at high prices. Butter, cheese, poultry, eggs, fruit, vegetables, jams, pickles, honey, arrowroot, hams — all found a ready market that kept the household busy from morning till night, while its bank account grew large and sound.

Mr Mazere set up a mill that became the pride of his life. He had always held that it would be more profitable to sell to the diggers who had money to fling about than to dig oneself.

Then the evils attendant upon gold rushes appeared. Things were stolen from fields and sheds, an annoyance from which the settlers had been free for the twenty years or more since they had come to those parts.

2

Bushranging broke out again in the district. People were stuck up around Gundagai, Cooma and Yass. Small affairs these, without bloodshed, and somewhat mystifying since the robbers seemed to get so little for their trouble. The troopers were out in force, but while they were scouring the neighbourhood of the attack, the next strike would be fifty or a hundred miles distant. The suspicion grew that it was local talent that was responsible — having a little fun on its own account and resting safe in the knowledge of how easily the settlers' households could be overcome.

As the gold yield at Coolooluk increased, the robberies in the area grew more daring. The actual bailing up was done by two men, a tall one and a short, broad one, but whether they were young or old their victims could not say, since their assailants wore crape masks and broad slouch hats pulled down over their ears. Their tactics were to wait until the men of the house were absent or, failing that, until the family was assembled at a meal. Then they entered, one by the back door and one by the front, a proceeding which was facilitated by the primitive design of the houses. They knew the exact membership of each household, a simple matter to determine in the bush, and the taller man would be left in charge of them while the short one did the ransacking. It was believed that they had assistants, for on one occasion when they made off hurriedly, it was in response to a peculiar, shrill whistle from outside. Also, when leaving on that occasion, they threatened that anyone who moved before half an hour had elapsed would be shot by a sentinel on watch. One man who disregarded this warning and emerged from his hut ten minutes after their departure had a bullet whistle within a foot of him. So the threat was clearly not an idle one.

The Stantons at Mungee were relieved of a tidy bag of gold which the provident Isabel had accumulated as a result of her dealings with the hawkers. The usual threat kept the household inside after the bushrangers' departure, but Isabel tiptoed to the back room and, in the dark, peered between the slabs. Thus she saw a rider disappearing on a horse with a long white mane and tail.

"He was just like the Waterfall," she told her husband.

"The fellow must have got away with Bert's stud horse, or else the moonlight deceived you."

"Deceived me! It was as plain as anything!"

"Well, we'll wait and see. Don't let on to a soul that we know anything, or it mightn't be safe for us."

When the Stantons found a chance of discussing the incident with Bert, he assured them that the Waterfall had not been out of his sight for a night, and that there was no other horse with his peculiarities within a hundred miles. "Must have been imported from somewhere," said George puzzled.

Thus it went for a year following the droving expedition.

3
Rachel wrote home that she hated Maneroo in the winter; the biting

winds and frosts gave her chilblains and made it impossible to grow things which flourished at Three Rivers. She also complained bitterly of homesickness and upbraided her dear Papa that he had not come to stay with her.

Mazere and Emily thereupon decided to pay a visit to Eueurunda, their visit to tie in with the New Year festivities which Maneroo had long been planning. Numerous young people from Bool Bool had been issued with invitations, for Maneroo had its heart set upon a gay New Year. On the 29th December, after spending Christmas with their respective families, the Bool Boolians set out for Maneroo. Mrs Mazere, not feeling equal to the journey, decided to stay at home.

Mr Mazere was chaperone to the party which included Mary, Agnes and Tim Brennan, Ned, Lizzie and Jack Stanton, Hugh and Emily, Maud and Tom Saunders, Martha Spires, as well as a couple of English guests who had been staying at Brennan's Gap.

Sixteen people in all set out on a heavenly summer morning, the horses all in splendid buckle and needing no urging. Clothing for the festivities — what could not be fitted into the valises strapped beside the girls or in front of the men — was put onto the packhorses along with the camp gear and sundry gifts for the matrons of the highlands.

The first day took them, by the bridle track that Philip had taken on the day when he went to recapture a bull and won a bride, to the head of the Jenningningahma. Here the gallants from Maneroo were to have camp pitched and everything ready for the Bool Boolians' arrival. Bert, accompanied by Louisa who was dithering with excitement at the prospect of seeing her darling Emily — and Hugh — again, was the leader of the welcoming party. Malcolm, Denny and Charlie Timson were waiting as well. Mrs Labosseer, still unprecedentedly free from impediment, had insisted upon meeting her family, so Simon accompanied her. Others would also have liked to come on this fair frolic, but had had to stay at home to help arrange the grand ball and races planned for New Year's Day.

As it neared sundown, the Bool Boolians saw above the trees the smoke of the waiting camp fires and Emily, recognising Bert's blackfellow signals of welcome, felt her heart lift. The tents were soon to be seen amid the timber on the rim of a little plain beside a musical stream. The men fired shots and cracked whips in a hullabaloo of welcome.

Two large tents were set apart, one for the ladies and one for the gentlemen, with a small one in between for Mr and Mrs Labosseer. But Rachel announced with spirit that she would prefer to be a girl again, and so Mazere and his son-in-law were disposed of in the little tent.

The Manerooites had everything ready and, the horses being speedily unsaddled and hobbled out, the young people gathered for tea and tucker. Though there were a number of candidates for Emily's company, they tactfully left her to her sister, who was delighted to see her after such a long separation. Emily was entranced to see Bert again and beckoned him over to join her and Rachel. She was elated to see how readily he was captured. Usually he would have busied himself with tents or horses in such circumstances, but tonight he left these jobs to his companions and stretched contentedly on the grass with the two girls, happiness illumining his handsome face. Emily tasted joy, too, to have him there beside her.

Mazere had rather given in about the Pooles of late, but not so Labosseer, who had all the uneasiness of an elderly husband in possession of an acclaimed young beauty in a community where cavaliers were rampant and fair ladies in a minority. And he felt he had justification for that uneasiness.

On Maneroo, Labosseer had noted that Bert was at Mrs Labosseer's elbow whenever an opportunity presented itself. Of course, he might merely have been pushing his social connection but...in any case, he was too infernally handsome. Of course it was a common, flashy kind of good looks, but currency lasses seemed to prefer them.

In fact, prejudice clouded Labosseer's perception of Bert's looks. The most belted earl in all the Queen's realm had not such an aristocratic brow, nose and hands and bearing as Bert Poole, who was presently lying in the land of singing rivers, sucking the sap from the stems of the seeding kangaroo grass as he listened to the girls' talk and very occasionally threw in a word.

The general talk was mostly of the bushrangers, who had been rather quiet of late.

"Wouldn't it be thrilling if we were held up!" said Martha Spires.

"I don't think they'd risk coming near Bert," said Louisa confidently.

"What would we do if they did come?" asked Emily as they were separating for the night, just to give Bert an opening. But Bert responded by saying to Rachel:

151

"I'll be on watch just back of your tent, Mrs Labosseer, and he'll be a dead man who tries to disturb you."

Overhearing this pronouncement, Labosseer went straightaway to his wife and, taking her aside, complained, "I think he might have left me to say that."

"That was meant for Emily, but he's too shy to say it direct."

"Shy! Bert Poole, shy! I'll tell you something that I don't like the sound of. Healey of Little River tells me that one of the families stuck up somewhere down the country saw the bushranger riding away on a dark horse with a white mane and tail."

"Old Healey is always putting about some nasty scandal behind people's backs and pretending to be great friends to their faces. He has such an evil mind that I wouldn't trust him an inch. He surely doesn't mean one of the bushrangers was riding Waterfall, does he — or that Bert is a bushranger?"

"Perhaps Bert knows who the bushrangers are, though."

Bert felt that it would not really be necessary to keep watch that night, but Malcolm and Denny thought otherwise — partly because of the opportunity to clank about as brave fellows in the sight of the girls.

Glistening, dew-dropped sunrise found them all safe and happy. A snake in the men's tent had caused a temporary flutter but the women had not been worried by so much as an ant. A little later, all dressed bravely in high, holiday spirits, they rode off towards Gowandale and Eueurunda, Bert galloping along beside Emily and Rachel.

That it should be Emily who was the object of Bert's fancy was certainly preferable to it being his wife, but the Poole connection would always be distasteful to Labosseer. And it seemed to him that if Bert was cultivating his wife as a channel to Emily, he was overdoing it a little. He decided to set a trap for the unwary Bert. It was easy, for the youth was three parts unconscious of his state. Totally unsophisticated, he was not lusting after his neighbour's wife in order to possess her or do her dishonour; marriage was an insuperable barrier and had finished any hope of romance in Rachel's direction, but he was in the toils of a more elementary force than he understood or even was conscious of.

Labosseer separated Emily from her sister and devoted himself to her so cordially that Emily, usually a little in awe of her aristocratic brother-in-law, was flattered. Labosseer's next move was to leave

Emily unattended and to himself squire his wife. Though he repeated this manoeuvre several times, not once did Bert seem to notice Emily's position. It was always Malcolm, Dennis or Tim who were on the alert. But let his wife ride for one minute with her off-side free and immediately Bert's big bay mare — the Waterfall, being no company beast, was absent on this occasion — would be seen neck and neck with Mrs Labosseer's chestnut, as surely as an iron filing gravitates to a magnet. Bert was young and infernally good-looking, if only to the crude colonial taste. His wife was young too and, so far, untrammelled. Labosseer was impatient for those trammels.

CHAPTER XIV

1

It was New Year's Day up the country, a beautiful New Year's Day with not a cloud in the sky. Signs of activity could be seen on Little Plain very early. About three miles from Gowandale homestead, it was one of those round, timberless plateaus that distinguish the region, with a crystal stream singing between perfumed shrubs all in bloom and a carpet of flowers girth-high among the tussocks.

For the past few days, the curious eagles, kookaburras and magpies had watched a marquee of bushes being erected, and had noted other signs of human invasion. The kangaroos and wild turkeys had retreated from the spot, and the plovers expressed their indignation volubly. Some of the flowers were trampled, and a bushman would have discerned quite a track, circular, for about two miles. Aha! a virgin racecourse, to be sure! In full view of a little knoll near the marquee where blackbutts and snow gums afforded shade, a finishing post had been erected.

The young men had set their hearts on a race meeting, the women on a picnic, and thus took place the first picnic races of the district, which occasions, started so informally among neighbours, these days sometimes command special trains, the presence of vice-regality, and an atmosphere of exclusivity.

This wonderful gathering, which had been in the air ever since the cattle exodus, had been bruited abroad by the coach-drivers from Koruya to Araluen, and from Goulburn to Yass and Tarago. Inquiries had been received as to whether the races were open to all comers. They were, and the prizes grew and multiplied. There were to be all sorts of races — from the "Ladies'" with a beautifully fashioned bridle to be won by some blade to present to whom he willed, to the "Sweep Stake", for which every entrant had to pay a "canary" and the winner to scoop the pool. Then there was the "Squatters' Race", each squatter giving five pounds towards the prize, the "Gentlemen's Race", and the "Diggers' Race".

Some of the big squatters from Yass and Goulburn had sent word that they were coming, and in due course had received cordial invitations to stay at one or other of the Maneroo homesteads. Men from the new diggings at Coolooluk, from the old communities of the south coast, and from Gundagai, were also attracted by the prospect of the horse races. The gambling attached to the sport is perhaps a vice older than the love of gold, and the diggers, especially, were eager for a little holiday involving the society of, or at least a sight of, the renowned belles of Bool Bool and Maneroo.

A couple of days before the races, camp fires were to be seen around the course as men arrived to try their horses.

When, on the day, the leaders saw what proportions the congregation was assuming, they went apart and held a conclave.

"I'm afraid," said Healey of Little River, "there will be trouble before the day is over."

"We must take precautions to avert that," said Mazere firmly.

"The only trouble would be likely to come from the Coolooluk crowd and the Eagle Hawk Gullies lot," said Labosseer.

"Sure, are they here?" inquired Healey nervously.

"Logan, Burn, their friend Erroll, and most of the others are over on the hill opposite."

"Och, musha, God help us," exclaimed Healey in a tone of deep foreboding.

"We need a committee and stewards," said Mazere, after looking curiously at Healey.

"Then Mister Mazere, it's yerself is the right man for leader in that," said McEachern. As Mazere and the others were of the same opinion, so it was, and the ad hoc committee set about the task of appointing stewards from amongst the elders of the visiting squattocracy.

155

"We'll want stewards representing all parties, so that their rulings will be accepted as fair," said Mazere. "There must be some experienced men from Eagle Hawk and Coolooluk included."

· "Those be wise words, Mazere, and I move that some of us go over and put it before them."

"We'll need to keep a sharp eye out for trouble between that Eagle Hawk Gullies assembly and the Coolooluk gaffers," murmured Healey.

"A free field to every visitor here, man, woman, black or child. But order must be maintained — let every man we enrol understand that quite clearly," said Mazere.

Healey said he felt suddenly unwell, so Gilbert was left with him while the others made their way over to the crowd, holding up their hands to signify that a word was to be said.

" 'Tis Mazere of Three Rivers himself," observed Burn of Eagle Hawk as Mazere and the others approached.

"A fine magistrate and a stirring old blackguard when his paddy's up," chuckled Logan.

"And that's McEachern of Gowandale — 'tis high society yer in this day, ye ken."

"Yes, ye comport yerself according, Sandy Burn. An' God help us, who is that? Labosseer of Eueurunda, or is it the Almighty? 'Tis the latter, I do believe. An' why, can ye tell me, is that stravagin' Healey not here, him that's usually more consequential than a recruitin' sergeant?"

"Haw! Haw!" guffawed Erroll, adding slyly, "Perhaps you can tell us that yourself. And further, why has Healey taken to a long beard and shady hat like some other gentry?"

"Sure, ostriches when they cover their heads, I'm told, think they're hidden entirely."

But the call for stewards was received with cheers. The request had special weight emanating from Mazere, who was well known as a just magistrate and a man who, though straight in his judgements, was always against brutal sentences. Many volunteered; a number of them had had good training as wardens on the diggings and realised the necessity for order. The task appealed to their feelings of self respect and gave them an opportunity for promenading within sight of the ladies.

2

The flutter of skirts on the ridge opposite raised a ripple of interest among the women of the Gowandale-Eueurunda party. In those days, precious though ladies were to the opposite sex, it was as nothing to the joy with

156

which their own sex hailed and welcomed them.

"I'd like to go over and ask those ladies to come join wi' us for dinner. It would be more neighbourly, I'm thinkin'," said Mrs McEachern.

"I wonder who they can be?" said Mrs Healey.

"Keep away from them entirely," whispered her husband hoarsely.

"The more the merrier," said Maria Brennan.

"We should go and speak to them now, before the racing starts," said Mrs Labosseer. "Oh, but isn't that the Pooles' carriage?"

Mrs Poole's conveyance was now seen to be approaching, bumping and dancing over the virgin tussocks, and soon Poole, with a fine sweep that commanded the attention of all those assembled, brought his four-in-hand to a standstill. Mrs Poole held the sacred infant, Raymond, in her arms.

Mrs McEachern greeted her neighbour with great cordiality, and while Raymond was received into one of the half-dozen pairs of arms that reached out for him with appropriate renderings of "Oh, the ducky little down diddlums, pretty little thing," his mother was curiously regarded by the onlookers. Rachel Labosseer was titillated to be at last face-to-face with this woman, connected to her own family by marriage, ignored socially by her husband, and the subject of gossip both curious and ribald from Maneroo to Goulburn.

It was now that she made her stand, within the hearing of her husband.

"I would have been over to see you when Raymond came," she said, "but I knew you were too ill to be bothered with strangers, and being new to my duties. . ." Emily looked and listened, enraptured by the fine lady her sister had grown into under the influence of Eueurunda.

"I ought to have been over to see you before that," said Harriet Poole in reply, seeing the young matron's attitude was cordial.

"But now, while my sister" (no mere Emily, mind you, but "my sister"; Emily felt really grown up at last) "is here," Rachel continued, "I want you to come and stay with me." This was one in the eye for His Nibs. She turned to him now, as poised as a duchess. "Have you met my husband?"

"Not yet," said Mrs Poole, holding out a hand which he could not refuse. He gamely rose to the emergency by bending over it in a stately bow. Staggered by his wife's total disregard of his wishes, in full view of his circle, he began to suspect that the influence of Bert was more insidious than he had supposed.

Mrs Poole beamed upon Emily, the next to be presented. "I want to borrow Miss Mazere from you. Louisa will never be happy until she has her at Curradoobidgee."

"Miss Mazere!" Emily glowed with delight. Never, never had there been such an exciting New Year, since the world had begun all over again under the Waggon Star!

The Poole family and the others had left Mrs Poole free for these pleasantries. She had the old-country expectation of being deferred to.

"We were just about to go over and call upon those ladies yonder," said Mrs McEachern, "but maybe ye'd prefer to rest a wee while."

Malcolm, whose duties at this moment brought him among his womenfolk, exclaimed, "*Ladies*, Mamma! There's only Polly Lowther from McGinty's pub at Coolooluk and a couple of her friends." He and Dennis had earlier learned with relief that the Eagle Hawk Gullies women were not present.

"Ye seem to be so well acquainted that maybe ye'll bring them to us, laddie. I want that the friends of my bairns shall be mine," said Mrs McEachern quickly.

"Better leave them where they are," said Malcolm, but his mother persisted.

"There's too few womenfolk for us all not to be neighbourly."

Malcolm found it politic to hasten away. Mrs Poole observed, "The difficulty is that if we show ourselves friendly to women like that, the young men will be marrying them before we know where we are."

"They'll be doing that in any case," said Mrs McEachern, "an' we might just as well be neighbourly on an occasion like this."

Miss Lowther and her companions were surprised to be honoured instead of slighted by such highly respectable members of their own sex and accepted the invitation to the midday picnic effusively. However, they did not stay long. Finding the welcome from Dennis and Malcolm unusually constrained, they escaped as soon as possible.

3

The intrusion of the digger element rather detracted from the pleasure of the racing for the squatters, but they carried off their frequent defeats by the outsiders in a sporting spirit. There were no disastrous mishaps and any incipient disturbances were detected immediately and capably dealt with by the stewards.

Old Healey lay down for a good part of the day on an improvised couch under a spring-cart. "It's just a touch of the sun," said Mrs Healey.

"Sure all he's got to do is lie quiet till sundown. I'll take him a peck or two and stay by him."

The peck or two was a thumping meal.

"Perhaps it's the mean things he says about other people that are making him bilious," observed Rachel. Bert found this such a super-witticism that his chortles caused Emily to call out, "What's the joke?"

"That's a secret," replied Bert, to Labosseer's annoyance.

The Squatters' Race, with prize money amounting to nearly a hundred guineas, was the big race of the forenoon and was won by the Coolooluk visitors with The Digger. He had been carefully trained and had the advantage of being a professional among amateurs.

Except in the heavyweight gallops, Bert didn't get nearer the post than second or third. Malcolm and Dennis, a couple of lighter weights, carried off between them many of the prizes with their mounts, Currency Lass and Holey Dollar. Jimmy and Harry Poole, a daring young pair now sixteen and fifteen respectively, won everything they were allowed to enter, both with their father's big bay mare and their own nags, who were relatives of Black Belle. Harry was sure he could have beaten The Digger in the Squatters' Race had he been allowed to ride the Waterfall, but that had been forbidden owing to the beast's uncertain temper.

Though the course was strewn with loose boulders and, here and there, ridges of rocks as sharp as picks, it did not cause difficulties for horses trained in the chase of wild cattle around precipitous sidelings riddled with wombat holes. Every beast and rider tried his utmost to win, for nothing was to be made by "pulling".

Among the ladies, interest was keenest in the little gallops with prizes of bridles, since these prizes were inevitably presented to the riders' favourites. One bridle, already mentioned as fit for a princess, so splendid the material, so finished the workmanship, called out a big field. Bert allowed brother Harry his big bay for this, and Jim was to ride the Waterfall, at this stage of the day sufficiently tamed after winning the Gentlemen's Race for heavyweights to be safe for the boy.

"If I lend you my nags, the bridles are mine if you win," said Bert to his brothers. This was agreed to. Thus Bert had two chances, and Mary Brennan's, Emily's and Jessie McEachern's hearts fluttered deliciously. Louisa prayed Hugh Mazere might win, without much hope, for his riding was not up to the Maneroo standard. Hugh mounted thinking that if he won the bridle it would be polite to present it to Jessie since he was quartered at Gowandale for the holiday. Meanwhile, Tim Brennan

159

wanted that bridle for Emily as much as Emily wanted Bert to present it to her.

With so many hearts fluttering on the outcome, it was no wonder that the race was one of the most exciting sprints of the day. Off they went, helter-skelter, Harry coming in first on the bay, with Jim a close second on the Waterfall.

The boys dutifully brought the bridles to Bert who looked them over and, with a chuckle, handed them back. "Give them to anyone you like. I was only funning when I said I wanted them." The boys asked for advice. "Oh no, you must give them to anyone you like."

"There you are, then, Jen," said Harry to his little sister with a swagger, "no girl can ride like you!"

"Well done!" the others exclaimed, and the delighted little girl ran off in high feather to put the bridle on her horse.

Jimmy longed to give his to Bella Timson, but was too shy to run the gauntlet of the chaffing he was bound to receive. He handed it to his stepmother. "I reckon it will be a nice little bridle for Raymond," he said, and there was a general laugh.

"There'll be plenty of bridles by the time Raymond wants them," chuckled Bert.

"That won't be so long if the bairn takes after his daddy," said kind Mrs McEachern.

Only Mrs Poole did not smile, treating the tribute seriously, in the manner in which it had been offered. She took the bridle. "Thank you Jimmy, we'll put it by for him and you shall teach him to use it."

"Yah! Yah! Yah!" said Raymond, seizing the gift and slobbering upon the sweet new leather.

It was not a particularly happy day for Polly Lowther from McGinty's pub, what with Denny Healey buzzing around Emily for all to behold. But Polly was paid to distribute her favours, not to lose her heart to curly-headed Denny of the glib tongue and as reckless a rider as was ever accoutred in high boots and spurs.

4

The best of this splendid day was yet to come in the ball. The McEacherns were the hosts, and never before had the old hand-made house on the edge of the plain been racked with such violent preparations. Such bakings and washings and scourings and paperings and sewings on the part of the women, and such killings and carpentering on the part of the men — the preparations were fit to rival the Labosseer-Mazere wedding.

The McEacherns and their assistants hurried home early from the races to put the final touches to the preparations. With them went Mr and Mrs Healey. Mr Healey quite recovered en route, a fact which he attributed to the approach of sundown.

The dining room, drawing room and bedrooms adjoining had all been emptied of furniture to afford room for dancing. One of the verandahs had been closed in with tarpaulins to make a supper room. Sleeping accommodation was provided only for the babies and very young children, for the dawn would be danced in, and there were no old people. There were a few tables in a little room with a fire for any who wished to play cards, and there were seats by the wall of the ballroom for the lookers-on (who wouldn't be the matrons, considering the scarcity of maids compared with men).

When all the guests had returned from the races, a picnic meal was swallowed in the kitchen, and the ceremony of dressing began. In the bedrooms of the men's quarters, placed at right angles to the main house like the foot of an L, and where the babies would eventually be put to bed when the commotion flowed to other rooms, the men talked of razors and collars and studs and bootjacks, while in their own quarters the women exchanged curling irons and borrowed needles and thread and hairpins. The desired effects were achieved at last, with the aid of tallow candles and little square mirrors. There was no artifice, except that attained by the very obvious means of a little squeezing into tight waists, and no artificial complexions. The flowers the women wore in their hair were all from the dear old Gowandale garden, planted with flowers and shrubs from faraway England. The sheep and cattle browse in that garden now, and the stately scrub has crept down again avidly to reclaim its kingdom.

A rose bush leaning against a kitchen verandah post bore the darkest red flowers that ever bloomed. The curling velvet petals were almost purple, delicately powdered and smelling like paradise. Mrs McEachern called the variety "Prince Charlie", but Jessie said it should have been named "Flora MacDonald".

Since her arrival at Gowandale on the previous evening, Emily, who had the ineradicable hankering for red that is born in the fair-haired, had set her heart on one of those magic blooms for her hair. The rose, of course, was for Bert. At least, she hoped that he would

161

ask for it. The signs were propitious; he had been more in her vicinity than in that of any other girl during the day. Poor little Emily — how was she to know, she whose experience of life had been encompassed by the regularity and simplicity of the Three Rivers routine and the spartan respectability of Bool Bool's four first families, that marriage did not necessarily mean the end of amorous attraction for the two people concerned.

Finishing her toilet betimes, she stole outside to the rose bush, nearly colliding with Tom Stapleton, who was also spending the night at Gowandale. The working men were as welcome to the hospitality of the kitchens as were their masters to the drawing rooms, and Tom had taken up a position in the dark in the hope of a glimpse of the splendid gathering. As an oblation to his self-respect, he was dressed in his suit, faded in crossway stripes, strangely crumpled and having in its vest pocket a hairpin. The coat was tight and short, and his unmentionables, as they were designated in the polite society of his day, bulged queerly on his rump, but the kindly night hid such peculiarities.

Emily started, as did Tom to have startled her. "You be like an angel, Miss," was the tribute jerked out of him.

She was, in truth, a heavenly picture in her white, diaphanous tulle — or jaconet or organdie, or whatever it was. Laces and frills billowed around her lovely young form on the hoops that Hugh had carried for her from Bool Bool, all folded in his valise, and her ringlets were of angel gold. Her eyes were as blue as summer skies, her cheeks like England's lilies and roses, and gladness and youth and chastity enwrapped her as an aura.

"I've come for a rose," said she.

"Will I be making a light for you, Miss?"

"No, thank you, Tom. I can see two beauties, just here." Well she knew where they blew.

Encouraged by that tender embracing night with its summer zephyr from old Kosciusko to render it divine, he ventured, "I do be thinking those the prettiest roses I ever seen, Miss."

Moved partly by the kindness of her heart, burgeoning like the rose bush, and partly by a feeling of self-consciousness — it seemed to her that the universe must be proclaiming that she was seeking a rose for Bert Poole — she said, "Would you like one, Tom?"

"Aw, that I would, Miss!"

"Well, there it is, Tom, with good wishes for a very happy New Year — and no more broken collar bones!" And, lifting her finery, she seemed to Tom to float away like an angel, back to her own sphere.

Tom, who hardly knew who his mother was and certainly had no idea who his father might have been, stood there with glad New Year wishes ringing in his ears, and a rose — could it be real? He pressed it to his nose in the middle of his funny possum-like bushman's beard and smelled it and felt its velvet petals. Yes, it was true. He had a whole rose, a red, red rose, a perfect half-blown blossom all for his very own, handed to him by the princess herself!

5

McEachern was a great mon the night, ye ken, supported on either side, as by seraphim and cherubim, by Healey of Little River, bedad, and Gilbert of Maryvale, and Timson of Wombat Hill. Labosseer of Eueurunda was likewise there, and Poole of Curradoobidgee, and several visiting squatters of Goulburn, as well as Mazere Himself, J.P., of Three Rivers. Dignified in frock coats, all had their faces washed and their hair — as yet ungreying — neatly trained about their ears. Stiff collars and voluminous stocks were about their necks.

A greater man than any that night was Rab McIntosh, the chief musician. And since Simon Labosseer, Mazere and a couple of the English guests could play charmingly on the flute, Tim Brennan and old Healey and several others were decent fiddlers, and a larger percentage than can play the piano today could manage the concertina, there was no lack in the orchestral department. But Rab, the Eueurunda shepherd, was the boss cocky of the musical department and had been specially borrowed for the occasion. Rab knew so much of the hearts of the men and women on Maneroo that he was accredited with second sight, but perhaps it was only the keen observation he employed as musician at the balls when folks forgot his presence. He was a natural musician to whom every instrument was a friend, whether it was the Jew's harp, the concertina or the fiddle. He was a genius at the ballads, reels and strathspeys of his own country, and the airs of other countries had only to be hummed for him to add them to his repertoire.

Amid a storm of applause and some indulgent chaffing, he was conducted to the great fireplace where his toes would be safe from the dancers. Tom Stapleton, watching from afar, was consumed by regret.

163

Oh, that he had only learned to play the concertina — then he, like Jake Brannigan, a shepherd on hand to relieve Rab, might have had the chance of participating in so great an occasion.

Rab, after tuning up with tremendous elan, dashed into the introduction to the first quadrille. The men bowed, the ladies curtsied, and there they were!

CHAPTER XV

1

It was that slack hour before midnight, and while the little girls in short skirts, like Jenny Poole and Flora McEachern, were thrilled to be asked for a dance by Mr Mazere and Mr Labosseer, the current did not run as smoothly for some of their elders. The black-red rose was still in Emily's hair and beginning to wilt a little. She had had only one dance with Bert. It was bliss to be swung in his steel-strong arms, but he did not linger a moment with her after their dance had ended. Jessie McEachern, with a pale blush rose in her glossy black locks, was in the same plight; it seemed to her and Emily that every man in the room but the right one coveted their roses. Mary Brennan's posy of forget-me-nots and mignonette was also safely guarded from the many that wanted a sprig from it and she, like Jessie, wondered who it was that Bert really favoured. He spoke mostly to Mrs Labosseer, and the fact that he protected himself with a matron was interpreted by the three girls as his still being fancy free, and each having as good a chance as the next to attract him.

Things were equally at cross purposes with the men. While Jack Stanton wanted Mary's forget-me-nots, he had to dodge instead the rose that Agnes Brennan would have given him. Louisa's rose was waiting for Hugh, but he was hankering after Jessie's. And Malcolm, Tim and Denny all wanted what they were not invited to have. Emily provoked them with eyes that were for no one but Bert — couldn't she see that Bert enjoyed dancing with his sisters, his stepmother, Mrs McEachern, Mrs Labosseer and the other married women as much as with any girl in the place?

Malcolm, Bert, Tim and Denny went out to take a look at the kitchen fire and general supplies, and to see that the horses were safe, the night fine, and so on. Malcolm had taken a couple of nobblers during the afternoon, and now he took another. He had become a little brash, as sometimes a young man can at race meetings and balls.

"Tell you what would be a good lark — let's put on masks and bail the party up," he suggested.

"What for?" asked Bert.

"We'll make the girls give us a kiss."

"Wouldn't they do that without us bailing up the whole shoot?" asked Bert.

"The wrong ones might..." began Malcolm.

Denny cut in. His mother sometimes said sly things, the import of which had not escaped Denny. "Would Mrs Labosseer give you a kiss, Bert, if you asked her?" he said, seemingly innocently.

"She might if it was the only thing to save my life," responded Bert good-humouredly, but there was a furrowing of his straight, clean brow that warned Denny to go no further.

"Are you on?" asked Malcolm.

"I am," said Denny.

"It might be good fun, but it doesn't seem quite nice," said Tim, torn between his desire for Emily and his natural kindliness.

"Bert can favour the married women," said Denny, "while we go for the others."

"All right. I'd rather kiss Mrs McEachern than any unmarried lady in the place," said Bert carelessly, and his statement was quite true — as far as it went.

"Come along then and let's rig up."

"I don't know — it might scare the women. And if the men got their revolvers out, it might end badly," said Bert.

"Not it!" said Malcolm. "We'll just run in, kiss the girls and pull off our disguises."

They capered off and cut up a perfectly good pair of Jessie's black hose to make masks.

"How can we kiss anyone through this?" said Tim, thinking of Emily.

"All you need," replied Denny, who had evidently been considering this problem, "is to secure your lassie and then pull the mask off to kiss her."

"Maybe she'd prefer a bushranger," said Tim, a little wistfully.

"I think I'll go for Mrs Labosseer, just to put her old man in a sweat," said Denny.

"Better not," warned Bert shortly.

"Two of us go in the front and two in the back," said Malcolm.

"No, three go in the back and get on with the kissing," said Bert. "I'll stick to the front and do the bailing up." Bert foresaw danger, should any of the men get rattled, and determined to guard against it. He did not like the joke. It savoured too much of a burlesque of something that had been running in his daydreams.

A gasp ran through the party upon the appearance of three men at the back door. They turned towards the front, but there stood a tall figure holding a levelled revolver.

"Your life or a kiss," cried Malcolm to Emily, flourishing his unloaded weapon, for Bert had insisted upon balls being removed.

The revellers should have recognised the voice, but every mind was running on hold-ups. Labosseer, stubborn and fearless, strode towards Bert determined to come to issues. His wife watched him, alarmed; while she had no fear of bushrangers, the prospect of the menfolk fighting with them made her fearful. Alarm lent a startled look to her sweet features that struck to the marrow of Bert, and he leaned towards her, with no thought of any such familiarity as pressing his lips to hers or even to her hand, but only to reassure her.

"It's me, Mrs Labosseer, Bert," he said in an undertone, "and it's only Malcolm's little lark among the girls."

But Labosseer saw his wife about to be insulted by the intruders and, regardless of the danger to himself or to others, hurled himself upon Bert, striking him a heavy blow. Labosseer was a big man and no milksop, and since Bert would not counter-strike, he would have been felled to the ground had it not been for Rachel's intervention. She flung her arms about Bert, placing herself between the two men. "Stop! Stop! It's only our dear Bert. Don't hurt him!"

For one glorious moment he had her firmly in his arms. Oh, ecstasy at last! She was tight against his heart, her little cheek like velvet against his, her breath warm on his neck for a moment. Sweet-smelling as a rose bush and so small and delicate, she was all floating silken skirts and ruffles, like a little bird in a wealth of beautiful feathers. The rose in her hair was shaken loose and fell into the opening of his vest. Thus Bert came by the rose of his desire, a trophy from the field of chivalry.

It was all over, without further mischance. Bert had received a blow to stun an ox, but which, in his elation, he had scarcely felt. Labosseer was deeply upset, and Emily was disappointed that the kisses pressed hastily upon her had not been Bert's.

Mrs McEachern's voice could be heard in admonition, "Ah, laddie, what put such a callant notion in yer pate?"

"I'll not speak to you for a week," Emily was saying to Malcolm and Tim.

"Ye'll apologise at once to Miss Emily Mazere," continued Mrs McEachern. "I'd pull their stupid lugs if I were you, Miss Emily."

Thereupon the three young men went down on their knees and prayed loudly for forgiveness, till Mrs McEachern forbade them to make mock of sacred things. The dimples and colour came again to the girls' faces. In fact Emily had little difficulty in forgiving what had really been a tribute to her belleship. The other girls giggled with glee. They had adored every moment of the bail-up, and regretted its brevity. Larry Healey, blue with apprehension, shook his head and muttered something about "looking for trouble".

Mr McEachern called upon Mr Mazere to say a few words, and he responded pontifically. Being so deferred to on Maneroo — what with one daughter as mistress of Eueurunda, the other acclaimed as a belle and himself having been introduced by McEachern as Mazere, J.P., of Three Rivers — he was in full crow. Emily was clinging to his arm now, and from that place of safety threw enslaving glances upon her admirers as she threatened to ask Papa to take her home the next day.

"This joke, while undertaken in high spirits, might have ended in disaster," Mazere was intoning. "With people's minds preoccupied with bushrangers, someone might have got out his revolver and then..."

Bert felt sure that he could have handled that eventuality but he said nothing. He had a rose in his coat pocket which he could not stop touching with his beautifully fashioned fingers.

"I have laid down a procedure in case my own household should be stuck up," went on Mazere. In fact, it was Mrs Mazere who had formulated this procedure but that's neither here nor there. "It appears from what we hear that the robbers seek only money or provisions. If they are not interfered with, human life is safe — and what, may I inquire, are money and provisions compared with the lives of those dear to us?''

"It's good sense yer speakin', Mr Mazere. That's what I say meself," approved McEachern.

"If we allow the brutes to do whatever they like, they'll soon take the roofs from over our heads and insult our wives under our very noses," said Labosseer, glaring at Bert.

"Ah, but it's not for any one man to be venturesome," said Healey. "A deal of difficulty and trouble will be avoided if these fellows are left to the proper authorities."

"It's a little early, but who votes for supper now?" said Mrs McEachern, hoping to restore equanimity. This suggestion was received with enthusiasm.

"I hope you weren't hurt or frightened," Bert was taking the opportunity of saying to Mrs Labosseer.

"No, I'm sorry you got such an awful thump." Bert thereupon offered Rachel his arm to proceed to supper.

But Labosseer refused to be pacified. Sternly intercepting them, he drew his wife's arm through his with a commanding, "Come, Rachel!" Turning to Bert, he said harshly, "In this vulgar joke, *Mr Poole*, you have offered my wife an affront that I cannot overlook."

"But Simon," protested Rachel, "Bert did not insult me in any way. He was just trying to let me know it was Malcolm's little joke."

"I'm sure, Mr Labosseer," said Bert, "that Mrs Labosseer is the last lady in the world that I would ever think of insulting."

"The whole thing was my fault," said Malcolm gallantly. "I saw I'd never get a kiss from the ladies without gammon of some sort, and Bert volunteered to mind the door while we bailed the girls up."

Labosseer saw that he would make a fool of himself if he was not circumspect, so he said, "I was referring to the act of frightening frail women."

"I wasn't the least frightened — or if I was, it was only because I thought that you might hurt Bert before you found out it was a joke," returned Rachel promptly, which reply didn't help at all. Meanwhile Emily was holding back, looking for Bert. Pretending Malcolm and Tim were out of favour, she held her father's arm until Mrs McEachern paired him off with Mrs Poole. Then Mrs McEachern

169

said, "Now, Bert Poole, ye dinna deserve it, but ye take in Miss Emily Mazere and comport yerself according." Emily looked eagerly towards him. Bert could not refuse.

As he smiled at the girl and offered his arm, he saw over her head a tall figure with face hidden behind a crape mask, a slouch hat pulled down low over his forehead. He turned to the other doorway to see there a broader, shorter figure, similarly disguised.

Trapped! The real thing this time!

2

"Bail up! If any man stirs, he's a dead 'un!" said the short man roughly.

"Bail up!" repeated the tall man.

Two masked men stood behind each of the spokesmen, and others could be seen at the windows. The guests were easily trapped, since the house was of the usual pattern, with only two outside doors. The only sane policy was to follow the procedure promulgated by Mazere.

"All the men stand along the wall there," ordered the leader. The order was promptly, but sheepishly, obeyed. Larry Healey, trembling from head to foot, whispered, "The blessed Virgin preserve us, I hope no one will be fool enough to make trouble." When every man was ranged against the wall, the leader examined them for firearms.

"If it's money yer wantin', there's but a few shillings in the house," said McEachern.

"Hold yer jaw. This is ladies' night!"

"Then if that's it," said Mrs McEachern, as chipper as a cricket, "it's meself that's going to take a hand, and what is it ye're after?"

"Be easy now, Alannah! We're wishful for nothing but a little of yer society," he replied with a grotesque bow, rather like that of a performing bear. "Ye forgot to send us an invitation to this elegant assembly and be jabers, our feelin's are hurt."

"That was an oversight, Barney Logan, among neighbours, and I apologise, but ye have not shown yerself friendly since ye came to the district."

"So ye mistake me for Barney Logan."

"Maybe Barney Logan's the better man."

"That's neither here nor there, but here we are, and we've come for a little kick-up with the girls. An' the devil a morsel of harm will come to anyone — ye'll all be as happy as innocent children in their perambulators — if ye're willing to be agreeable."

"Well now, mind, Barney Logan, that ye stick to yer word."

"It's a bargain then, an' who is to open the ball with me. Won't ye step forward Mrs Labosseer. If ye be half the woman of yer ma, ye'll not be afraid of anything."

"I'm not afraid," said Rachel, stepping forward, a look of bewitching defiance on her face, "but I think you are a rude, bad man."

"Musha, musha, that's not a very friendly sentiment from ye, Asthore. Sure ye look like a little canary and speak with the manliness of a gander, and by that token I'll be easy with ye. Miss Emily Mazere, step out beside yer sister." As Emily moved forward, she glanced at Bert, but he was watching Rachel.

"Miss Jessie McEachern, Miss Mary Brennan, Miss Louisa Poole, Miss Ada Poole, Miss Agnes Brennan, Miss Spires, Miss Saunders, Miss Bella Timson." The girls, evidently well known to their assailants, stood together in the middle of the floor. Logan beckoned and four masked men came in from outside.

"Choose your partners, gentlemen!" Emily, Jessie, Mary and Louisa were requested with extravagant ceremony for the pleasure of a dance. "Now," proceeded Logan, "Mister Bert Poole Esquire will stand up with Mrs Labosseer and think well of me for the rest of his life. Mr Tim Brennan and Denny Healy and young McEachern will also step up. God Almighty Labosseer will enjoy himself lookin' on, and I'll enjoy meself lookin' on at him."

Labosseer grinding his teeth in fury and his host hardly able to restrain him, the taller ruffian put a bullet in the wall above his head just to larn him, and his companions advised him to be still. The musician was told to play and the dance went with a swing. It is doubtful if the girls ever had another dance in their lives so thrilling as that one with the masked ruffians, with their loaded revolvers. As for Bert, he was sure he never had. When the quadrille was through, the four intruders gave up their places to four others and Logan said, "This time I dance with Mrs McEachern. And then I play kiss-in-the-ring with Miss Emily and Miss Jessie and all the pretty girls."

Two or three sets went off in this way and then, during a lull, Logan took a seat. The trembling Healey saw him coming. Mrs Healey bore it more brazenly.

"Sure," Logan exclaimed, "now for a word with me old friend

Larry Healey. Sure he's gone up in the world an' it's lamentable that he's forgotten some things that he'd better remember. Sure the she-rogue he calls his wife has more pluck than himself. Sure she doesn't look as if she had repented the bargain, an' faith, there's not any woman within me reach that I wouldn't take a five-gallon keg of rum for any day. Now pluck yerself together, Larry, me old friend, like yer good Aileen, who passes for yer wife. Sure ye've got nothin' to be fearin'. It would be a sin cryin' to heaven for vengeance if I disturbed such pillars of society as ye've become — friends with Labosseer of Eueurunda himself. Hoo! Hoo! An' now why should ye mind the pleasantries of one like meself. Sure, remember what ye have said of yer neighbours duffing the very beasts ye planted yerself — and has it done them any harm at all, at all? Think now what a pleasant thing it is to say good of everyone like ye do. Ridin' round the country spreadin' sunshine every time ye open yer gob. But sure, this is more one-sided than I enjoy in conversation. Now, haven't ye a word to say in refutation?''

At this moment, when Healey was beginning to feel that his punishment was more than he could endure, Mrs Poole heard Raymond crying out, as he was apt to do during the night. She arose with calm dignity and said firmly to the speaker, "You won't mind if I go to my child? I hear him crying."

"Go on to yer child," said he with a bow. "We're very sentimental about childre. Safe passage for the lady! Now there is a lady," he continued, "if ever there was one. She takes a man and his family and turns them from wild scrubbers into as elegant a circus as there is to be found. Sure I wish to God she had taken me instead of Boko Poole." The company ventured to laugh at this. The leader then called for another set, but a cultivated English voice behind the mask of a man dressed as a digger called out, "We think the ladies have been very kind and we do not wish to intrude any further." The uninvited dancers thereupon withdrew and only the men on guard remained.

One of the men kissed Mrs McEachern's hand with a flourish as he passed, while others who were not so gentlemanly took rough kisses from Jessie, Emily and Mary. Jessie said with spirit, "There's plenty of good water on Maneroo to wash my face." She looked towards Bert, hoping that he would see that other men were not as slow as he was, but he was looking at Rachel Labosseer.

As a last act the intruders demanded the roses from the girls' hair,

172

and that is what became of the red, red rose, the pale blush one and the forget-me-nots intended for Bert Poole, who still fingered a pale pink rose, intoxicated by the revelation it carried.

"Barney Logan," said Mrs McEachern to him, "ye came uninvited but as a friend, not as a robber, and I'd like ye to have a bite, as no one has ever gone from here without hospitality. Come wi' me." He went like a lamb, after ordering his lieutenants with a nod of his head to take his place.

"Barney Logan, why would ye now, a man o' yer age be about wi' these tricks o' a callant, holdin' up the lassies for a kiss?" asked Mrs McEachern as she led the way to the supper table.

"Och! 'twas a little innocent jollity!" he replied with a sigh. "Sure I couldn't resist the temptation to lam down that God Almighty Labosseer — keep the lower orders in their places he would, in the new country like the old." Here spoke the old political malcontent, gone from bad to worse.

"And what is that wild talk about Mr Healey?"

"Sure, ask him if it's wild, an' remember it when ye hear him talkin' scandal about his neighbours."

" 'Tis New Year's day — why not turn now from your reckless ways?"

"Easier said than done, Jessie McEachern. If the world had been full of women like you, rather than strumpets like that one sittin' in there as elegant as a sack of flour, I might have been better off."

"It's a terrible thing to have a man's blood on yer head."

"I may take what's owin' to me by society, Jessie McEachern, but I'm no murderer."

"No, but ye will be, most like, before ye know it," she replied as she packed up a parcel of sandwiches. "Ye men are like a muckle of bulls in the spring, roarin' at each other in yer lunacy, an' one day a trigger will be pulled an' murder done afore ye know it, an' then no goin' back."

"Och, there's no goin' back now, I'm thinkin'. If I go forward, it's life or to swing that I can look forward to, an' if I go back, it's God help me from one of me mates."

"Poor man, I'll pray for ye tonight," said she, giving him the parcel.

"May the blessed Virgin preserve ye, Jessie McEachern. It is a good night's work, this for ye. If Gowandale is ever stuck up, ye'll be knowin' it's not my work. Sleep in yer bed content henceforth, as far as I'm concerned. Sure 'tis a proud man I am this minute to be discoursin' with ye an' 'tis a powerful queer world an' you an' me might be relatives yet.''

While Mrs McEachern was being entertained by this adventure, McEachern was considerably uneasy under the levelled aim of the revolvers of the invaders. ''I never can understand the leddies,'' he confided in an undertone to Mazere. ''Look ye now at Jessie — treatin' a ruffian and a robber as if he was one o' us.''

''My wife is just the same. She makes me tremble in my shoes sometimes, she is so utterly lacking in logic. But I suppose we can't expect that from the ladies.''

''It is no to be expected frae them,'' agreed McEachern. ''And though it seems indelicate to say it, they acted as if they veritably enjoyed the invasion. A shameless way to behave, indeed it was.''

''It's not just their shamelessness — they seem utterly oblivious of danger. Apparently they lack the reason to estimate the degree of danger.''

''They're strange kittle-kattle, I don't believe they know themselves what's in their heads,'' observed McEachern sagely.

As the intruders withdrew, they bowed elaborately to the ladies and thanked them. Then their leader, warning everyone not to leave the premises for half an hour, fired a shot or two through the back door as a hint.

3

A great babble followed their departure. The bail-up was judged to be a diggers' New Year night lark, led by the bushrangers. The number of men in digger apparel and the apologetic English voice seemed to suggest that some of the invaders, on seeing the refinement of the household, were ashamed of what they found themselves committed to and were anxious to cut it short.

But thrilling as the incident grew in retrospect to the women, it remained a galling affront to their men. A real robbery they could have borne with dignity, but this incident, they felt, lowered their prestige. They had been made to look ridiculous.

Even supper could not restore male good humour. The toasts and speeches had a fragmented character, and though the best of the night remained, the ball was over. The men were anxious to return to their homesteads to see that they were safe.

"We may find nothing but a few ashes," said Healey. "Sure, 'tis a strange thing that meself and Labosseer seem to have been singled out by them for abuse. It's given me wife a terrible turn." And thus did he dismiss the strange monologue of Barney Logan. The young men rode off in the light of a late-risen waning moon, leaving their families to follow at daylight. Labosseer was for starting there and then, but as he wanted to take Rachel with him, there was an outcry.

"Go yerself and leave Mrs Labosseer wi' us. 'Tis meself that has a safe conduct from Barney Logan henceforward," said Mrs McEachern.

"I prefer to keep my wife under my own protection," he returned shortly.

"It's no to be wondered at, she's a bonnie wee thing an' a sight for sore eyes," she said. But Labosseer would not be mollified, and insisted upon taking his wife, Mrs Millburn, and a maid in the carriage. Mrs McEachern, however, prevailed upon Mazere, Hugh and Emily to remain. "Ye'll stay wi' us, Mr Mazere, and cheer the good man after the bobbery. It's no so often he has a visitor that can give him the pleasure o' such a crack as yerself." Mazere was delighted to remain in the comfortable and appreciative atmosphere of Gowandale instead of hooting off in the chill air to Eueurunda with Labosseer, who, to his mind, seemed to be taking the whole affair unnecessarily seriously.

The women spent the remainder of the night discussing, with keen enjoyment, the raid. The men wished they would hold their silly tongues and let the thing drop. But they wouldn't, and eventually the story became known far and wide. It became embroidered with time and is a legend to this day. The men always dwelt on the fact that Labosseer, a proud man, had to be held down while the bushrangers kissed his wife — though in fact they did not kiss her at all. The women preferred to recount how Mrs McEachern lectured the chief bushranger and how Gowandale became immune to the visitations of such gentry henceforward, and how Jessie, her daughter, sauced them by saying she would wash her face clean in the thousand burnies of Gowandale. "Oh, Jessie was a lovely young woman in her day!" they would say. Listening youth would exclaim, "She beautiful — that queer looking old thing, all dried up like leather!" The reply would be,

"There's none of you young ones could come near her — and as for Emily Mazere, she was even lovelier — a lily and roses beauty with a kind word for everybody. All the young men were mad after her, but it never turned her head a bit."

4

Characteristically, Labosseer waited until things had settled down after the bail-up before speaking to his wife of the affront he had suffered at the ball. He put this in the forefront of his grievances in order to conceal the demon of jealousy that was tormenting him.

"Rachel, there is something I wish to say to you. Are you listening?"

"Yes."

"I don't like the part the Pooles took in that so-called joke — and I am also suspicious about the strange coincidence of those ruffians arriving so soon after that shameful episode."

"It was Malcolm's joke — no one knew anything of the bushrangers coming."

"I have no doubt young McEachern thinks it is his joke, but I'll be bound he never would have thought of it but for Poole." Rachel looked at him in surprise. It was beginning to dawn on her that a husband — a tall, stately husband at that — could be jealous. Silly!

"There was one very sinister circumstance connected with the incident in my mind."

"What was that?"

"When Mrs Poole heard the baby crying, they let her go out of the room without question. They would not have trusted anyone else to leave the room, I am sure."

Rachel laughed merrily. "So you think dear old Bert is the chief of the gang — what a joke!"

Labosseer's brow clouded. "You are too free with your *dear* Bert."

Seeing his anger, Rachel adopted a conciliatory tone. "Well, he's like a brother to me — because of Charlotte, of course. And, but for Bert, Mamma would have been drowned that night on the Yarrabongo. I shall never forget how splendid and brave he was."

"But for his flashness, your mother would not have been able to risk her life for small cause."

"What about Mrs McEachern going off with Barney Logan for

176

half an hour — what do you make of that?'' protested Rachel.

"The McEacherns can do what they like — their integrity is above reproach." Rachel was silent, but there was a smiling radiance on her little face and the demon whispered to Labosseer again.

"And what did that ruffian mean when he said, 'Mr Bert Poole will dance with Mrs Labosseer and thank me for life'?''

"Perhaps you looked so grumpy that he thought dancing with Bert would be a nice change," she said with a merry peal of laughter.

"Now you are light. Bert Poole's society will give you the reputation of a wanton woman and I'll have no more of it, do you understand?''

"I've never had any of his society. He's never been here and I've never been there."

"And indeed you never will. That is my wish."

"I have already promised to go and see Mrs Poole. And if she comes here, what am I to do — shut the door in her face? Make a scandal in the neighbourhood?''

"Anyone who comes to my house shall be treated with hospitality, but you will not go to other houses when I do not wish it.."

"*Your* house! When you took me away from home, you said this was to be my house! I wish I had never come to this horrid, windy old Maneroo! Papa might have been hot-tempered sometimes, but he was never cold and horrid!'' And Rachel, bewildered, burst into tears.

Not proof against the tears of his wife, he gave way in part. He would accompany her on one formal visit to Curradoobidgee. Rachel was content for the present, for the proposed visit would relieve the awkwardness she felt about the Pooles.

5

Bert rode away from Gowandale into the perfect night through country which paradise might equal but not excel. He splashed into the singing streams and galloped girth-deep in flowers across the dew-drenched, tussocked plains. He eased up on the timbered ridges where the snow gums stood like brides in veils of perfumed lace, and threaded his way through shrubberied gullies. As the sun rose, he laughed in company with the kookaburras, and sang with the operatic magpies that were sweetly intoning matins. Ah, but it was good to be alive, with the Waterfall invincible on the bit, and in his pocket a withering rosebud that had made a world-shaking revelation. At last he knew why his life hung upon Rachel Labosseer's every movement. Marriage, after all, need not be a barrier to his feelings for this lady. The birds, the streams, the splendid ringing clatter of the Waterfall's hoofs on the ridges — all sang the refrain of beautiful little Rachel. That she was Labosseer's wife could no longer stem the intoxicating revelation. Sufficient to the hour was the glory thereof.

Good Mrs McEachern kept most of the young people about her, and the work of reducing Gowandale to order was as merry as a circus. Bert was absent, but he had left behind him three maids all convinced that joy and adventure depended upon seeing him again as soon as possible.

The way to Bert was through Curradoobidgee, and the surest way to Curradoobidgee was through Mrs Poole. And since the way to Mrs Poole's heart was through the prodigy, Raymond, that young panjandrum, though he had not inherited the Poole beauty, did not lack petting and kissing and attention in general. Emily was anxious to get to Curradoobidgee without delay, and Mr Mazere unwittingly became a pawn in her game. He had much enjoyed talking about England with Mrs Poole and had instantly recognised her as being socially congenial. In return she invited him over to Curradoobidgee, on the pretext that she needed advice about her garden and orchard.

Thus Emily and her father descended upon Curradoobidgee on the third day of the New Year, and Labosseer was chagrined to hear that his father-in-law was established with the Pooles before he could intervene.

Mr Mazere returned to Three Rivers with the men of the party at the end of the most enjoyable week he could remember. The Brennan, Stanton and Saunders girls returned to Bool Bool after a month, and Emily was permitted to remain for the winter at Eueurunda to keep Rachel company.

Those were enchanted months for Emily. Bert did not seem to be won, but there was always the hope that he would be at the next meeting. She did not get many visits to Curradoobidgee; Bert was only too anxious to be her escort to and fro, rendering Labosseer increasingly hostile.

Nevertheless, Emily had Mrs Poole on her side as well as the infatuated Louisa, and Labosseer, much as he disliked his family's connection with the Pooles, was willing to extend it if he could thereby get rid of Bert. In his calm moments he wondered if his jealousy was not without foundation, but the proof seemed to be obvious. While it was plain for all to see that Emily was completely infatuated, it having become as near to a pursuit as the girl's modesty and inhibitions permitted, and even though it would have been an ideal match for Bert, he hung off, as unresponsive as stone. It seemed clear to Labosseer that Bert merely used Emily as an opportunity to hang around his wife. After some deliberation he wrote a confidential, man-to-man letter to his father-in-law. He explained Emily's infatuation and Bert's indifference. He thought, speaking as Emily's brother, in deepest affection and with her welfare at heart, that it would be better to remove her from Maneroo for the present. Emily would not have forgiven her brother-in-law had she known, but the secret was kept by the two men and her mother. The latter wrote that she needed Emily at home and, as Hugh Mazere had formed an attachment for Jessie McEachern, he was only too delighted to go to Maneroo to escort his sister home as soon as the longer days came.

CHAPTER XVI

Young Tim and Mary Brennan were relieved to hear that Emily was back in Bool Bool; Mary waited quietly for what she might hear, while Tim gave his trusty steed, Kilkee, such a grooming as did both man and beast a world of good. Next he turned to every buckle of his gear, then to his own person until his locks were trained to the right curve about his ears, his face was razored to a velvety softness, his immaculate collar points were high about his chin, and a voluminous neckcloth was arranged as if he feared a chill or had a goitre.

He was presently walking in the Mazere garden in the cool of the evening, smelling the flowers, looking at the little loquat trees and the famous baby sweet briar, and hoping that Emily would give him a buttonhole.

"Sure ye should see his room!" his mother had exclaimed to his father, after watching him ride off. "It's like a whirlwind has hit it, the rejected collars and things strewn about like hay. An' Kilkee, polished like for a horse fair, an' himself shining like a brass candlestick an' ridin' off as manly as a young gander who's found out he's a swan an'..."

"By the hokey, it's a drake without the curl on his tail he'll find himself any minute."

"An' why would ye be so sure? Where would a princess find a handsomer young fella than our Tim?"

"Handsome begorra! He's about as handsome as my old strawberry bull, and why would a beauty like Emily be lookin' on this side of the road? It's got to finish, I tell ye, Maria. Never a bit of good ever came of these mixed marriages."

"They could be very happy."

"Och, musha, it's all very fine till the childre come."

"Sure let them divide, an' we can pray maybe that they'd all take after ye an' be boys."

"Sure Maria, what would ye be meanin' be the like of that? Sure ye haven't the hang of logic at all."

In the Mazeres' front garden Tim had manoeuvred Emily into giving him both a rose and a sprig of the sweet-scented verbena bush which had been planted in front of the Old House at the time of Emily's birth. "Did you leave your heart behind you in Maneroo?" he asked. "You'll be eighteen next week, you know. Time is running short."

"Mamma would rather we didn't marry till we are twenty-one." Emily was guarded by Fannie, Rhoda and Philip, Fannie walking with her pet crane. Rhoda and Philip insisted that Tim should see their bantams, descendants of the ones that had hatched at Mungee at the time of Charlotte and Philip's wedding. The children were fond of Tim, and would not be dismissed. They liked to be carried on his shoulders, holding on by his thick, red locks. Tim was satisfied by his finding that Emily was still free. He still had as good a chance as anyone else — many hearts could be won and lost in the space of three years.

Their mutual interest in Maneroo gave them plenty to talk about and Emily was as sweet and genial as of yore, so Tim thought he was progressing.

On his return to Brennan's Gap, Mary, who had lain awake unable to sleep, went to his room. "Has Emily any Maneroo news?" she asked, with a simulated yawn of indifference. "Did you give her my love and tell her I'll be over tomorrow?"

"Yes, she's expecting you. By the way, Charlie Timson is mad after Ada Poole now. He's forgotten Maud, apparently."

"It's wonderful how some seem to forget," said Mary pensively. But she was content with the knowledge that Bert was still free. Tim's bearing was not that of one who has heard that his love is engaged to another.

181

In the following weeks, while Bool Bool was at its busiest with the lambing, maize sowing, and with the wool-washing and shearing approaching, Tim's pursuit of Emily came to a head. The wholehearted fellow was in a volcanic state until it should be settled one way or the other. He at last found Emily unguarded by the children and pleaded his cause, without reservation and bravely, as becomes the natural gentleman before his princess. His heroic youth and vigour could hardly have failed, but for that previous engagement of Emily's affections. Pressed, Emily would not in her maidenly modesty confess what was clear for all but Tim to see.

"Tim dear, I love you as brother, but not the other way."

"Couldn't you love me the other way in time? I'll wait," pleaded Tim.

"I don't know yet whether I want to be married at all," said the girl, desperately seeking to gain time for that laggard at Curradoobidgee.

It was trying to the maid. It was tragedy to the man.

"Emily, you don't hate the sight of me?"

"Oh no, Tim dear, I love you very much as a *brother*." His hand, all covered with red hair and big freckles, a mightily honest, capable hand, closed over hers. Its warmth and gentleness fluttered her tender heart. It was dreadful to hurt her dear playfellow, who had always been ready to give all he had. Her gentle tears fell upon her pretty pink cheeks, and Tim was cut to the core.

"Don't cry, Emily, ma chree. My heart is yours always for ever. Whether you want it or not, it is yours to play with or trample on."

"Oh Tim, how can you say such a terrible thing? I could die to think of hurting your dear heart. Your mother and father will hate me for hurting you."

"Oh no, they won't. No one dare hate you or I should hate them. And sure, cushla ma chree, if you can't stand me, I'll up and go away to Queensland."

"Oh no, I couldn't bear to think of you not being here! Please don't love me in the wrong way, but in the old way — like a friend."

There were three years, and she did not hate him. She could not bear him to leave Bool Bool. He would win her yet. The tenacity of a lover's hope is supramundane.

Yet the strain on him became plainly visible. He lost weight till his mother was full of brooding grief. His father, observing the reckless

182

feats to which Kilkee was driven, feared for his son's neck or spine.

"Maybe if I threaten him with no quarter if he marries a Protestant, that might cure him," suggested Tim Senior.

"Ah now, don't be foolish Tim, mavourneen. Sure if by one flick of yer eyelash ye hurt that child when he's goin' through what he is, an' it rakin' the flesh off him before our eyes, it's meself ye'll have to reckon with."

"Murder, woman, I'm not goin' to do anything but put up with the lovesick gander till he plucks himself together. But sure if I were in his shoes, I'd win the girl!"

"Would ye now, ye struttin' old gander yerself!"

"Sure, didn't I cut out young Desmond O'Kennedy, and he then driven to be a priest."

"Och, me jewel, don't ye get cocky. Sure I took ye meself as the least of the two evils, an' it's often I'm thinkin' ye the greater." This crusher reduced Tim Senior to his proper place, as escort, it turned out, to Maria who went over to spend the next day at Three Rivers as ambassadress for the fevered Tim.

Tim, standing up to his father on the point of religion, had turned stubborn as a mule. "I don't care if she's a Protestant or a Hottentot. The church can do what it likes. Emily Mazere is the girl for me...if I can get her," he added wistfully. His wistfulness brought his parents firmly down on his side. They were warm-hearted, generous souls with a deep affection for the Mazeres. Brennan Senior secretly felt that the girl was worth it, and his mother wondered how any girl could find it in her heart to refuse Tim.

Mr and Mrs Mazere talked the situation over amicably with their old friends, expressing their deep affection for Tim. There was, of course, the question of religion, but even that problem was not insurmountable. It was a matter entirely for the young people.

Her parents did not divulge Emily's preoccupation with Bert Poole. They were loyal to her in that. Even so, the girl's infatuation was known to them all and sensed in the background. "Och, musha, they could be as happy as paradise if only they would let us do the pickin' for them," said Maria to Rachel when the interview came to an end.

She sought Emily privately, trembling at her temerity before the regality of youth, but valiant and humbling herself for her dear boy's sake. "Ah, Alannah, what are ye goin' to do with my beautiful boy?"

she demanded. "Sure ye have him ragin' after ye as mad as a gander. He's pinin' away before me eyes with the ravages of his tender heart."

"Oh, Mrs Brennan, please, don't say such terrible things. He only thinks he wants me, and I hope there will soon be someone nicer."

"Sure who could be nicer than the pair of ye, mavourneen? Don't ye think ye could love him? A little to begin with would be enough. The rest would come with the childre."

Emily melted in blushes at the mention of childre. "Oh no, Mrs Brennan. I love Tim as a brother. He'll soon forget — look at Charlie Timson who was raging about Maud."

"Och, but my boy is no Charlie. Tim will never change. Sure ye've had all of him since ye crawled upon the floor, an' he givin' ye everything he ever had. Devil a morsel of harm would it do some of them others, but my poor Tim is kilt entirely with the burden of his love."

"It breaks my heart to hurt him and I'd love to marry him because he's your son, but I only have a sisterly affection. I can't help it."

"Sure, I don't know what's comin' to ye young people. There is Jack Stanton wild for Mary and when I ask her what she is goin' to do with him, she says to me, 'Maybe, Ma, I'd rather take the veil than marry just any gossoon that's walkin' about on two legs.' 'Sure, do ye want one specially constructed with three legs?' says I, an' we left it at that."

It was bad enough to be rent by compassion for Tim, but to have dear Mrs Brennan pleading and to have to hurt her was more than Emily could bear. But for Bert, she felt she could not have resisted the mother's appeal. It reduced her to sobs. Mrs Brennan wrapped the girl to her.

"Now, Alannah, I'll tell ye a secret that no one knows, not even my own, an' ye'll keep it safe, won't ye?" Emily promised. "Well now, when I was your age there was a boy I loved, och, I was wild for him, but I never could get him to consider me, but there was my old Tim as lovin' as your Tim is today. Sure I could never get rid of him at all, at all. But the devil a morsel of encouragement would the other fellow bestow on me, an' sure at last he went for the priesthood and that finished it for certain. But I had me senses with me and managed so 'twas thought he was takin' orders on account of meself, an' though

I thought me heart was breakin' I turned to me faithful Timmy, an' now, musha, he's dearer than me own heart to me, Asthore, an' sure he never knows he's not me first love. Sure I've forgotten it meself mostly, an' would not have it otherwise. An' we'll say nothin' now, but maybe someday it might be like that with my boy, an' sure he'd be happy anyhow, an' us women will have this secret together, that way we'll get the best of the men on one count. The blessed Virgin help us, they have it on us in too many others."

"Thank you, Mrs Brennan for telling me, and you don't hate me for hurting dear Tim's feelings, do you?"

"Ah!" and she folded the girl more closely to her warm heart, "Alannah, ye needn't fear that yer old friend Maria could ever find in her heart anything but love for the Mazeres. Besides," she added with a kiss, "life is young for ye yet, and ye'll remember what I've said."

CHAPTER XVII

1

It was nearly three years since Charlotte had left Three Rivers. A year had passed since the ball at Gowandale, a troublesome year for all the Southern District. The diggings at Coolooluk, and others rising like pustules all about the ranges, had changed the old order. These days the hills were full of fossickers and cattle duffers. Land was being taken up by a new breed of squatter, some of whom were of questionable stamp and without doubt cover for the gang which operated from Eagle Hawk Gullies.

Nearly every settler had been stuck up, some more than once. Timson of Wombat Hill, his son Charlie, who at Christmas had married Ada Poole, Healey, Brennan, Stanton Senior, Saunders Senior, and Richard Mazere at Nanda — all had been relieved of valuables or provisions or firearms. Only four houses remained unmolested — Gowandale, Eueurunda, Three Rivers and Curradoobidgee. The immunity of Gowandale was attributed to the compact with Mrs McEachern that Barney Logan had entered into on the night of the ball, that of Eueurunda to the fact that there were many hands about and generally a number of male guests invited for the good shooting that the neighbourhood afforded. And people said the bushrangers were afraid to tackle Curradoobidgee because there were now four dead shots in the family. Three Rivers was supposed to be

186

safe because it was not a compact dwelling and, like Eueurunda, always sheltered a good number of male hands and guests.

Many were suspected of sympathising with the bushrangers and presently the vague suspicions that had been gathering about Bert Poole gained momentum. Larry Healey did all in his power to foster these speculations. In fact, he knew nothing against the Pooles, but feared they knew too much of him. Uneasy about Barney Logan's tirade on the night of the New Year's ball, he would have given his soul to know if any of it had stuck in the minds of the hearers. Coward that he was, he thought the way to clear himself was to throw dirt at others.

Even so, more than one robbed settler testified that they had seen, as the robbers rode away in the moonlight, a dark horse with a white mane and tail. A beast so marked was as conspicuous as a speckled crow, and the only one known from Gundagai to Goulburn and back to Maneroo was Bert's far-famed stallion, Waterfall.

Labosseer gave willing credence to these rumours. Bert was still uncommitted, despite the fact that there wasn't a girl who knew him but was anxious to lure him from his bachelor condition. The reason for their failure was there in his eyes for all to behold when Rachel Labosseer was around. She now had in her arms the trammels for which Simon had longed, but it did not allay his jealousy. He saw a sinister reason for the immunity of Three Rivers and Eueurunda — Bert spared these households because of his wife.

Other factors seemed to point to Bert. Whenever Malcolm, Denny or one of the Gilberts went to Curradoobidgee that year, they nearly always found Bert away from home. Denny reported this at Little River and his father made much of it. Mrs Healey, who never said much and that little rarely expressing faith in her fellows, once said to Bert slyly, looking the other way as was her habit, "I hear you've lost Waterfall, Bert."

"No, I haven't lost him. What makes you think so?"

"Only that so many people who have been stuck up say the bushrangers have a horse with a white mane and tail."

"They're barking up the wrong stump," was Bert's only comment. He did not explain that the Waterfall was at stud. But Mrs Healey manufactured the bullets that old Larry Healey fired, he thought, and if these were her present brand, there must be some queer yarns around. Indeed there were.

"If Bert isn't a bushranger, the makings of a fine one are

wasted," said Labosseer one night to his wife when his irritation got the better of him. His comment was apt. Had Bert turned highwayman and had there been a price on his head, he would soon have been a figure of romance for whom there would have been not a girl in all the countryside but would have risked her honour to shelter him.

Labosseer wrote to Mazere about the rumours and "the unfortunate Poole connection". Mrs Mazere, deeply distressed, stoutly said she didn't believe a word of it. Then Isabel confessed to her mother that she herself had seen one of the bushrangers disappearing from Mungee on a horse with a white mane and tail.

Mazere favoured Tim Brennan as a corrective for Emily, but it was all to no purpose.

"Tim is nice, Mamma, if he wouldn't persist in bothering someone who doesn't want him. I can never, never love him," Emily said when her mother tackled her on the subject.

"Is it Bert, my child?"

Emily paled and flushed and said in low voice, "Yes, Mamma."

"But my dear, he does not ask you to marry him. They even say he is mixed up with that Polly Lowther gang from Coolooluk."

Emily burst out sobbing. "Mamma, I don't care what they say. I just don't believe it."

Mrs Mazere, recalling the valour of the young man on the river crossing, was loath to believe it herself. "It's not nice to believe evil of anyone, but there must be someone he cares for."

"I can't help that, Mamma. I shall love him always, and no one else, till my dying day," said the girl passionately. Her mother comforted her and said no more. Emily had always let her mother see the letters she received from Dennis and Malcolm, which were couched in ardent terms. Ned Stanton and Tim Brennan were equally devoted. What could be the reason, Mrs Mazere wondered, for Bert's aloofness? There had to be some other attraction.

She had never seen Bert paying special attention to Rachel, except on the night of the flood, and she then had been too preoccupied to note what Charlotte suspected. Such a thing would never have occurred to her, in any case, any more than it would have to Hugh or his father. But Rab McIntosh, the Eueurunda musician, could have told her, as could Labosseer, if he had not been too proud to admit such a thing.

Poor Emily never for an instant doubted her hero's integrity. In great distress she felt at last compelled to write and put the whole case before Charlotte. Her letter concluded:

> Do come home and help me clear him. I am the only one who believes in him. It is terrible, and breaking my heart to hear such things. I wrote to him to come and see me and tell me all about it and prove that what they say is not true, and he never answered. Mamma is longing to have you home and Papa is getting quite angry that Philip doesn't come and be forgiven. He wants to take Mamma home to see Grandpapa in England, and he can't unless you and Philip mind Three Rivers. There is a diggings right near here now so Philip can't have that as an excuse to stay away any longer and baby Philip will be a man if you don't come soon.

2

The up-country *Courier*, voicing the opinion of its squatter subscribers, called on the rich and aristocratic relatives of the bushrangers to come out on the side of law and order by assisting the troopers to put down the outlawry. Labosseer was sure that this exhortation was especially intended for him, and it wrung his withers unendurably.

Knowing Mrs Poole to be an ambitious woman, he humbled his pride sufficiently to ride over to put the case before her privily. She appeared genuinely upset about the evil suspicions clinging to her stepson, but at the same time she was indignant that such rumours should be given credence. Her explanation of Bert's frequent absences was that he must be enamoured of one of the pretty girls of the Eagle Hawk connection. This was the case with Malcolm McEachern, as many knew. But Labosseer felt that the explanation lacked plausibility.

Then the McEacherns asked Bert to help the mounted troopers in clearing out the Eagle Hawk Gullies crowd. It was a hopeless task for the troopers to try to dislodge anyone from those fastnesses. Bert had a supreme contempt for even what the Eagle Hawk crowd knew of the land. He could have led them a dance and got away every time, had he so desired.

Mrs McEachern pleaded with him. She had already forbidden Jessie to associate with him any more than necessary, which had aroused in that brave lassie the desire to do something so spectacular that all the world would know that she cared not a fig for the rumours.

She wrote a letter to Bert embodying this sentiment, which Bert burned carefully along with the one from Emily, and another from Mary Brennan, so that no one should see them.

"Laddie, ye've brought suspicion on yerself. Can ye no do something to clear it up? Can ye no help the troopers?"

"It would be a waste of time trying to help such a pack of old hens. Might just as well send out a bale of wool on a wheelbarrow to catch the bushrangers," said Bert in his quiet way. "All it would do would be to bring the gang down on us again. We'd find Curradoobidgee burned over our heads, and all our best horses done in like poor Black Belle. I know a trick worth two of that."

"Well, laddie, ye must do something."

"Perhaps I will, presently."

"Can ye explain why the robbers have been seen getting away on a horse like the Waterfall, and there no other like him between the Upper Murray and the Murrumbidgee?"

"I expect that mystery could be cleared up pretty easily," said Bert shortly. He had long since known that the horse in question was a ewe-necked, hollow-backed mare who spraddled the off hind hoof. She had been ridden by the destroyer of Black Belle three years before.

"We're blessed to have been free from bloodshed hitherto. If Barney Logan and his friends could be taken without murder and put safely under lock and key for fifteen years, it would be well. I've seen ye grow from a wee laddie. Ye're dear as one of my own bairns — can ye no do something to help us now?"

"I'll do my best presently, Mrs McEachern," he said calmly, and rode away towards Eagle Hawk to do a little scouting.

On these expeditions he rode a small yellow bay with a dash of Timor, hardy and sure-footed as a goat. She knew the country as well as Bert did, and though seemingly dwarfed by her rider, she carried him up hills so steep that no amateur could have remained seated on her, nor any girths but those of sheer greenhide have stood the strain. Then down again, by a series of props.

The day after his talk with Mrs McEachern, Bert took her up a seemingly impassable gully neck to where he knew of a wonderful limestone cave. It had an arched entrance like that of a great cathedral and, inside, was large enough to hold all the troopers and bushrangers of Maneroo and their horses. Its entry camouflaged by a springhead and a clump of ti-tree, inside it was dry and firm. Anyone not familiar with the place would have turned away at the springhead, the water of which immediately obliterated all tracks.

Bert left his pony tethered in the centre of a dense clump of ti-tree and muzzled with a handkerchief so that she could not betray him by neighing. Then, under cover, he crept to the opening of the cave and listened, his hand on one of the six-shooters in his belt. There was no sound. Cautiously, he entered and investigated. Horse dung, hay and other odds and ends showed that horses and men had been quartered there. The cave stretched away into further caverns, and he heard the sound of dripping water and an underground stream.

The clatter of hoofs was presently heard and Bert had time to secrete himself before the figure of a man was silhouetted in the opening. His eyes now adjusted to the semi-darkness, Bert recognised Barney Logan, Sandy Burn, their friend Tom Cane and another man. On previous occasions, safely hidden in a hollow tree or other shelter, Bert had heard scraps of their plans, but now he was at a real conclave. For this moment, he had long been watching and waiting.

Eueurunda was to be stuck up the very next night. Bert was triumphant as he heard the simple plans. It seemed that Labosseer had until now been left alone because of the well-armed nature of his household. But tomorrow night, Bert learned, the household was to be only slightly manned. Labosseer had only one guest, old Dr James from Bool Bool, who had been sent to Eueurunda to recover from one of his bouts, and the trustworthy hands would be away with sheep that had recently been sold to other stations. Two of the Eagle Hawk sympathisers had lately been hired at Eueurunda, and tomorrow night were to betake themselves to a shepherd's hut to play cards, leaving the place unprotected and also thereby clearing themselves of any charges of complicity.

The raid was timed for the dinner hour, when Labosseer, who always preserved table ceremony, would be in the dining room with its one door and small windows. Sandy Burn was to guard the back, the other man the front, Cane to keep the family at bay and Barney Logan to ransack the premises. They expected considerable booty and planned to take a couple of packhorses to carry it away. Should the sentinels give the warning whistle, each man was to make off as hard as he could go.

"No bloodshed if possible," said Burn. "So long as we pluck these fowls without hurtin' them, we can have all the friends we need, but if we pot anyone, every man's hand will be against us."

"No bloodshed if possible," confirmed Logan, "and we're all polite to the ladies."

"But if that God Almighty Labosseer wants to resist, and if it's a question of him or me, God help him," said Cane.

3

Next morning Bert was so unusually lively that he attracted the attention of his stepmother. He whistled and burst into bits of song as he cleaned his bits and buckles, boots and spurs. Now and again he practised shrill, ear-splitting whistles with his fingers. Special attention was given to his revolvers and he took pot shots out the back door at the domestic animals, eventually puncturing the comb of a strutting rooster and bringing Louisa down on him for his brutality. Then, without explanation, he seized half the dough Louisa was rolling out for a pie and put it in a handkerchief. Straight after lunch he rode off on Black Belle No. 2.

Louisa frankly stated her belief that he had gone mad. In the light of Labosseer's recent call upon her, Mrs Poole felt disturbed and expressed her fears to her husband when he came home at sundown.

"What horse was he on?"

"Black Belle No. 2."

"Did he say where he was going?"

"He said he was going to meet Tom Stapleton, but he went towards Eueurunda."

"I reckon I'll wait up for him tonight and see what time he comes in — and what he looks like," was all that Poole said.

Meanwhile Bert dashed on his way with the elation of a cavalry officer whose military strategy is at last about to bear fruit. An adolescent dream fed on the great romances his stepmother had read to him was about to blossom into action. Ridge and plain were taken at a rattling pace and with song and shout in anticipation of the promised adventure.

She is won. We are gone, over bank bush and scaur;
They'll have fleet steeds that follow, quoth young Lochinvar.

"My oath they will, old girl!" he added, letting the good mare stretch herself.

Dusk found him and the faithful Tom Stapleton in a clump of

trees overlooking the more covered approach to Eueurunda. Bert, in deciding that he could scarcely manage without an assistant, had chosen Tom for his quietness and obedience. Brother Jim was a little too green and heady.

They watched the twinkling lights come on about the homestead. The lantern in the awning between the house and kitchen was plainly visible. That meant dinner was due, and they waited tensely. At last they heard horses approaching and passing on towards the house. Pinching their own horses' nostrils so that they should not neigh, Bert and Tom waited till the robbers were well past and then, fifteen minutes later, followed circumspectly to the cow-yards. Here they tied their nags, muzzled them and proceeded on foot.

Things seemed to be progressing without a hitch. The bushrangers' horses were tied up to the palings at the bottom of the orchard, a spot affording a clean getaway from the premises. One was the ewe-necked, hollow-backed mare, with a white mane and tail.

The dogs that had barked vociferously at the approach of the strangers settled down contentedly after announcing Bert and Tom, who were known to them.

Tom stood by while his master reconnoitred. In the light of the rising moon, Sandy Burn could be seen guarding the back premises. Bert drew back a few paces, mewing like a cat, and at that signal Tom Stapleton crept up. Bert made sure of his tackle and, in stockinged feet, the two men crept forward. What young Jimmy Poole had lately undergone as Man Friday to his brother's practice bore fruit in the next instant. Before Sandy Burn knew what was happening, he had a noose about his shoulders that rendered his arms useless, and was thrown violently to the ground, Tom in charge of the rope and Bert with his gag of dough ensuring that no sound issued. In about three minutes Burn was tied securely to a tree.

So far so good. Bert looked to his further tackle and proceeded according to the plan he had devised. He was masked and dressed much like the bushrangers, a ruse designed to confuse the bushrangers and to gain time in case of surprise. The second sentinel was at a short distance from the front of the main house, his attention not so much on the house as on the road from Gowandale and Wombat Hill. This man, Erroll, was put out of action in the same way as the first, and with less risk of being heard from the house.

The task ahead promised to be more difficult and if Bert's plan failed, he meant to use the bushrangers' own warning whistle which would call them off. This was the moment to send Tom Stapleton off for the troopers who, he knew, were not far away that night. Tom had instructions to lead his beast quietly away from the house, and then gallop like hell. The faithful Tom, though anxious to remain, obeyed like a well-drilled soldier. Bert now turned his attention to Logan and Cane. If the bushrangers were working according to plan, Tom Cane would be bailing up the household in the dining room while Barney Logan ransacked the other rooms.

If the house had been of the usual bull-run layout, Bert could not have operated single-handedly, but the front door, as has been previously recorded, opened onto a square hall. Bert gained this safely through the front door, which had been left open. Bert was well acquainted with the plan of the house, since there wasn't a neighbour who had not constantly inspected it during its building. After listening for a moment he crept softly back outside and along the verandah, and looked into the Labosseers' bedroom, where he saw Barney Logan at work. A little further around, he could see through the dining room window that the family was bailed up, as he had expected, by Cane, masked and with a brace of revolvers. Then he returned quietly through the entrance hall to the bedroom. This was easy as Barney Logan was making a great noise in his hasty search and Cane, concentrating on Labosseer, was depending on the sentinels.

The room was in a state of considerable upheaval. The contents of drawers and boxes were strewn about, and Barney was putting a selection of articles through the open window preparatory to carrying them away. Some of Mrs Labosseer's fine silk dresses and many of her husband's best clothes had been chosen. Standing in shadow and watching through the open doorway, a feeling of elation overcame Bert. He had the drop on Barney now; if Barney caught sight of him, he would mistake him for Cane or Erroll.

Near the doorway was a heavy footstool, used by Mrs Labosseer when nursing the baby. As Barney filled a bolster cover with articles of jewellery, silver-backed brushes, hand mirrors, candlesticks and silver-topped bottles, one of his revolvers on the mantelpiece, the other in his belt, Bert lifted the footstool, crept up behind Logan and felled him to the ground. The elderly man went down without a sound and lay quite still. For a horrified moment, Bert thought he had killed him, and his impulse was to call for help for the man, the noise of whose

194

ransacking had made the thud of the blow pass unnoticed through the thick stone walls. His heart was pounding like a sledgehammer and disturbing his judgement. He decided that to attempt the capture of Cane was too risky. A stray bullet might touch Rachel. He ran swiftly out the front and from the garden gate gave the warning whistle.

4

Until Bert's intervention, the raid at Eueurunda had gone off smoothly. Dr James, Labosseer and his wife, Mrs Millburn the companion, the baby's nurse-girl, the housemaid and the cook had all been quickly lined up along the wall. The remaining shepherds and stockmen, with the exception of two men employed about the premises who had been "squared", were out of hearing. Mrs Labosseer was in agony, since her baby's crib was in a little room adjoining her own. So far she had not heard him cry. He was a fine child who slept well and sucked with gusto. Following the precedent of Mrs Poole, she asked the bushranger to let her go to him, but Cane told her to hold her jaw if she wanted to be safe. Labosseer was also told to slew his head and not look at his jailer, unless he wanted a bullet between the eyes.

This confrontation had continued tensely for perhaps thirty minutes, until they suddenly heard the shrill whistle which all the Southern District knew meant that the men were disturbed. No sooner did Cane turn to bolt than Labosseer, with all his wits about him, leaped to his firearms.

Bert stood outside the garden gate awaiting Cane, and as the bushranger fled he fired in the hope of cracking his thigh bone. But Bert was a trifle rattled and, in the uncertain light of the moon, the shot went wide. Presently two horses could be heard departing at full gallop. Then Labosseer, pursuing the robber, saw Bert and though Bert had torn off his mask, recognition in this case did not save him. Labosseer fired directly at close quarters. Bert reeled against the gate post. A second shot might have done for him, but for a scream from the house from Mrs Labosseer. Though Labosseer had been quick to leap to his firearms he had not been as swift as Rachel had been to go to her child and on entering her room, the unprepossessing figure of the bushranger had startled her.

Labosseer bounded back to the house and into the bedroom, followed by Bert, for it had flashed through Bert's pain-benumbed mind that, after all, Logan had merely been stunned and might have arisen to injure Rachel. Labosseer turned and lifted his piece.

"Steady, Mr Labosseer, I'm after the bushranger too. It was me who caught Logan, and Burn and Erroll are tied up outside!" cried Bert, but it was too late. The trigger was pulled, and this time Bert went down and lay still.

Rachel, seeing that her baby was soundly sleeping and unhurt, laid him down again and ran to look at Bert. "Is he dead?" she cried.

"I don't know," said Labosseer. "If he is, he deserves to be. I hope you now are satisfied that. . ."

"It can't be! It's terrible! You're mistaken — didn't you hear what he said? Poor Bert — doctor, doctor come quickly," she called, running to fetch him.

The doctor and Labosseer extricated the two men and laid them side by side on the back verandah where the big lantern afforded the best light. And so it came to pass that Bert, who had dreamed of strutting nonchalantly about as a saviour in the eye of his lady-love, as the single-handed conqueror of the gang which had kept all the Southern District on the qui vive, was laid out as a criminal specimen along with Logan.

"This man is only stunned," Dr James presently observed of Logan. "You had better bind his hands and feet, or he'll get away."

While Labosseer hurried off for rope, the doctor turned to Bert. "I'll hold the lantern," said Mrs Labosseer, lifting it higher when it was seen that a trail of blood led to the back door.

"This is more serious." The doctor went to get his bag and started ripping the clothing from Bert's shoulder. "What a splendid specimen! A pity he should come to this," he remarked as he proceeded. He had seen Bert once or twice but did not recognise him. He found the source of the blood in the fleshy part of the shoulder.

"This is only a flesh wound — the bullet has gone clean through. Not enough to knock out a man of his physique. I'll have to make a more thorough examination and must ask you to withdraw, Mrs Labosseer," he said, baring Bert's splendid chest, clean as a woman's. "God, what a pity — like a Greek athlete!"

Labosseer returned with a collection of greenhide leg ropes. "Doctor, there's a man outside tied to a tree — he sounds as if he's dying. Come quickly!"

"Better make this one safe first," the doctor replied, nodding in the direction of Logan. "He'll come to any minute now. This fellow is safe enough."

"Doctor, you've mistaken him for a bushranger," said Rachel from the doorway, "but it is only our dear Bert Poole, my brother-in-law, you know."

The doctor hurried away with Labosseer, shaking his head. The colonies produced some strange social paradoxes, he thought. He had always thought the Mazeres of good family but...well there he was himself, an F.R.C.S. poking about the scrub. He sighed.

He discovered that the strange noises were coming from Burn, choking on Bert's gag. After this was removed, he quickly recovered. Promising him a drink of water, the doctor returned to the house. During his absence, Rachel had tenderly washed Bert's face and tried to staunch his wound with bandages of old linen. He lay with his eyes closed, the long black lashes resting on his cheek as silkily as those of a sleeping child.

"Bert! Bert, dear Bert! Do open your eyes and say you're not dead!" pleaded Rachel, tenderly holding his head in her hands. As he regained consciousness, Bert wondered if it were lips sweet and soft as rose petals, or only fingertips on his lips and cheek — or merely the dream that was constantly with him.

"Don't let them get away," he murmured, lifting his head as the doctor and Labosseer entered the room. Struggling to his feet, he staggered and the doctor helped him to a chair.

"It's Bert who's saved us," said Rachel, "and Mr Labosseer has shot him by mistake."

Labosseer was appalled, as the full realisation of what he had done came to him. The momentary taste of triumph he had experienced in exposing, at last, the treacherous character of the boy, was now as ashes in his mouth.

"I must find where the second bullet went," said the doctor.

"I feel as if I'm going to be sick," complained Bert.

"Ah, your head!" Dr James found that the second bullet had grazed the temple. Meanwhile the blood from the shoulder wound was making a pool under Bert's chair.

"We must put him to bed and staunch that wound," said the doctor and, as the women hastened to prepare a bed and produce old linen, Labosseer and the doctor between them supported the patient.

"I'm sorry about this, Poole," said Labosseer awkwardly. "Can you tell us a little of what happened?''

"Tom Stapleton has gone for the troopers — don't let the others get away. Put them inside somewhere. Don't trust any of the men except Tom Stapleton and Rab McIntosh.''

"The others! We've found only Burn, tied up on the way to the cow-yard.''

"Erroll is out the front, tied to the blackbutt near the orchard fence,'' said Bert. But Labosseer, after making a search, found only the ropes. The man had got away.

Bert made one more effort to speak before lapsing into unconsciousness. "Mr Labosseer, you'll find Logan's old mare — got up just like the Waterfall — hanging on the orchard fence. Will you please leave her just as she is and hide her in the stable where no one can see her.''

"Anything you wish, my boy, but keep quiet now.''

"Don't let the troopers get that horse, whatever you do, Mr Labosseer,'' urged Bert. "Hide her now and tomorrow send her over to old Healey with Barney Logan's compliments.''

Bert was put into bed by the two men and given over to the ministrations of the women. Logan was brought inside and, as Rachel stood by with a levelled revolver, which she did without a tremor, he and Burn were removed to the dining room where they were securely bound. Logan had now returned to consciousness. Seeing his grizzled beard and fearing he was suffering like Bert, Rachel put a pillow under his head. The doctor gave them each a draught of water, but nothing else. They drew the blinds on the window so that should any of the men return to spy, they should not see them. The three servant women were put to bed in an inside room under the watchful eye of Mrs Millburn. Bert, by this time, was sleeping easily and his wound was bleeding less freely.

The doctor and Labosseer, armed to the teeth, kept watch in case of surprise before the troopers should arrive. Labosseer went on a tour of inspection and found the old mare disguised in a false mane and tail of white hair, ingeniously and securely attached. It was flashingly clear to Labosseer how the evil suspicion had been fastened on Bert by the crafty Logan. And now there was Bert, lying helpless and wounded by his — Labosseer's — own hand. He was smitten with shame to be on the level of old Healey whose integrity of soul he had long since begun to doubt. He determined to make retribution to Bert Poole and, while

198

he could not fathom Bert's part in the capture of the bushrangers, he decided to trust him and to carry out forthwith his request about the disguised horse. Putting her in a room in which rock salt and hides were stored at the far end of the stables, he provided her with hay and a bucket of water to keep her content. Then he left her as he had found her, with the exception of slipping the bit out of her mouth.

5

Bert's exploits caused a sensation throughout the Southern Districts and far beyond.

For reasons that have never been made clear, the troopers did not arrive to take charge of the prisoners until towards noon the next day. Before their arrival, Labosseer had decided to act upon Bert's request by sending one of his stockmen, Heffernan, over to Healey with Logan's mare. This man, lately engaged by Labosseer, Bert knew to be a member of the Eagle Hawk fraternity. Labosseer was on the alert for him when he arrived at the homestead early in the morning. Bert had told his host what he had heard about Heffernan on the day the attack was planned in the cave.

"Where were you last night, Heffernan?" inquired Labosseer.

"Me and Robinson went over to Rab McIntosh's for a game of cards, sir." The reply was suavely respectful.

"Ah. What time did you get back to the hut?"

"Well sir, to tell you the truth, we got playing so late we turned in there."

"Ah. Well, don't turn your horse out. I have a job for you. In the salt room you'll find a mare saddled. Take her at once, just as she is, to Mr Healey at Little River with this message, 'Barney Logan presents his compliments and the mare to Mr Healey as he has no further use for the beast'."

Heffernan was clearly nonplussed, and Labosseer estimated that the man had no idea how the affray had ended. "Did I get you right, sir?" Heffernan asked slowly.

"Repeat the message and I'll see."

"I'm to take a mare out of the salt room to Mr Healey with Barney Logan's compliments, as he has no more use for her."

"Excellent. Get away at once."

But the man still lingered. "Does the mare belong to the bushrangers, sir?" he asked boldly.

199

"Evidently. Start at once on your errand and make good time."

"And — er — may I ask, sir, if the bushrangers has been caught and where the horse came from?"

"The horse came from Barney Logan. Further than that I have nothing to say."

The man saw he could not be too inquisitive without bringing suspicion on himself. He contented himself with, "And after I take the horse to Mr Healey, what shall I do then, sir?"

"Perhaps Mr Healey will tell you."

The man rode on his way seeing he could get no further for the present. His impulse was to go to Eagle Hawk and, since Little River was in the same general direction, he enjoyed the thought of going to old Healey with the mare first.

Though Bert's plans had gone somewhat awry, he was on the whole content. He was alive, without permanent injury and had Rachel as head nurse. When Labosseer whispered to him that the mare had gone to Healey, he was delighted. It was a great honour to feel that Labosseer was a pal. And further, though he did not understand why it should be so, it was the act of discomfiting Healey rather than the capturing of Logan that seemed to wash away all the bitterness he had felt in those years since the loss of Black Belle. The arrival at Little River of Logan's ewe-necked mare, complete with false mane and tail, would bring to an end Healey's whispering campaign against the Pooles. Bert smiled. It was his crowning triumph.

6

Old Healey was getting ready to set out on horseback when Heffernan rode up with the mare. His eyes fairly bulged with apprehension of trouble when he realised the significance of the mare's disguise. Heffernan delivered the message as instructed by Labosseer, and with a touch of malice.

"Begor'!" Healey said, at first bravely. "Logan has his knife into me and I take it as a compliment. Where in the name of the devil did ye get the beast at all, at all?"

"From the boss."

"What boss?"

"The boss Boss of Eueurunda, God Almighty Labosseer himself."

Healey's knees trembled so much that he gave up his attempt to mount. This was too much. He could not trust himself to speak. How much did Heffernan know or believe of what Logan said?

"Sure," he said. "I'd like Mrs Healey to see this. I'll go get her." He ran to his wife as a small boy seeking refuge. "Aileen!" he called, and shuffled with her into their bedroom, shutting the door. "Sure it's all come out.We're done! There's Heffernan right in the backyard with Logan's..."

Mrs Healey had difficulty in rendering him coherent, but as soon as she got the hang of the story she put on a fighting front. "Pluck yerself together, Larry. Sure ye're pullin' the cat out of the bag with your own hands by these capers. I want to see the mare." She swept out with a curiosity which at least was not assumed.

"Good morning, Mr Heffernan, and where did you get that animal — from Logan, ye say?"

"And Mr Labosseer." The man watched the effect of this.

"Sure there's matter for sifting there, but this would explain why horses with white manes and tails have been in two places at once."

There was nothing to be got from this woman, Heffernan realised. She had the guts, as he expressed it admiringly afterwards.

"What shall I do with the mare, Mr Healey?"

"Sure if she's Logan's mare, she belongs to the troopers. Have ye any explanation why a man like Mr Labosseer should play a practical joke like that? Take it back to him with my compliments. Sure, if it had been one of the young fellers like Bert Poole playin' such a trick on Denny, I could easier understand it. Even then it would need to be April first."

"Very like we'll find it is not from Mr Labosseer at all, when it's all sifted," said Mrs Healey.

"Well, that's where I got the mare — upon my oath and no two ways about it," said the man.

"But there must be something at the back of it. Perhaps someone is playing a trick on Mr Labosseer at our expense," said Mrs Healey and, her courage rising in the teeth of danger, she added, "Mrs Labosseer and the baby well, I hope?"

"Take that beast away — it's really a matter for the troopers," said Healey. "And I'll — I'll sift it with Mr Labosseer himself when I have more time. I must be off now to give Denny a hand."

He did not, however, feel as grand as he feigned, and when he saw Heffernan disappear from sight, apparently on the return journey to

Eueurunda, he crept back to the comfort of his wife. Denny, arriving home in the middle of the afternoon and sore about his father's failure to meet him at the Twelve Mile Stockyards as they had arranged, found his parent bordering on collapse.

"What have ye been doin', Denny, to bring this upon me?" he spluttered.

"More like, what have you been doing to bring it on me?" Denny retorted, none so easy himself. "We've been a little too wide in the gob about Bert Poole and the Waterfall. I reckon to shut up tight now will help us more than anything."

It was not as simple a matter as that to his parents. They long had been confronted with the necessity of breaking a certain piece of news to Denny. His father blurted out now, "See here me boy, I hear ye're traipsin' after that Nellie Logan, an', och, that's...well Denny, ye can't touch her. Sure Denny, ye must know this now and keep it to yerself, as tellin' is yer own disgrace. Sure, well, me boy, I was a little wild in me young days and Nellie is, sure can't ye guess, well, she's yer half sister. Now ye see."

This was a gallant lie on the old man's part, the girl being in fact his wife's child and she never divorced, but they had decided on this way out of the difficulty. Mrs Healey knew nothing of spiritual integrity, but she had made an industrious and plucky fight for respectability and was not going to surrender it now.

"By gob!" exclaimed Denny.

"God help me, boy, ye're not goin' to tell me..."

"It's all right as far as that is concerned. It's Malcolm...but you're a nice one to be lecturing me."

"Well, me boy, ye see why I was anxious. Now if Malcolm wants Nellie, sure that would be fine, fine! Help it on all ye can."

"Good gawd!" exclaimed Denny, further speech dried up.

"An', me boy, I'd like to see ye runnin' off with Emily Mazere. Sure the old man has pots of money an' she's a nice girl with no airs, I will say that for her. An' it would be the devil's own revenge on that damn Labosseer. I'll get even with him some day in a way he won't like."

"It's no good anyone thinking of Emily. She's like all the rest of them, mad after Bert Poole, and he with his tongue out after Mrs Labosseer."

"Sure I wish they'd run away together. That would please me entirely."

202

"He's got as much hope of running away with Queen Victoria. The Mazere girls are not like that."

"Sure, then, Denny me boy, silence an' mindin' our own business is the tip."

But things get out where news is precious and where every neighbour's business is known, even to the number of coats he may have in his wardrobe. And since old Healey had been industrious in circulating the inferences he had drawn from the descriptions of the bushrangers' mount, the going home to roost of this chicken contributed greatly to the joy of the wits in the district. Other rumours accompanied it; for example, that Bert Poole had been shot while bailing up Eueurunda and was lying at the homestead in a critical condition and guarded by a couple of troopers and a doctor until he was fit to be removed to the lock-up. Some such story even got into the up-country *Courier* and though it was speedily suppressed, it was not before it had reached the diggings in Victoria, where it persisted long after Bert had become a hero, not only to maids but in the eyes of grown and grizzled men.

7

For some time Charlotte had been anxious to remove Philip from the diggings. She had never had much hope of his striking it rich and now she decided that it was foolish to indulge his dreams of riches any longer. It had taken her some time to adjust herself to the change in her husband. A bald-headed, broken-mouthed man with granulated eyelids had replaced the pink-cheeked boy with the golden curls who had won her maiden heart. Even sadder to tell, she had found she had a drunkard on her hands, though this discovery she had loyally kept to herself. She wanted a place where she could rear domestic animals, as allies in the battles of life. She had woefully missed the amiable cow, the loyal hen, and Emily's letter appealing for help for Bert was the last touch needed to fix her determination.

Leaving her sons in a special category, there were two men inalienably dearer than life to her, her husband and her brother Bert. Younger than herself and at an age when youths are not always a benediction to their sisters, Bert had never been anything but a comfort. He had stood by her more like a sister than a brother in her two great campaigns, for love and education. Her thoughts strayed fondly to her last meeting with him at the Three Rivers wedding, nearly four years ago now. Was there anyone, anywhere, to compare with him in looks, ability or disposition? How daring and splendid he had been that night on the flooded river with Mamma! Charlotte's heart swelled with indignation to hear that he was suspected of aiding the bushrangers. Emily's loyalty became precious.

She showed the letter to Philip, for whatever her husband's failings, when sober he never lacked in sympathy and understanding. He had all his mother's sensitivity. But when Philip read Emily's letter, he had his doubts — Bert was such a horseman, such a superlative shot, so well acquainted with the uttermost fastnesses of the countryside. And men could, and did change — what about himself, a man who had once said his prayers and who had been unacquainted with the taste of alcohol? He recalled his first impression of the Poole home before Charlotte's determination had affected a metamorphosis. He remembered the hobble chains lying behind the old stable and his doubts grew. But the quality of his comradeship with Charlotte was such that he did not express his doubts.

Charlotte found her husband amenable to the proposal of returning to his old haunts and the land. In fact, he was tired of the diggings and relieved to have his wife take the initiative about going home.

Matters, however, so shaped themselves that they could not leave the diggings in a hurry, and it was there that they received the newspapers containing the false report of Bert's connection with the bushrangers. Charlotte never wavered in her faith, however, nor did Philip ever let her know of his doubts.

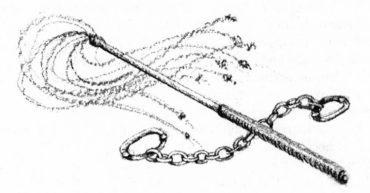

CHAPTER XVIII

1

Logan and Burn were tried at Goulburn. The case aroused tremendous interest throughout New South Wales and Victoria, and anyone of any importance in the Maneroo and Bool Bool districts was there. The hotels were packed and the town as lively as a beehive.

In summing up at the end of the trial, the judge referred to the specially high character of the witnesses that had appeared. There was Simon Labosseer and his lovely little wife, the latter of whom all eyes sought out. The cultivated accents of Dr James, carefully kept sober, were most impressive, and Mrs Millburn, in rustling black silk, was convincingly respectable and refined. The native-born maids of Eueurunda were as pretty and perky as you please, and the English cook presented a solid character. Tom Stapleton was there too, or, more correctly, he was in heaven, being yarded among the witnesses and in constant contact with Miss Emily, who wrung him by the hand in her excitement and delight. Tom was wearing his striped suit, still with the talismans of the hairpin and pressed rose in his vest pocket. The most important witness was Bert, or, as he had become in the press, Herbert Poole, Esq., son of James Poole, Esq. of Curradoo-bidgee, one of the earliest and most highly respected settlers in the Maneroo district. In fact, had Bert desired two "ees" to conclude his surname, they would have been readily accorded him.

205

No less impressive were the supporting cherubim and seraphim. Among these were Poole the elder with Mrs Poole and Raymond, Mr and Mrs McEachern and, needless to say, Malcolm as one of Bert's cronies, as well as Jessie, who would not be left behind. Mazere J.P. of Three Rivers, Mrs Mazere, and the beautiful Miss Emily Mazere attracted much attention. Tim Brennan's fine, big face, topped with its stiff red locks, shone out among the crowd. Tim, who felt that Bert was too devilishly lucky for anything, and that a girl who had stood by him in adversity would not be able to be wooed from him by any power under heaven, was not letting this realisation tinge his hearty manliness with spleen or melancholy.

Representatives old and young of the other families of Maneroo and Bool Bool were to be found in the gathering, though Mr and Mrs Healey of Little River were not present. Denny appeared, probably because he feared that it might seem strange if he absented himself. The recent knowledge he had gained of his relationship to the daughter of the chief criminal had poisoned his soul and lately rendered him uncharacteristically inconspicuous. With Bert victorious, Emily was rapt in elation and, though she was kindness itself to anyone who addressed her, the young men felt that she was now quite beyond their reach.

Nearly all the ladies in attendance were wearing gorgeous dresses, specially made for the occasion, of the beautiful silks of the day, and the rustle of their voluminous folds was to be heard on every hand. They wore elegant bonnets richly ornamented and so shaped behind as to make the crown seem as if it were falling off. Why a crown, in order to be elegant, should need to appear to be falling off was a puzzle to the men, but it entertained the women, and little it mattered what was perched on the top of a head composed of ringlets and eyes and lips of a consistency to bewilder the senses.

Bert, with lovelocks, neck arrangements, unmentionables and all such details right up to the knocker, was the very deuce of a fellow and the darling of society. The Poole connection was no longer deplored as unfortunate — in fact, people who had the slightest acquaintance with the Pooles now traded on it. When the young pressman representing the *Sydney Morning Herald* referred to Mr Mazere as Bert's father-in-law, he laughed good-humouredly and said, "Not yet, though his sister is my daughter-in-law." When Labosseer was called Bert's brother-in-law, he accepted the description without emendation.

2

Most of the elite put up at the Royal Arms Hotel during the trial which lasted over a week. The evenings were spent with Mr and Mrs Oswald of Goulburn Plains, the Three Rivers of its district. Mrs Oswald had been waiting for an opportunity to return the hospitality extended to her husband and son by the McEacherns at the time of the New Year races on Maneroo.

It was an enjoyable meeting for the leading pioneer ladies. Mrs McEachern and Mrs Mazere were able to thrash out the good points of Cochin Chinas and Brahma Putras, and Mrs Oswald presented each lady with a clutch of guinea-fowl eggs. Mrs Mazere contributed her recipe for preserving eggs, and Mrs McEachern was an authority on knitting socks. Mrs Poole took the opportunity of laying a few bricks in the path of Raymond's career. The judge was impressed with her education when they met at dinner at the Oswalds. Afterwards, while she played the piano in the drawing room, he enjoyed himself singing several of Moore's melodies. She told him that she had dedicated Raymond to the law and the judge laughingly said he would look out for the young gentleman when he began.

As for Mr Mazere, he was simply "it", as some of the more irreverent young people present expressed it, and enjoyed himself in full crow.

3

The high point of the trial was when Bert entered the witness box. Ushered to the box with the deference extended to conquerors, his sensation of discomfiture exceeded that of exultation as he found himself the focus of all eyes. His dark, sunburned skin hiding his blushes, for a moment everything seemed a blur but then he found one little face, its starry eyes fixed on him — and life, so sweet, so fraught with pain, became grand in that moment.

He gave his name as "Herbert Poole", his age as "twenty-five", his residence as "Curradoobidgee, Maneroo". While he was no philosopher and had not consciously thought about the narrow chance that had put convict weals on poor old Logan's back while his own, stripped, was a sight to make a sculptor cheer, some such awareness touched his easygoing consciousness with regret as he was called upon to identify the men in the dock. He was glad, at that moment, that Erroll had escaped with Cane.

"Mr Poole, you will tell the court what happened on the night of…"

Barney Logan, remembering what he had done to the boy's beloved horse, expected implacable revenge. As to how Bert happened to be on hand so opportunely on the night of the raid, he listened with curiosity.

"I happened to be passing and my attention was attracted by the horses hanging on the orchard fence, especially the one with the white mane and tail. I rode up to have a closer look at it and my suspicions were aroused. Tom Stapleton was with me and I thought I had better have a look around and see what it all meant…"

It was the aim of the counsel for the prosecution to lead Bert into telling a graphic account of the incident. But Bert, simple and unselfconscious, resisted the self-aggrandisement of describing the capture of the bushrangers as the result of his own daring plan. Mrs Mazere, looking at him across the court, mused on his physical similarity to Charlotte. He had her clear, kindly, straight-eyed gaze. Even his poor ailing mother, with a flock of others elbowing him from babyhood, must have found joy in him.

Emily's eyes were fixed on Bert with such complete adoration that her mother's heart was wrung, and Jessie McEachern wept into her handkerchief tears of sheer hero-worship. She was thinking of babies too, as was Mary Brennan — but what does it matter now what was in these hearts, now dust, as are their floating silken skirts and ensnaring ringlets. Other gowns and coiffures have taken their place; other hearts harbour other — no, the same sweet dreams of youth and love.

The prosecuting counsel continued: "Did you meet with any resistance? Did the prisoners employ their firearms?"

It is a decent instinct to avoid stepping on the face of a fallen foe. Bert said, "I think it was because they were careful in their use of firearms that I was able to take them so easily. They have not shot anyone in our district."

Something of hope or relief passed over the prisoners' rough faces. They were aware of the generosity of this statement, and that they had, at least, been outdone by a man deserving of his status.

The defending counsel made the most of Bert's statement in his address to the jury, but the tide was against the men. They had been a pest in the southern districts for too long. The jury did not want them at large again, with opportunities for revenge. The record was black

208

against Logan. He bore it on his back, if nowhere else. It came out that he was a "lifer" who had escaped years ago from a chain-gang near Albury. He had lain low until the gold rushes when he made his way to the diggings, but eventually he had been forced to retreat to Eagle Hawk Gullies. Both men were found guilty and received the maximum penalties of life, and twelve years, respectively.

Bert refused the reward of two hundred pounds which had been offered by the government for the apprehension of Logan. Bert was not avaricious, and it seemed to him like blood money. Of course, there were those who called him a fool, but his stepmother firmly supported him, considering this act of self-denial an action befitting a gentleman related to her son, Raymond. Bert's one bit of crowing took the form of riding the Waterfall for all to behold. The legend of the bushrangers being seen with a similar beast was so widespread that he surely had a right to this indulgence. The showy beast, groomed until he shone, his conspicuous mane and tail just a little too long for the fashion, became as familiar as the winning flag in a tournament, and if an unnecessary touch of the spur put him on his hind legs when the girls looked his way, well, the Waterfall was rampant in any case and enjoyed the thing as much as anyone.

4

Though many people considered Bert a fool to refuse two hundred pounds in cold cash, his refusal nevertheless put the seal on his popularity. A move to give him a purse of sovereigns was started there and then by McEachern, and there was a rush to be on the subscription list. Treble the government reward was quickly promised. In fact, the real story behind Bert's capture of the men was known to all, and some of the big squatters about Tarago, Yass and Goulburn who had been harried by this gang and relieved of their best horses and firearms, promised substantial sums. The list was held open so that everyone around Maneroo and Bool Bool who had benefited from the cleaning-up could contribute. Even somewhat shady people came forward and subscribed with a flourish, lest they should be under suspicion as sympathisers of the fallen gang. Driven by fear of trouble, and feeling enormous relief that his early connection with Logan had not come out publicly in court, Healey of Little River went a guinea better than McEachern, remarking to his wife, "Devil a bit of good may it ever do young Poole!"

Maneroo organised a ball in the hero's honour, which was held at the McEacherns'. It being leap year, the young people sought to lend variety to the entertainment by having a leap year ball. A special innovation was introduced in the music by a set of bagpipes which Mr McEachern had long promised Rab McIntosh and upon which he performed in addition to the fiddle, the concertina, the Jew's harp, etc.

Though one ball is but a repetition of another, each is entirely new to lovers, for whom they are principally designed. One to whom it brought great disappointment was Emily Mazere. One to whom it brought signal humiliation was Jessie McEachern.

Mrs Mazere was not at all strong that year. The turn of life held unspeakable perils for many pioneer women, and she made her health the excuse to keep Emily at home. Although she had still not discerned Bert's preoccupation with Rachel, she was startled by the obvious intensity of Emily's feelings, and by Bert's total indifference to the girl. Something had to be done to shore up the girl, or her self-respect would be in danger. But, sympathetic to the girl's bitter disappointment and understanding it in the face of the public excitement about Bert, she made Emily a promise of compensation, of which more anon.

Hugh went up to Maneroo with the Brennans and other Bool Boolians. With typically Mazere single-mindedness, he had been patiently pursuing Jessie ever since he had met her. He was not her only wooer, Jessie being trim of form, light of foot, bright of cheek and eye and famous for her virtue and domestic abilities. She was, in short, a belle, and a catch second only to Emily Mazere of Three Rivers.

It was Bert's ball, and a rule had been laughingly proclaimed that all programmes should be held open until Bert, like royalty, filled his. A gentle, gracious sultan, he was merciful to Labosseer, though the latter had ceased to show whether he felt any jealousy or not. Bert asked Mrs Labosseer for only one dance, the first, which was quite fitting. The choice was received with applause. He insisted on Mrs McEachern giving him the supper dance. Jessie McEachern and Mary Brennan came next, in honour of the letters they had written him, and which, after the capture of the men, he had acknowledged with excessive formality. These dances engaged, he then opened his programme to the leap year field. Jessie was first off the mark and was given the two numbers she palpitantly requested.

At last she screwed up her courage to take her chance. Halfway through their second dance, she complained that someone had trampled on her toes, and sought a seat on the front verandah. But this

210

spot being well lit by lantern, she said a splinter in the boards was endangering her gown and moved to a spot lit only by the stars shining above a bower of old climbing roses. She picked one for Bert and, fastening it in his coat, said, "Well Bert, how many proposals have you received tonight?"

"None," he replied, suddenly sensing danger. But it was too late. Jessie rushed on.

"It would be too bad, did you get none. Will you answer me a straight question if I ask it?"

"It depends what it is," he said cautiously, wondering guiltily if his secret was out.

"Why aren't you married?"

"There's time yet, isn't there?"

"You're the oldest unmarried man that I know. Is it because of Emily Mazere?"

Relieved by this, Bert fenced a little. "How do you mean, because of Emily Mazere?"

"That's my question. Do you care very much for her?"

"Emily is one of the nicest girls I know, and one of the best looking. I expect she'll be marrying a swell like Labosseer one of these days."

"I thought maybe there was something between you and her."

"Not a thing except a Maneroo wind, and I expect it would blow as cold as Cootapatamba from Labosseer's direction if I forgot myself with Emily. He's only just come round a bit to me lately. And you know old Mazere kicked Philip out for marrying Charlotte, don't you?" In fact, as Bert well knew, the Poole stock had gone up since those days. But Jessie took heart, as the love-deluded will.

"Then, Bert," said Jessie tremulously, "what would you think if I proposed to you myself?"

"Just to cheer me up! It would be very nice of you, but — ah — don't you think you might catch cold out here? We'd better go in."

"But Bert, I'm not joking, I'm in earnest," she said desperately. Then, utterly dismayed by the situation, she broke into tears. Bert was the one to be startled now. He wished that he could be away engaged in some easy and happy enterprise, like capturing bushrangers.

"But Jessie," he stammered, "I love you just like a sister. I couldn't think of anything else. You must have some fine young fellow, not old brother Bert. Besides, I think I'm cut out for an old bachelor.

211

Tell me you were only joking, there's a brick.''

"Perhaps I was," she said and, trying to hide the sobs of humiliation that were advancing, she turned and fled. What now to do? Bert felt none of the elation of the lady-killer. His only desire was to conceal the incident from the other guests. Surely Jessie would never mention it. The ball was spoiled for him. Here was the supper dance for which he was committed to Mrs McEachern, thank heaven, but next in order was Miss Oswald — horrors, supposing she proposed too!

A little later, Hugh Mazere found Jessie pretending that the supper table needed a finishing touch.

"Oh, Jessie, it's our dance!"

"Someone has stepped on my toes. I hope you don't mind not dancing this," she said. Her embarrassment his thumping heart interpreted as a response to his own agitation.

"No fear," he exclaimed, "not if — if, Jessie..." He halted, remembering the embargo on males proposing. "Jessie!" He looked at her ardently. A look from her, and she might have been tightly clasped in his arms, his lips upon hers, no need to say anything. How eager the wrong man was, Jessie thought bitterly, and how deadly unresponsive the only man in all the world.

"Now, Hugh," she said, feeling a pang to think she had made him suffer as another had made her, and seeing here a way to retrieve herself, "I'm not going to propose to you, and have people saying I had to depend on leap year to get a husband, but tomorrow..."

"Oh, Jessie!"

Hereupon, the supper dance being over, Mrs McEachern entered with Bert. "I do hope we have not intruded," said that good lady who was most anxious for the match with Hugh Mazere, having cannily estimated Bert's indifference.

With Jessie's allusion to "tomorrow" elating him, Hugh said gaily, "I'd never say that you had intruded, Mrs McEachern, but I had yarded Jessie here in the hope that she might pop the question. There's no telling what another ten minutes might have done."

"Ye must give her another chance, the night is young yet," said Mrs McEachern, well pleased with Hugh's triumphant demeanour. Bert, on the other hand, gazed at Jessie disbelievingly. Had she really only been joking? He felt cheered, if somewhat bewildered.

Daylight was danced in to the skirl of the bagpipes; then all the

212

guests from those parts departed, including the Pooles. Gowandale was packed with guests, many of whom had come from afar, including the Oswalds and Gilmours from Goulburn. The household turned in for a few hours' sleep, Jessie utterly dejectedly. She awoke at about nine o'clock with a depressing sense of misfortune. With full consciousness came a searing sense of humiliation. She arose and went to breakfast on the verandah, the dining and drawing rooms being as dusty and desolate as her heart. But Hugh was not going to let opportunity slip through his fingers. He was awaiting her, looking as fresh as the morn. A slender young man about five feet ten inches tall, fair and fresh complexioned, his emotions, which were quick and warm, were mirrored on his face.

"Jessie, did you mean what you said last night?" he began eagerly.

"I've forgotten that blether," she said listlessly, hoping that someone might wander on to the verandah to interrupt them.

"Oh, you know, about leap year — will you?" Jessie sighed and looked away. "Don't you care a little, Jessie? I'll wait till the end of my days if you'll only give me a little hope."

"I'd rather not have the whole country thinking it the outcome of leap year."

"If that's all, I'll go home and write you a letter — I don't care if you put it in the *Courier* as long as you say yes now."

So they became engaged, to the great satisfaction of Gowandale and Three Rivers homesteads. Emily wrote an effusive letter of congratulation. Her absence from the ball had not had the terrible consequences she had been fearing. Mary Brennan's letter was equally cordial. Only gentle Louisa Poole's eyes were often red with weeping, for no cause that she would confess. She took refuge in fervent and frequent prayer. Poor Jessie was hardly less unhappy and wondered, as Hugh pressed her to him fervently and tenderly, that he could not feel how her heart sank. Bert was so astonished that he lost his bearings entirely. So he simply maintained his customary silence.

CHAPTER XIX

1

Thus Charlotte, who was returning to Bool Bool in order to be at hand to defend her brother from calumny, did not arrive until after he was the hero of the colony.

The senior Mazeres had been in a fever of expectation about Philip and Charlotte's arrival for weeks. They had once gone all the way to Gundagai to meet them and, disappointed by their non-appearance, possessed themselves with what patience they could muster to await the wanderers at home.

Charlotte and Philip suffered various delays on the homeward route which made it impossible for them to arrive on schedule. One delay, unfortunately, was caused by a drinking bout on the part of Philip in Melbourne. Another was due to the baby suffering an attack of croup in Sydney. But at length Mrs Mazere, who each afternoon went up on to the ridge to observe the coach coming in, saw the vehicle coming on towards Three Rivers.

Papa and Mamma stood together, trembling, to welcome their firstborn and his family. Emily grabbed her nephew Philip and ran with him, crying, "Come, your Daddy and Mamma are coming!"

With a deep murmur of joy Charlotte was presently crushing her child to her in her strong, brave arms. Little Philip was startled at first and refused to leave Auntie Emily for either of his parents.

There was much to be seen and said. Charlotte went about the houses, noting the changes. Philip was astonished by the maturity of both the new orchard and the line of ornamental trees that stretched beside the track from the back gate to the edge of the township.

Ellen Slattery was no longer in the kitchen. Convinced that her husband must have been made away with on the diggings, she had finally acceded to the importunities of Bill Prendergast. Now they were running an accommodation house situated between Gundagai and Coolooluk; Bill had risen to be proprietor as well as being the driver of the connecting coach. As to the Mazere small fry, Joseph was a sturdy boy now, though not fair like his elder brother and lacking his geniality. Fannie and Rhoda had grown quite beyond the baby stage, and Emily was in the full glory of her young maturity.

The sweetest moment for Charlotte and Emily came in the evening when, after putting all the young fry to bed, they drew chairs up to the fire that had been lit for the bathing of little James, and Emily went into the exploits of Bert, the beloved of both.

"I wish you could have seen him, Charlotte, in the witness box. He is so brave and good! You can imagine how everyone felt after their silly suspicions. I never had any doubts for a moment, did you?"

"Dear me, no!"

"I don't know how people could have been so silly. You only have to look at Bert to know how wonderful he is — look at the way he took Mamma across the Yarrabongo. And when the trial was over, more than six hundred pounds was collected and presented to him along with a beautiful gold watch and chain." The girl was silent for a moment. "I haven't seen it yet."

"Doesn't Bert come down this way much?"

"No, but I hope he will now that you are home," Emily said wistfully.

Charlotte, after kissing Emily — so bright and glowing and unaffectedly adoring — produced a present she had bought for the girl in Melbourne. It was a beautiful shawl of finest Indian cashmere, worked to an ancient design.

"Oh, Charlotte, how lovely! I'll wear it to my twenty-first birthday party. Mamma has consented to have a big ball for me. It broke my heart not to be able to leave her to go to the ball for Bert at Gowandale, so Mamma is giving me this one instead. Isn't it heavenly?"

215

Charlotte had never seen anything as lovely as this joyful girl as, wrapping herself in the bright shawl, she curtsied and flitted about in delight. How could Bert resist her? Emily looked so much like Philip used to before he met misfortune, Charlotte thought sadly. Rachel Labosseer now had two children; surely she did not still hold the young man's heart? As eager to see Bert as Emily was to have him come, she determined to await his confidence.

After Emily had gone to bed, Mrs Mazere had a little private conversation with her daughter-in-law. She, too, touched on the projected ball and confided that she was mystified that Bert did not return Emily's affection, seeing that he favoured no one else. Charlotte, the quiet observer, could have enlightened her but was too wise. She simply murmured, "I expect it will all come right presently, Mamma. I am longing to see the Curradoobidgee people."

2

Saddened by the changed appearance of their firstborn, the senior Mazeres were anxious to have Charlotte and Philip settle at Three Rivers, in the actual homestead. Hugh was engaged to Jessie and Emily was likely to marry at any time so, anxious to fill the looming void, his father offered Philip his beloved mill and a farm. Philip, however, had other ideas. He did not trust his father's uncertain temper and wanted his inheritance to be safely separate, so that it could not be peremptorily recalled due to a difference of opinion or policy. Charlotte, likewise, wished to be independent. It was due to her efforts at Mount Alexander that they now had a comfortable nest egg. Philip had come to agree with her that the diggings were institutions from which a competence might be made, rather than a fortune.

There was land to be had between Mungee and Coolooluk, and here Philip meant to establish a mill, just on the fringe of the mining operations. Charlotte was to have cows, poultry and pigs, so that when the diggings were played out they would have a comfortable grazier's plant to fall back upon. On the diggings Philip had noted the need for heavy horses suitable for transport work, and now he proposed to breed such from Shire stock. His father supported him enthusiastically in this venture, for he had been preaching for some time that horses would be swifter, stronger and altogether more profitable for the great carrying trade, inevitably developing with the increase in population, than the slow and unwieldy bullock. Stock, both men prognosticated, must rise in price. The difficulty in securing shepherds and stockmen was being overcome by the continual arrival of immigrants in search of work, and also because a number of men who had had their fling on the goldfields were now anxious to settle down, either as workers or owners of land. As well, the advance of fencing was doing away with the need for so many shepherds and stockmen.

Thus Philip went ahead, his whole family lending a hand to the end that his new home should be in working order as soon as possible. Hugh fancied himself as a builder. Bert prided himself on his shingled roofs. George Stanton was an authority on sheds, yards and fencing, and Mazere Senior busied himself with the establishing of gardens and orchards, taking Grubb along as executant.

Thus was launched another undertaking which added zest to life and afforded social opportunities. Bert sometimes came down to Three Rivers on Saturday night and spent Sunday with Charlotte. Emily was radiantly happy; Bert's name was not connected with that of any woman and she was confident that he would turn to her presently. But she was weary of defending her single status and now, in the year that she was to come of age, the dictum of her mother that no girl should marry till she was twenty-one was beginning to ring a little hollow.

It was decided that the promised ball in honour of her twenty-first birthday should also celebrate the return of Philip and Charlotte, and the whole of the Poole family were consequently invited to Three Rivers for a long stay covering the event. Mrs Poole rose to the occasion with her usual efficiency. She, Poole, Raymond and Louisa, who was mopey these days, took a trip to Sydney beforehand, putting up at Petty's Hotel where they cut a considerable figure. Thence, after patronising the shops, back to Goulburn by coach and on to Bool Bool, by four-in-hand. Jenny, Harry and Jim Poole were to come to Three Rivers by horseback with the other young folk from Maneroo, Tom Stapleton being left in charge of the homestead. Mrs McEachern would not be present; she felt the journey would be too much in the cold weather. Mrs Labosseer was also prevented from coming by the expected advent of another infant.

3

So once more a great gathering was imminent at Three Rivers. The preparations had reached an advanced and enthralling stage, and the famous four-in-hand was hourly expected. At length it could be

217

descried at the punt. Most of the township came out to watch the boss of cattle musters and droving expeditions tooling his beasts up the slope of the main street. His team for this adventure had been enlarged to five beautifully matched bays with black points. Well fed, well groomed, well caparisoned, they passed by at a gait that was more of a hand gallop than a dead run.

"By damn! Sure there's a man for ye!" exclaimed McHaffety.

"A flash old buck!" said Isaacs, "at his time of life..."

"Sure his missus sittin' up there with the child — where did he get the likes of her, at all?"

On they came to the white back gate where the whole household, including the guests already arrived, went forth from verandahs, kitchens, cow-yard and barns to welcome them. Raymond was tossed into the arms of Bert and thence to Charlotte. Emily gurgled with glee over Louisa. Mrs Mazere led Mrs Poole inside, and the men went off towards the stables with the steaming beasts.

Raymond was now five years of age, neither large nor robust, but exceedingly well grown in his own importance. He was rapturously received by both Fannie, now getting on for ten, and Rhoda who had passed her seventh birthday some months previously. Raymond promptly biffed the latter on the nose and seized her doll, which masterful tactics probably enabled him later in life to carry off the good-natured little girl as a bride. But for the present she fled bawling from this iniquitous monster, who made off unrepentantly with his booty.

Louisa was the centre of attraction among the young people. Her trip to Sydney lent her special distinction and raised her to the level of Martha Spires, who had been there several times. She had the latest thing in sleeves, chemisettes, bracelets and millinery and was quite lively, more than she had been for a long time. Mrs Poole was well satisfied with these results.

Emily was enthralled by the presents Louisa had brought her from Sydney, several of which were to enhance her person at the ball. Mrs Poole was installed in state in the Big House and was soon being consulted on all manner of subjects. She had the great gift of being able to impart her knowledge without giving offence, and even Mrs Mazere, on occasion, referred to her.

4

It was the night of the great ball and all the actors in the drama were dressed and in position. Charlotte and Philip were receiving many kindly words of welcome, and Emily was blushing like a rose under the congratulations, kisses and presents, compliments and chaffing showered upon her.

"Sure now, Miss Emily, if ye don't announce this night who is the lucky young feller, we'll have to be sendin' home for one of the princes of the blood," said Terence McHaffety who, having been invited to the wedding, albeit at the last moment, could not be shut out from the birthday party.

"Yes!" said Tim Brennan Senior. "Sure, I'll have to be after runnin' off with ye meself if none of the young fellers can please ye."

"Alannah, sure ye'll keep two or three dances for Timmy," said his mother, embracing the girl and presenting her with a wonderful brooch in the pattern of an acorn and oak leaves.

"If he asks me," said Emily happily, "of course I will." Tim's hopeless suit was as familiar to Bool Bool as Mazere's temper, and was just as respected. Tim was of so vigorous and honest a character that he was able to lend dignity even to an unrequited love affair.

Emily's first dance was with Bert. All the forces of gravitation ensured that. He had no other attachment, and he could not flout the belle of the district at her own coming-of-age party. They made a wonderful pair, striking in the contrast of their physiques and colouring. Emily was wearing one of the loveliest dresses that had ever been seen up the country, with its appurtenances chosen by the infallible Mrs Poole in Sydney.

All eyes followed the pair to the top of the room. It was confidently expected by some that there would be an announcement following the ball; after all, Bert was free, and Emily's preference was no secret even among outsiders. There had once been rumours that Mrs Labosseer held his youthful fancy, but that lady now was an established and expanding matron, producing the regulation infant at intervals. Mrs Mazere wondered again why Bert should be indifferent or dilatory. So did others. The air was full of expectancy.

Jessie was dancing with her faithful Hugh. Tim Brennan led out Louisa. Jack Stanton captured Mary Brennan; Denny Healey, Malcolm and other young men and maids sorted themselves out.

After the first dance with Emily, Bert was seen to relapse into his time-honoured custom of dancing both with the matrons and with such a vast galaxy of maids that there could be no particularity imputed to his choice. Jessie and Mary, with hope that would not die, noted this

219

immediately, as did Tim Brennan, Malcolm McEachern and Denny Healey, who put their heads together in a corner of the apartment set apart for masculine refreshments of drink and tobacco.

"It is as plain as dirt that Bert has no more thought for Emily than he has for poor old Jess, or his stepmother," said Malcolm.

"That being so, she must fall back on one of us soon," said Dennis. "She can't hold out much longer without being an old maid. We must bring her up to scratch."

"God knows I've done my best, but she cares no more about me than Bert does for her," said Tim wistfully. "I don't want to persecute the girl any more."

Malcolm and Dennis were of different kidney. To relieve the pangs of love rebuffed, they had eased themselves — if rumour spoke the truth — with favours purchased of Miss Polly Lowther and her colleagues at McGinty's pub and other Coolooluk haunts. Tales that trickled through even to maidens' ears now branded these two young men as "fast" blades, and certainly the deterioration ensuing from such a course had become evident in their speech and manners. They had long since been entirely frank between themselves as to their failed pursuit of Emily, and with this mutual acknowledgement of failure had died their jealousy of each other.

"Let's go and ask her one more time, and then be done with it," said Denny. "After that I'm going to have a good fling and then settle down with someone else — if I feel that way."

"Let's draw lots to see who goes first," said Malcolm.

"I don't like it," protested Tim.

"Rats!" said Malcolm. "You'll be popping the question anyhow the next time you're alone with her."

Tim came first in the draw. "All right, boys, I know it's no use, but I'll go through the form." He went back to the ballroom and Malcolm and Denny mixed themselves a couple of fortifying nobblers.

"This is my dance," said Tim to Emily, who came to him radiant and good-natured.

"Yes, and I just love this polka." They careered off together, Tim steering her with vigour and dash, his mother watching him with pain in her eyes. After a turn or two, Tim capered with the girl right out through the doorway where the initials had been carved five years before. They continued to dance on the verandah for a moment until Tim, seizing her shawl from where he had seen her lay it, wrapped it about her and took her towards the back gate.

"Now, Emily, I want to know if I can have the next two dances."

"They are promised to Malcolm and Dennis. You'd have to ask them."

"They would give their places to me under certain conditions, and you know what they are." Though he was merely going through a form with the gentle Emily, his heart thumped like to suffocate him.

"Now Tim, if you are going to propose again, you'll spoil my birthday party. Do please say that you don't really care very much and are only doing it for fun." Tim, being a brave man and the worthy son of his mother, replied in the way she wanted him to.

"Well, I felt I ought to propose to the belle of the whole country on her birthday night, just so that when you're an old lady you'll be able to count my name among the gossoons of good taste."

"Tim, you are a dear to say such nice things. But it could have been risky — I might have accepted."

"Sorra a bit of hope of that!"

"I don't know, with such a dear!"

"Am I dear enough for just one kiss on this night? And then I'll never bother you again, unless I stand up as best man to the luckiest fellow in the world at your wedding." The look of love and relinquishment, paling his freckled face and darkening his appealing Irish eyes, smote her.

"Oh, yes, Tim, if you want me to. I love you dearly, you know that — but not in the way you want me to."

In the dark shade of the lauristinus shrubs where she had listened tremulously for Bert on another frosty night, she put her arms about his neck and kissed him generously, wondering at the velvety warmth of his cheek, her first contact with a lover. But that was all Tim got, and when she left him in the cool dark to treasure the moment under the blazing stars, he stayed looking at the Southern Cross, unmindful of the cold. Malcolm, a little over-fortified, went in search of Emily.

The watchful Mrs Brennan saw Emily return alone, and heaving her bulk from her seat, went in search of Timmy. As she went out into the garden, carefully feeling her way with her two sticks, she heard the murmur of voices near the Old House. It was her Mary and Jack Stanton.

"It's no use, Jack. I thank you very much, but I don't want to be married. I'm going to take the veil."

"That's wicked. You should leave that for old maids blighted in love."

"Perhaps that's what I am," said the girl gently.

"Why can't you love me? I'll do anything you want. If it is religion..."

"No, Jack, it's not religion. If I loved you, I wouldn't let that stand in the way."

"I don't know what to do."

"Please go away and think of someone else, there's a darling."

"Well, come back inside. You'll catch cold here."

"I want to stay awhile, thank you. Please leave me. I feel a little upset."

Eventually she persuaded him to leave her and, standing in the shade of the naked cape jasmine and spiraea bushes, said a short prayer. Then, looking up at the sparkling skies where the old woman had left her snow-white road to heaven, she wondered whether she would find peace there.

Her mother presently found Timmy standing alone on a back verandah. "Alannah," she said, putting her arm through his. "Come ye in to the warmth, darlin'. Never ye grieve. Life is not begun yet. Who knows how the tide will change."

Malcolm's approach to Emily was very different to Tim's and betokened both the influence of Polly Lowther's kind and the effects of alcohol. He began gaily enough.

"Well, Emily, this is your last chance. Are you going to become an old maid, or are you going to marry someone now that you are twenty-one?"

"I might as well ask if you are going to be an old bachelor! You're older than I am."

"I like that! I'd get married tomorrow morning, if you'd help me. Here I am waiting to be knocked down, and to your bid. Aren't you going to bid, Emily?"

"You musn't make fun of me like that. Someone will hear you."

"They'll only hear what the magpies know — that Malcolm McEachern is fool enough to propose to Emily Mazere once again, and it's as much use as a possum barking in a green tree because she is dead nuts on a man who doesn't care a rap for her, and she's the only person in all the countryside too blind to see it."

Emily's heart fluttered to hear such rough words. "What do you mean?"

"What do I mean! All the crows on Maneroo and all the magpies at Bool Bool know what I mean. Just listen to them and you'll know."

"I don't want to know some things, Mr McEachern," she said reprovingly. "You can't be quite yourself to speak so."

"Ah," ejaculated Malcolm, reckless now that he had nothing to lose but his good manners. 'When the wine is in, the wit is out.' "So I have no hope of winning your hand, fair lady?"

"I should hardly think so," said Emily, her colour high.

"I have no more hope of catching you than you have of that fellow the crows and magpies are chattering about. Well, well, goodnight! When you're an old maid, I'll have the satisfaction of knowing it's not my fault."

"Is it my dance?" inquired Dennis Healey, hurrying up.

"It is! It is!" said Malcolm, whereby Dennis knew where he stood. Malcolm withdrew with an over-elaborate bow and, bumping into Mary Brennan, who had just come onto the billiard room verandah, swung her willy-nilly into the dance. Bert was dancing with Charlotte, and a wonderful pair they made, both so tall and commanding. People turned to look at the brother and sister, together again after their long separation.

Emily was beginning to feel nervous as Dennis led her onto the floor. Dennis's alcohol-laden breath was not reassuring. He had had another stiff dram after Malcolm left him and was in a nasty mood. His animosity was directed against Bert, whom he felt was hogging attention, and he vented it on Emily, who was so exasperating as to idolise this long-legged black gorilla. The Healeys had not recovered from Bert's very decided score in sending Logan's disguised horse to them at Little River, for they found out eventually about Bert's part in that exercise. Denny knew he had no hope with Emily, but was determined to go through with the compact. He began conventionally.

"Well, Emily, my beauty, many happy returns."

"Thank you very much, Denny. When is your birthday?"

"April first."

"Not really, is it?"

"Yes, that's why I'm such a fool as to say what I'm going to say now."

"Oh, please don't say anything," said Emily apprehensively. "We can't talk and dance."

"There's something I must say. Is there any chance of you marrying a decent man who loves the very ground you walk on, or are you determined to be an old maid?''

"I think I can wait a little longer without being a *very* old maid,'' said Emily, anxious to stave off unpleasantness.

"You'll wait a hundred years if you wait for Bert Poole to look the same side of the road as you're on,'' said Denny, straight out.

"Who said I was waiting for anyone?'' Emily prevaricated, praying for the end of the dance.

"I thought maybe I'd better warn you not to waste any more time.''

"I'm sure it should not worry you, no matter who I am waiting for.''

"Quite! But as an interested spectator, I'd like to give you a hint, out of the generosity of my heart.''

"I don't need it, thank you.''

"But I've got it on my chest and must get rid of it. Bert's too busy hanging around the skirts of another man's wife to even look at you. Jessie Mac had the spirit to see it and waste no more time on him. You're the talk of the country. Why don't you put an end to it and leave Bert to his diversions?''

"Please stop talking to me. You forget yourself entirely,'' said Emily, with a brave show of indifference. The dance being at an end, she made her escape without permitting him to lead her to a seat. Denny fired a final shot. "Perhaps if you didn't set your cap quite so hard at that black brigand from Curradoobidgee...''

Emily hastened into the covering darkness of the side verandah, bewildered and stung to the quick. Was she a byword among men? Was Bert like Denny and Malcolm, "fast'' — the lover of a married woman? What was she to do? As the dancers passed by the window, she could see that Bert was now dancing with Louisa. It certainly appeared that he sought out everyone but herself. A cruel realisation flooded her being from crown to toe, and she crept away into the garden to hide the tumult of her emotions.

The night was hardly less trying for Hugh. He had had a home at Nanda for Jessie ready for some time and could not understand her reasons for delay, since she had attained the ripe age of twenty. He hoped that night to persuade her to set a definite date for the wedding.

Following the leap year dance, Jessie had sought only to hide from Bert, so searing was her humiliation. But gradually the sting had

224

lessened. Bert behaved so well. He did not absent himself from Gowandale, nor did he thrust his presence on her unduly. Subtly he let her know that she had only enhanced their friendship through her suggestion. She felt instinctively that he had not mentioned the matter to a single soul.

She was sure now that his heart had been given irrevocably to Rachel Labosseer. How well he bore it! She, in a similar situation, had eased her wounded pride by doing grave injustice to honest, earnest, affectionate Hugh. His embrace was becoming a terror to her, and each time she submitted to it her conviction of dishonesty deepened. Nevertheless she shrank from the ordeal of the break. The engagement was so suitable, so popular with both families that it could not be broken without a furore ensuing. But broken it must be.

She was a straightforward girl, unversed in subterfuge. Now she took one steady look at Bert's transcendent person as he moved through the dance with his sister. No other could ever take Bert's place. It must be him, or no one. She allowed Hugh to lead her out of the room without a backward glance, but she shivered.

"Are you cold, darling?" asked Hugh.

"I did not know there was such a wind — just listen to it."

"That's not the wind — it's the river as it comes around the bend. That's what it sounds like at Nanda, too. I don't think I could sleep without it, I'm so used to it." He led her to his father's office where there was a fire, and seated her, taking pleasure in the beauty of her person and her dress. She saw the glowing affection of his fair, expressive face, and a pang smote her. How to begin!

As Hugh stooped to kiss her, she put up her hands against his mouth and his kisses fell there. He looked hard at her, puzzled.

"Jessie, I'm not going to let you out of this room until you name the happy day," he said.

"Please don't! It's no use, Hugh. We have made a great mistake — at least, I have — and I want you to forgive me. Let me go my way, and you go yours."

Hugh gazed at her, nonplussed. "Aren't you well, darling? Shall I get Mamma's smelling salts, or a glass of wine?"

"Nothing, thank you, Hugh. I am quite well. But I have to tell you this, though I would rather die than hurt you. I just don't love you in the way — in the way a wife should, and I can't go on with it. I can't."

225

"But," gasped Hugh, "we've been engaged for nearly six months. How can that be if you don't love me, can you tell me that?"

The whole pitiful story tumbled from Jessie's trembling lips, her only reservation being that she had actually offered herself to Bert at the leap year ball. Honest, humble Hugh — he was very much in love and anxious in his turn to save his pride, so he said, "That need make no difference, Jessie, if only you'll marry me. I'll make you love me in time. Only give me a chance. Jessie, I can't bear to lose you now after thinking of you as mine all this time."

"Hugh, I've tried so hard." She looked up at him, comparing him with careless, all-conquering Bert, and her heart said no. "But I cannot, Hugh."

"Do you mean that you accepted me just to save your own face? Because like all the girls you were running after that long-legged creature? You can't all have him, you know, and he's shown pretty clearly that he wants none of you. You'd think your self-respect—"

"It's my self-respect that makes me see I can't go on deceiving you, dear Hugh. It would be wicked. I deserve everything you're saying, but I do pray that you'll be happy with someone else and will forgive me some day. I'm so unhappy."

"Do you mean that I'm to be made a fool of before the whole country?"

"It will be unpleasant for us both at first," sobbed the girl. "That's why I've been so weak about telling you sooner. But no matter what people think, it would be better than a life of unhappiness."

"Not as unhappy as I'll be alone. Jessie, for God's sake...I wouldn't make you unhappy, I swear."

"Alone, laddie, look around! There is someone much worthier than I. Look in her eyes and you'll see no need to be alone."

"Who?"

"It is not for me to tell a sister woman's secret, but if you are so blind, you don't deserve to be loved."

Hugh had the quick temper of his father. "You women," he burst out angrily, "you ought to be locked up and not left at large to ruin a man. You ought to be ashamed of yourself. Don't cry, I'm not worth that," he said, unnerved by her tears. "Shall I send Mamma to you?"

"Oh no, please don't tell anyone. I only want to be alone."

"I'll take my despised presence off then." Wounded and shaken to the core, he flung off into the garden. There he let sobs, half of grief,

226

half of anger, break from him, to the astonishment of Emily, who had not yet returned to the house.

"What is the matter, Hugh? Has something dreadful happened?"

"What's the matter with yourself, out here all alone?" he said, recovering himself instantly.

"I'm hiding from everyone. Oh, Hugh! I've had such a terrible time with Malcolm and Dennis — I think they're half drunk. They're not fit to be in a ballroom."

"What have they been up to? Tell me at once!" he demanded, anxious to divert attention from himself.

Amid tears, Emily explained what had happened. "It's not true, is it, Hugh? Bert isn't fast like Malcolm and Dennis, is he?"

To be called upon to defend Bert at this juncture was adding insult to outrage. "I don't know what the truth is — except that you girls have no more self-respect than paddymelons to be flinging yourselves at Bert when he doesn't want you. No wonder he can't tell the difference between you and Polly Lowther's kind."

Seeing he could not weep in peace in the garden, he flung off back to the house and began dancing boisterously with the first girl that granted him the pleasure. It happened to be Louisa Poole.

Emily felt her birthday party a complete fiasco, what with Hugh behaving in as ruffianly a manner as Denny and Malcolm, and she went farther down the garden to sob in earnest, with the music of the river as it fell around the bend as accompaniment.

The observant Charlotte, meanwhile, was beset with anxiety. This ball was being celebrated with altogether too much alcohol for her liking. Even the girls were to be asked to drink Emily's health at supper, and drinks were readily accessible all the evening. The effects were patent already in the behaviour of Malcolm and Denny. Charlotte had overheard a little of their attack upon Emily and, missing her from the ballroom, she told Bert what she had heard and sent him to seek the missing girl. Her own hands were full with Philip, his father and Dr James, all now visibly intoxicated, and she feared her husband's greatest weakness could no longer be hidden from his mother. However, supper was at hand and might steady them a little. During her five hard years at the diggings, she had learnt the value of food in these crises.

Bert had some difficulty finding Emily, but at length he descried her at the bottom of the garden. On hearing her sobs, he did not fuss concerning their cause but brought forth an enormous handkerchief and wiped away her tears with the long supple fingers that were equally adept at shaping a horseshoe or at sewing a possum rug. Since the vast area of a gentleman's handkerchief is unfailingly amusing to women, Emily was immediately cheered and of her own accord confessed her trouble.

"Bert, dear, do tell me it's not true that you're fast and nasty like Denny Healey and the others. It's not true, is it?"

"Is that what they say?" he asked imperturbably. "Perhaps it's like the white mane and tail on Barney Logan's old mare, all over again." He chuckled. Emily found this convincing. The dimples played in her pretty pink cheeks. The river sounded like a chant of confidence.

"You'll get cold out here in the wind."

"That's not the wind. It's the river. Doesn't it sound wonderful? I love it."

"Suppose you dance all those jossers' dances with me, just to show you don't believe those stories," said Bert.

5

People were gathering for supper which, it being winter and there being so many guests, was to be served in the great kitchen, especially decorated for the event. The drawing room in the Big House had not been considered large enough, and the verandahs were too cold.

"If your intended threw you over, what would you do?" suddenly inquired Hugh of Louisa at the end of the dance.

"If I was a girl, I suppose I'd have to grin and bear it and pretend I didn't care," replied Louisa, "but if I was a man, I'd look around and make a fresh start."

"Would you, really?"

"Yes, of course I should."

That put an idea into Hugh's head. "If you're not engaged for supper, may I have the pleasure?"

Louisa, astonished, consented and then realised that something must be wrong — either that or she must be dreaming and would presently awake. But it was not possible for her to request an explanation without being overheard, since they were being pressed along with the throng for supper.

Bert and Emily were seated in the place of honour, nearest the cake.

"Where are Jessie and Hugh?" asked Mrs Mazere who, with Charlotte, had arranged the seating. Charlotte herself was to have a prominent place at the table with Philip, and mighty thankful she was to find him still able to sit straight.

"I'm here," answered Hugh.

"Where is Jessie?"

"I haven't seen her for some time," he replied, his colour high and realising that he had blundered not to have carried the thing on past supper. He was in for it now, as he could not retrieve himself without embarrassing Jessie.

Jessie meanwhile, recovered sufficiently to realise that she must not make a scene, had set out to seek Hugh and ask him to be with her for supper as a mark of friendship. She saw him leading Louisa in and noticed the radiant look on the girl's face. She had long known how Louisa felt, but was astonished that Hugh could so quickly recover. At hand was Joseph, now going on for thirteen and permitted to stay up upon the request of himself and Emily, on condition that he went to bed without fuss immediately the supper was past.

"Come on, Joseph, you be my gallant for supper," Jessie said with brave good humour. Joseph was much impressed and offered his arm in winning imitation of his elders.

"Oh, there you are, Jessie my dear," said Mrs Mazere. "You and Hugh are to sit opposite Emily and help her with the cake."

"Go on," whispered Louisa quickly to Hugh. "You can tell me what's happened afterwards." Seeing the look of disappointment on Joseph's face as Jessie moved away, she took his arm. "Joseph, do have me instead of Jessie."

Overwhelmed to be in such demand with fine young ladies who were almost strangers to him, Joseph accepted the substitution happily, and thus the awkwardness of the moment went almost unnoticed. The embarrassed expressions of Hugh and Jessie, however, told observant members of the company that all was not right. It was a lovers' quarrel, no doubt. Only Louisa sat as in a dream. Were her prayers going to be answered after all?

CHAPTER XX

1

Following the ball, the news of the broken engagement distracted attention from the lack of any announcement about Bert and Emily, which had seemed imminent, going by the signs. Jessie's decision was received with astonishment by the neighbours, and grief by the parents who had set their hearts on this union between Three Rivers and Gowandale.

They tried to get the young people to reconsider, but Jessie having gained the spiritual relief that was her due for her courage, was not to be persuaded. Neither was Hugh. His pride had been deeply wounded by Jessie's use of him, and he found himself strangely soothed by the tender, unselfish Louisa, ready to give all and thankfully accepting as much or as little as came her way in return. Mrs Poole was delighted by this alteration in affairs; she much preferred Hugh Mazere to Larry Healey Junior or Alick Gilbert, the alternatives that had been threatening.

The sentimental Louisa moved as if in a dream. Five years ago, in her nonage, she had hitched her wagon to the Mazere star. When Jessie had accepted Hugh, she had actually prayed right up to the last moment that something might free him. Now here he was — free! Presently the two young people had no difficulty persuading themselves that this was their first real love.

Emily, on the other hand, felt she had not progressed and the rude truth hurled at her at the ball by Malcolm and Denny threw a blight on her spirit. Charlotte, who dearly loved the girl, was her strength in those days.

The great event at that time was the setting up of Charlotte and Philip's new home near Coolooluk in which Emily had a considerable hand, either going up there to work with Charlotte, or having the children with her at Three Rivers so as to give their mother a free hand. Before the spring came, the couple were well settled, though the building was not yet completed and was surrounded by heaps of shavings and chips that obviated the necessity of drawing wood for the present. The foundations of a mill were being set up on a limpid creek that entered the Mungee a little above the Stanton household, and that sang a lullaby to a wealth of ferns and shrubs.

2

One Saturday night a couple of months following the birthday ball at Three Rivers, Bert sat down to write a letter. It was a love letter, and he had called upon the aid of Charlotte, a fact which indicated that it was more a state than a spontaneous affair. The children were abed, Philip was absent at Coolooluk, and the sister and brother had the living room of the new home to themselves. Awaiting the shrinking of the slabs, the walls had been papered with periodicals, and very cosy and cheerful the room was with its beautiful fire of boxwood blazing on the wide, white hearth.

With writing materials laid out on the hardwood table that he had made, Bert was waving his quill in a circular movement above the spotless paper, rather like a rooster flaps his wings before he crows. After waving his hand about several times, he came to a standstill, laid down the quill and took off his coat. Again he waved the quill, equally ineffectually, and then rolled up his shirt sleeves, showing his tanned muscular forearms where many a girl had wished to press her fingers or try her teeth.

"Charlotte, when are you coming to help me?" he called.

"You make a start," she replied from the next room, still unboarded, where she was tracking down little boots and socks and placing them in pairs. "I'll be there in a minute."

The truth was that the hero of two districts and beyond found the prospect of penning a letter an entirely daunting prospect, despite the instruction he had received from his stepmother. Not that he was lacking in other skills. He could glance at a forest giant and tell which way it would fall to his axe and how many slabs it would yield. He could flay a beast and tan its hide and make from it harness and many other things. He could snare a wild horse of the plains and convert it to a domestic ally, for there was no outlaw ever wrapped in hide that could shake him off while buckle and girths would stand. His love of horses was rooted not in gambling, but in personal friendship for a noble fellow animal. He could canter over a stretch of country and estimate how many acres it contained, and how many beasts per acre it would graze. He could make a fire when the country was girth deep in snow or sodden under pouring rain, and cook his meals at it. There wasn't a beast from the Upper Murray to the Lower Murrumbidgee that he didn't know by the cut of its jib, and no bird could call to its mate nor outline its wing on the sky at dusk without his reading it like the alphabet. He could not be bushed while the stars shone at night or the sun by day. But he would have thought any duffer could do all this and much more, but that the fellow who could cover a sheet of paper quickly with a letter was no end of a gun.

"How far have you got?" asked Charlotte as she came to him, rolling down her sleeves and taking off her apron.

"Nowhere." His eyes strayed up towards the inside of the shingled roof — his work — of which he was justly proud. "Those rafters will soon be shrunk enough for me to nail the calico on for you — and then the room will begin to look ship-shape."

"No good putting it up too soon," said Charlotte, coming to stand by his elbow. "Bert, you haven't even begun."

"Aw! Do you think I had better do it at all?"

"Why don't you just ride down tomorrow and see her — she would like it twice as well."

"Oh no, I must write," insisted Bert. The standing of the princess he was about to invite to share his throne was such that he felt she should be approached formally, through a dignified letter. Anything else would not be meet. But it was an effort, verily.

The proposed letter was the outcome of Charlotte's advice to him following the ball, after Emily had confided to her sister-in-law all that she had suffered at the tongues of Malcolm and Dennis. Charlotte felt it time to act, for the sake of both Emily and her brother. It was not advisable that Bert should delay any longer in choosing a wife. He was a splendid fellow and a fit bridegroom for the daintiest lady in the land, but if he hung around footloose much longer, he might get into wild habits like Denny and Malcolm. Charlotte shrank from even envisaging such a fate for Bert — Bert who had never failed or hurt her, and whose mistakes had always been the result of inexperience and never of flawed disposition.

"Bert," she had said one Saturday night, "when are you going to get married?"

"I hadn't thought about it. There's plenty of time."

"You can't keep a girl hanging about until everyone's talking about her. Poor little Emily has waited ever since she first set eyes on you. It's not fair."

"Emily! I've never said a word to Emily."

"Haven't you! Well, then, you're too slow to catch grubs."

"But I don't want to catch Emily."

"Don't you! Who do you want to catch?"

"No one that I know of."

"Don't you like Emily?"

"I like her all right but—"

"Do you like anyone else? What about Jess McEachern?"

"Oh no!" The answer was firm. Charlotte did not pursue the question.

"What about Mary Brennan?"

"Mary is the dearest girl I have ever known, but I don't think about her in that way. She's too big. She'll be an elephant like her mother when she's a bit older, and anyway, they wouldn't have me because of the religion."

"They might overlook that if you really wanted her."

"I don't. I hope she'll get some fellow that's worthy of her."

"What about Martha Spires?"

"She's looking out for some swell Englishman."

"If you went after her good and strong, she..."

"I don't want to. Her teeth stick out too far and I can't stand her staring eyes."

"What about Joanna Healey?"

"Wouldn't touch her with a roping pole! She's as mean and sly as the old woman."

"What about Flora McEachern?"

"That kid!"

"Or Catherine Timson?"

"The old woman flings her at my head too much."

233

"Or Georgina Gilbert?"

"Don't like the breed."

"Well then, it must be Emily."

"The old man would raise a dust just like he did about you."

"You're only trying to get out of it now. We're as good as anyone these days, since the Missus brought us on."

The idea of Emily, thus presented, began to rather appeal to him.

"What do you think Emily would say, if I asked her?"

"There's no doubt about what Emily would say. I don't know how you can hang back — you'll lose her, you know. She's as pretty as a picture and as good and loving as she is beautiful. I can't tell you how loving and kind she has always been to me."

"Would you like me to marry her, Charl?"

"I would just love it! There's not another girl I've seen who can touch her. Why do you hang back?"

"Oh, I don't know. Perhaps I'll think about it one of these days."

"Now is the time, this very day. Neither of you is too young, and you have the money to offer her a good home."

"But I couldn't start off without coming up to it a bit gradually. She'd think I was drunk, like Denny."

Charlotte chuckled. "You've been as gradual as the grass in a dry season. You just ride down tomorrow and see what she says."

But Bert shied away from this prospect; only a letter could satisfy his notion of the fitness of things. It was not until a fortnight later that Charlotte finally brought him up to scratch.

"How are you going to start?"

"Oh, I don't know. What do you think?"

"My darling Emily!"

"That's much too bold and forward! Suppose I say 'Miss Emily Mazere. Dear Madam'."

"She'd think the letter was from a lawyer."

Bert laid down his quill again and Charlotte came and stood close to him. He put his arm around her, despite the fact that caresses were rare among the Pooles. They had not been reared to them. Then Bert said one of those things which sisters treasure in their hearts forever. "Oh, Charl, old girl, I wish I could marry you. That would come so easy and I wouldn't have to write a letter."

A letter was not essential even now, but Bert had set his heart on it and she would not nag the point. Instead she said, putting her arms around the great fellow, "You and I have been like a married couple ever since we lost poor mother and had to worry along somehow, but now you must have the real kind of marriage as well. It will make you very happy."

"Will it, Charlotte?"

"Yes, it will," she said simply. Bert chewed the quill in his strong white teeth. "Hurry along, or Philip will be home." She leaned down and put her lips against his ear. Great silly baby, he was so beautiful, so desirable — there wasn't a girl from Maneroo to Melbourne who wouldn't jump at him. His hesitancy made him adorable to his fond sister. His innocence about women enveloped him like an aura; he was as unspoiled as women would have their husbands, their fathers, their brothers and sons. As such Charlotte determined to keep him, as far as lay in her powers and with Emily Mazere as her indispensable ally.

Bert shaped up to the letter once more. "What did Philip say to you in his letters? If only I could see one."

"I'll pick one out," said Charlotte. She knew her budget by heart and chose one therefrom. Bert studied the document with furrowed brow. The Mazeres were all accomplished letter writers. Their proficiency ran that way. Bert's lay more in hitting a blowfly at an incredible distance.

" 'Miss Charlotte Pool'. Ah, I knew I didn't ought to be bold and forward!" said Bert triumphantly. With Philip's letter as his model, he re-applied himself. This time he took off his stock and collar, unbuttoned his shirt and really began.

Miss Emily Mazere, Three Rivers Homestead, Bool Bool
Dear Miss Emily,
    I have the honour to take up my pen to write to you these few lines hoping they find you in the best of health as they leave...

"Charlotte, what shall I say after 'they leave'?"

"Say they leave *me*!"

"All right!" She left him, as unselfconsciously absorbed in his task as a child, a lock of his glossy black hair falling over his forehead. What did it matter how he worded the letter, as long as he worded it somehow? What girl in her senses could resist him, thought Charlotte, enfolding him in a tender glance and going about her tasks. The next part of the undertaking was the approach to Mazere Senior, also to be made by letter. There would be no casual carrying off of *his* property! Charlotte had been privileged to know the contents of the stately Labosseer communication to Mazere in like case and could repeat bits of it like a poem, but its adaptation being beyond the scarcely literate, Bert and she decided to consult Philip.

When he reached home that evening, Charlotte was thankful to see him quite himself, in spite of an alcoholic breath. He was well pleased to aid Bert's enterprise. "I expected to hear of this long ago, Bert, old man, but I am glad you have waited till I could be at the wedding." As a return for past favours, Philip agreed to ride down to Three Rivers on the morrow to see his parents and deliver both the important missives.

It doesn't really matter what the parents said, or what Emily read in that stilted, hard-wrought letter. In fact, she read into it everything that her loyal loving heart had ardently desired and awaited. She laid it gently beside Bert's other letter, the one thanking her for her support during the days when suspicion rested on him. Gathering a sprig of sweet-scented verbena from the bush planted in front of the Old House at the time of her birth, and now out-topping the eaves, she placed it between the folds of her reply. For good measure, she stood before her little mirror and clipped a long, soft curl of bright gold and sent that too.

Very late on Sunday night, the curl clung around Bert's slim, dark finger like the finest silk and set him all a-tremble.

"What's the proper thing for me to do now?" he asked Charlotte. "I don't want to make any blunders."

"Get on your horse and ride down to see her as soon as it is daylight. Otherwise it might seem as if you don't have any real blood in you, and that disgusts a girl."

Bert's life fluid being what it was, he started out long before it was light. He reached the back gate of Three Rivers a little after breakfast time, but not a moment earlier than he was expected. Emily had seen him approaching and had fled to put on another gown.

After his interview with the parents in Mr Mazere's office, Bert was sent to Emily, who was awaiting him in the drawing room. He entered the room with far more trepidation than he had felt at the time when he had stolen up behind Barney Logan, now doing time at

Berrima. But he was speedily intoxicated by the magic of Emily's welcome. To have ruffles of perfumed silk floating all about him so that he had to remove his spurs for safety, to be clasped about the neck, his kisses returned with interest and a flood of tender names — this was like something out of a fairy story for Bert.

His old daydream of love had fled, as insubstantial as the wind, banished by this sweet reality. Before the day was out, he could no longer remember what the dream had been.

All household duties were abrogated for the happy girl and she and Bert spent a long day together, interrupted only by meals. Before his departure following family prayers, they walked together by the sliprails on the ridge, Bert with one arm around his love and the Waterfall's curb rings held firmly in his other hand. Emily could not be allowed to return to the house alone, so they retraced their steps to the back gate where Emily had stood with her pulses in a whirl five years before. Here they had a great many last words to say.

"How the old curlews are wailing tonight, and the plovers too," said Bert, "and the river more like wind than ever, though it's so summery."

He had to tear himself away eventually, or Papa would be coming to seek his daughter. Spring was everywhere in the air and coursing through the Waterfall's veins. Freed from that capable cruel twist of the bit rings that had held him quiet, he reared on his hind legs as Bert swung across him with the thrilling clink of bit and stirrup iron. As Bert turned the beast he saw the shadow of his lady's gown by the big gate and swung out of the saddle again for just one more kiss, just one more testing of reality.

"I just can't get away," he said, the vibration of his tones finding response in all her being.

Then he really had to go. She heard again the thunder of hoofs on the stony ridge, the clatter of rails thrown down, and the wail of plover and curlew in the new graveyard. But he had left his heart in her keeping this time, while hers went bounding with him under the starry sky by singing river and flowery ridge.

"Emily, my dear, where are you?" called Mrs Mazere from the back door.

"I'm coming, Mamma," said the happy young voice out of the shadows.

"You'll catch cold, my dear, out here so long without a shawl. There'll be other days, you know."

"Oh yes," said Emily, a catch of joy in her throat.

3

Charlotte was astonished when Bert told her that he was not going to be married for a year.

"Why wait so long? You've wasted too much time already. Won't Emily consent to marry sooner?"

"It will take me all that time to get ready. I can't dab a girl like Emily Mazere down in a shepherd's hut. I want everything nice for her."

He set about fulfilling this ambition without delay, taking himself off to Curradoobidgee the next day. His father and he rode all about the run, discussing the merits of partition as against partnership, and Bert chose a beautiful site for the house. He next chose the timber and directed the sawyers.

His stepmother was delighted with the news, and he found her a tower of strength. There was no aspect concerning making a home upon which she could not advise him, and they became warmer friends than ever.

The announcement aroused the dormant ache in the heart of Jessie McEachern. She had idealised Bert as at least being true to an unattainable love, but now she knew that she had made a mistake. He had not been indifferent to her because of Rachel Labosseer, but because he preferred another. For a fleeting moment she wished she might recover Hugh's affections. But that was impossible now, for it was known to everyone that he was to marry Louisa come New Year. His house was all ready and Louisa, brimming over with happiness, was getting her things ready.

"Why not make it a double wedding?" suggested Charlotte to Bert. But Bert said he couldn't possibly have the place fit for Emily by then, what with the wool-washing and shearing intervening. And Hugh could not be persuaded to wait a moment longer than necessary.

CHAPTER XXI

1

Louisa was visiting Charlotte, and Emily was keeping her sister Isabel company at Mungee. It being Saturday, both Hugh and Bert also found their way to the district, and the four young people gathered at Mungee for midday dinner.

The season was well advanced, the lambs had been tailed and marked, and it was the last time the men would be able to go gallivanting before wool-washing and shearing was upon them. The day was unprecedentedly warm, the air heavy and oppressive with the threat of a thunderstorm.

"By George, the fish ought to bite like billyo today," remarked Bert. "I saw them plopping up in dozens as I came along."

"They'd make a lovely change for tea," said Isabel. "I'm so tired of mutton. Why don't you try and catch some?"

The idea found favour. "Bert could cook them on the bank, and then you and George come down to eat them at tea time," said Louisa happily.

Lines and hooks were brought out, supple wattle saplings were cut for rods, and worms were procured from the end of the kitchen drain where it emptied into the blossoming orchard.

"It's so hot I think I'll take a towel and have a bogey," said Bert, and Emily and Louisa decided to do likewise.

239

They made their way to the upper side of the fish-hole where the crystal water ran clear and deep, treading over a carpet of spring flowers and warding off the attacks of nesting magpies. All around was a wealth of golden wattle, indigo woodbine, ti-tree and senna. They lay on the warm rocks, the girls crushing the little heath for its perfume, and the men lazily estimating the height of the river gum, towering like a marble column, that marked the spot.

The fish bit splendidly for a while and the sun came out burningly between the great thunder clouds. Then a sentinel cockatoo sent up a screech from a tall tree across the stream. "Not another bite today," announced Bert, furling his line. "Cocky says so and he always knows."

At first the girls disbelieved him, but after their corks had rested unmolested on the clear cool surface of the fish-hole for a while, they realised that Bert was right. Truly, he knew the most wonderful things.

"There's only enough fish for Isabel," said Emily. "Let's have a swim and then go home and go for a ride."

"All right, but be very careful not to go beyond that rock," said Hugh. "It's very deep under the bank."

"We'll be careful," said Louisa.

"We'll come back when we hear you coo-ee," said Bert.

The men took their towels and went further downstream where the current was stronger, leaving the smooth reach, sheltered by the high, overhanging bank and embowered in ti-tree, for the girls. Mixed bathing was unknown in those days, as were bathing suits up the country. Men and maidens frequented separate pools and dipped in all their fresh beauty, unclad as nymphs.

The girls unrobed and entered the pool with delight; the clear water was seductive and the perfumed shrubs enchanting. The water was cold, however, running as it did down from the ranges. They soon climbed out and warmed themselves on the great flat rocks, hot as ovens. While the little lizards blinked at them and angry magpies protested their presence, they exchanged confidences about love and life, so sweet and wonderful.

"Let's dive in and race to that big tree over the other side, and then we'll dress and coo-ee for the boys," said Emily.

They stood together, comely in contrasting ways, the Mazere form fair and rounded, the Poole form tall, straight and a little too thin.

"Now off!" A laughing squeal, a splash and they were swimming — Louisa for dear life, since Emily always outdistanced her. But this time she reached the bank first and, stepping out in triumph on to the beautiful water-smoothed stones, looked behind her. There was no sign or sound of Emily. The Mungee flowed on without a scar on its crystal surface. Louisa paused a moment, expecting her friend to appear laughing from behind some tree or shrub. She ran up the bank, calling. There was no reply. She struggled into her garments, coo-eeing wildly in desperate panic.

2

At first the men thought Louisa's coo-ee was the prearranged signal and prepared to take a final plunge. But Bert's quick ears detected a screaming note of terror. Hauling on his trousers, he fled through the bush, Hugh struggling into a garment and following.

"It's Emily! We dived in there together and she hasn't come up," cried Louisa piteously.

Bert asked exactly where they had gone in, made his way to the spot, and took a long, deep dive. Louisa waited in agonising suspense, fearing that he too had gone, he was so long under water. He came up far down the bank — alone! Hugh dived too, though he was not nearly as good a swimmer as Bert.

"Go up and get George, without letting Isabel see you," they commanded Louisa. Isabel was awaiting her fifth child and could not be alarmed.

Louisa, now booted and in most of her garments, sped away breathlessly, returning soon on horseback with George and two of the stockmen. Bert, winded for the moment, lay on the rocks. George, an intrepid diver, took his place. Then he told Louisa to go on horseback to the new house — a good seven miles distant — and ask Charlotte to come over to be with Isabel, and to tell Philip to bring the blacks, who were camped around the diggings.

Calamity entered their souls. There was no hope of Emily's life. The struggle would be to find her body.

Louisa went off at full gallop on her errand. Hugh, exhausted by the diving, was sent off on the Waterfall, now rising nine but better in wind and leg than a colt and never before ridden by anyone but his master, to break the news to Three Rivers and to bring Tim Brennan, who was a champion swimmer and diver. One of the stockmen, who knew the country, was sent up to Maneroo mounted on a tireless ninety-miler to take the news to Eueurunda and Curradoobidgee. The other stockman watched the river with Bert, while George broke the news to his wife. Her mother's daughter, she set about preparing food for the men and was soon upon the bank with a sheet and certain other things.

As soon as Bert had recovered his breath, he dived, and dived, and dived again until his strength gave out in exhaustion. The fish-hole, sly and serene, refused to give up its prize. The clouds had disappeared, the sun came out again bold and bright, and a delicious zephyr laden with perfume tempered the air. The Mungee moved silently through the fish-hole, falling away at the lower end with a divine song that filled the beautiful afternoon like a sigh from the gates of paradise.

In what seemed an incredibly short time, Charlotte and Louisa appeared, each with a small child in her arms and a larger one sitting behind her, to be with Isabel.

Philip arrived at dusk with Bert's three faithful friends who had never failed him, Nanko, Yan Yan and Lac-ma-lac. The blacks had a consultation with Bert, the only white man they considered worthy of such. Under the upstream bank, he had found a swift current, coming evidently from a strong underground spring. Bert thought that the body would be in the unbottomed reach, held under the curve of the downstream bank.

Nanko and his colleagues made a canoe and, having launched it, peered into the depths. When the cool starlit night came down, great bonfires were lighted on the banks and the blacks used fishing flares. But still the fish-hole refused to divulge what lay in its limpid depths.

Tim Brennan arrived there before midnight on Kilkee, who was steaming and blown from the screwing gallop of over thirty miles with a heavy weight in the saddle. At earliest dawn he and Bert dived, dived, and dived again, but Tim's strength, like Bert's, eventually gave out in defeat.

Before morning, the suffering parents had arrived with Hugh, after riding fast, too fast, for people of their age. A little later the senior Brennans came and, with them, Mary, to stand by her mother for whom the journey was like to be fatal. But old Mrs Brennan would not forsake her dear Rachel Mazere in tragedy.

"Ah, Mother of God, by the sacred crucified heart of Jesus help the poor mother to bear this," she prayed. "And my poor Tim, and Bert. Och, alas!" she said to her husband. "It's neither of them will ever have her in this world now."

In less than forty-eight hours came Labosseer, supported by Poole and McEachern seniors, all the young men having preceded them, riding furiously. Men came from everywhere offering to help, for the news that beautiful Emily Mazere, the bride-to-be of Bert Poole, had been drowned in the Mungee fish-hole and that the body could not be recovered had spread like wildfire.

The body! Thus had lovely Emily become in one cruel moment. Alas, alas! That youth and happiness could not prevail!

But no one could help, and though the night birds for miles around heard the clink of stirrup and bit as strong men rode swiftly from afar, their energy was to no avail. The cruel fish-hole held its prize.

It was decided to send to Gundagai for grappling irons, but these too proved unavailing. There was nothing now but ghastly waiting. At the request of the family, strangers returned to their affairs, not to reappear until the funeral. The blacks kept watch night and day. Mrs Mazere walked up and down the bank, praying for strength and lamenting her beautiful child, and her husband was well-nigh prostrate. The carpenter, brought up from Bool Bool, tap-tapped on a coffin lined with oilskin. Dr James also waited to do his duty.

It was dear, kind Maria who then took charge and waited with her winding sheet, supported by Charlotte, controlled and dauntless.

"Mother of God, give us strength!" she wailed. "Charlotte me girl, 'twill not be endurable to the mother, and Timmy and Bert must be right out of their minds."

Isabel and Philip walked much with their mother. Tim Brennan Senior loyally supported his old friend, his loving, Irish affection poured out in an uncontrolled grief that was very comforting to the stricken father. The gentle Mary and Louisa administered support and sympathy to their brothers, the two young men equal now in the loss of their beloved. They were dull with exhaustion following on their superhuman diving efforts and the emotional shock. They sat much together in the sunlight where the wattle trees shed a golden glory above the fish-hole, and it seemed to them that they must be haunted for ever by the divine song of the cruel Mungee filling the tortured and terrible hours.

On the ninth day the fish-hole gave up its prize. Maria, with the understanding and tenderness of an angel guarding from agonised or curious eyes a beauty that lately had been, had her way in the fitness of things. Alas! Alas!

3

"We brought nothing into this world and it is certain we can carry nothing out. The Lord gave and the Lord hath taken away; blessed be the name of the Lord."

It was the voice of Malcolm McEachern Senior, reading the order for the burial of the dead. Straight-backed, he stood bareheaded in the afternoon sunlight in his suit of black with crape upon the upper arm, and his high white collar and black stock. He was stern with self-control and dignified in his self-respect and neighbourliness in his filling the office of clergyman for his friends, and was a man to honour as he read from the big prayer book given to Mrs Mazere by the Bishop on one of his visits. He was glad of the large, clear print though, not because his eyes were failing — many of the old pioneers loved large print for the same reason that children love it.

Having reached this far, McEachern's kindly voice wavered. He coughed, and struck at an imaginary fly and brought out an enormous handkerchief, of the kind that had amused Emily but a matter of a few weeks before. But no one smiled today. Sobs rose all around, sobs from strong men unashamed of their grief.

At the funeral was a gathering such as had never before been known up the country. The romance of the dead girl and her bridegroom had been known far and wide, and the tragedy of her passing had brought together hundreds of horsemen, many of them practically strangers. Every neighbour and friend who found it possible to appear was there to show sympathy with the bereaved parents and families.

Tim Junior, standing between his mother and Mary, sobbed unaffectedly. Labosseer stood stiff and straight, the tears coursing down his cheeks. Mr and Mrs Mazere stood together, with Isabel and George Stanton on one side, and Tim Brennan Senior and Hugh on the other.

Tom Stapleton, wearing his funny crumpled suit and sobbing into the crown of his old slouch hat, stood on the outskirts of the crowd. The sun had been blotted out for Tom; though he had never caught

244

anything but a stray gleam of it now and again, the loss was one to rack his soul. The young people, appalled, let their grief have its way. The impossible had happened. One of their number supremely fashioned for life was dead in the flower of her youth.

Bert, alone, stood cold and dry-eyed while Charlotte clasped his arm tightly in sympathy.

McEachern was continuing: "Man that is born of a woman hath but a short time to live, and is full of misery. He cometh up and is cut down, like a flower; he fleeth as it were a shadow, and never continueth in one stay."

Again he halted, overcome, and sobs broke out like a storm, sobs of strangers, sobs of relatives and friends. Denny and Malcolm stood together, ashamed now of their unworthy behaviour on the last occasion that they had seen the girl. She had been so lovely, so kind in spite of her failure to appreciate them as they had felt was their due, and they had been so rude. Now it was beyond recall.

Bert remained numb, wondering what could be the matter with him. He could not seem to feel anything at all. He recalled his grief when Black Belle had been attacked. The tragedy of Emily's death, though so stupendous, did not seem to register. The ceremony of the day did not seem to concern him. He noted little details with a clarity that bespoke unreality. Poor old McEachern, a good old buffer, was getting a bit of the flour bag in his whiskers. Poor Tim Brennan was terribly cut up. There was no doubt he had loved Emily deeply. The Brennans were the kindest people that Bert knew; a fellow could always be sure of their sympathy and help. He could hear the dogs barking in the deserted township, the ewes and lambs bleating on the ridges at the saltshed above the graveyard, and the sweet song of the Yarrabongo as it fell around the bend.

"...earth to earth, ashes to ashes, dust to dust..."

The clods were falling on the coffin that was double wrapped in new tarpaulin, the coffin of beautiful Emily Mazere of Three Rivers, belle of Bool Bool and Maneroo, the joy of her family and friends, bride-to-be of handsome Bert Poole, the idol of his contemporaries.

Now the men were replacing their crape-draped hats and moving away over the trampled flowers, leaving Emily alone in the cemetery at the far end of the hollow that stretched between Three Rivers and Bool Bool proper. They took their grief away with them from that place where the violets were blue amid the grass, the golden soldier buttons nodded in the sun, and the noisy magpies and plovers, anxious for their nestlings, savagely threatened the intruders. But their grief was inappropriate for Emily, and flowed only from their sense of shock. Hers was the triumph — to be forever young in their memory, unwearied and well pleased with love. Hers was the privilege — to be mourned in the splendour of her youth and beauty by the community as if she were a public personage, to have a small army of brothers and brothers-in-law as pallbearers, and to cause to weep, unashamed, half a dozen stalwart lovers, and her own desired the most desired of all.

When the night fell, the curlews wailed an angel requiem and the great stars smiled on her primaeval place of rest where she went like a queen to blaze the highway.

As soon as it transpired into the ether that a story of the old hands up the country was to be compiled the space about my ink-pot became congested with a throng of the elect. They hurried up from rivers and ridges, the plains and gullies and peaks in all their actuality and inevitability, keen to escape oblivion. The old hands who had outlived their mates, the lonely ones from graves that never were fenced, with none to know or mourn their passing, the little ones that snuffed out before they were christened, all were there, reproachful if overlooked.

They flock around with the endearing sociability and zest of the early solitary days, unbored, uncritical, unanalytical, no posing, no humbug. Appealingly, patiently they press about me with so many essential details of surroundings and incident that even a selection of those calling for record, and painted with utmost economy, would fill a three-volume novel.

"Why not?" they cry. "Many times three volumes are written about the absurdest fancies, and we are *real*."

"What is reality and what is fancy?" I parry.

Derision and arguments of detraction spread indecision in the pathway of determination. Among that press of genuine people, where were action and plot to compete with conventional novels and stir the debauched post-war imagination? Where the great rivers, the arctic snows, the dashing Indians which North America provides as background?

Research among the printed fiction of the time of the early Australian pioneers — forgotten stories like the unfenced graves, stories lacking sufficient literary value and fact to survive — shows that their writers magnified bloody affrays in the attempt to supply action, plot, thrill.

"Not one of you," I assert, "ever blew out another's brains or had your own interfered with except by alcohol, or a touch of the sun, or too much solitude; none of you was murdered or committed murder, or rapine, or mutiny, or political intrigue, or took any part or felt any interest in the big wars (American and European) that raged in your day!"

They persist earnestly, emphatically, reassuringly, that they have only to be kept true to life to make a book. They are equally insistent that they must be transcribed, day by day as they lived, possuming back and forth and up and down as simply as life itself. They contend that where a history lacks epic incidents it is not legitimate to supply that lack by drawing a picture out of focus or by clutching at elements outside the rightful frame. Tenderness these characters are entitled to, as are all that have gone their way to silence after gallant discharge of life, but it is not meet that they should be subjected to caricature or exaggeration.

An enriching recognition of the quality of the antipodean Old Hands is born of contact with the world's savants, which London bounteously provides for all. The Old Hands here of antithetical environment, rich in erudition by command of the priceless storehouses of human knowledge, and living association with their compeers, may be heard arguing the import of a phrase in some treasured folio; or tracing the parentage of a word through a dozen languages; or interpreting the inscription on a prehistoric coin, the hall-mark on ancient handicraft. "Ah," I have sighed, "if the Old Hands up the country, in exchange for a modicum of their experience of reality, could have only a little of the erudition of these rare souls, how refreshing it would be for both parties!"

There are, too, those other old-world denizens for whom space is found in the daily papers, gorged though these are with the world's distresses, needs, greeds, chicaneries, and abnormalities, to announce their rapture at the first primrose or the first note of the cuckoo each spring, or to draw attention to obscure literary reference to similar events. Here, my eyes having been opened, I see both schools of Old Hands well furnished for intercommunion. By their appreciation of the seasonal return of the cuckoo and primroses as momentous occurrences, the old-world Old Hands realise for me the opulence of culture to be imbibed from the environment of the early pioneers.

Flinders, recording his observations upon the day of 9th December 1798 in the lone and mighty waters that lap Australia's southern shores, has bequeathed us this gem:

> A large flock of gannets was observed at daylight to issue out of the Great Bight to the southward; and they were followed by such a number of the sooty petrels as we had never seen equalled. There was a stream of from fifty to eighty yards in depth, and of three hundred yards, or more, in breadth. The birds were not scattered, but flying as compactly as a free movement of their wings seemed to allow; and during a full hour and a half this stream of petrels continued to pass without interruption, at a rate little inferior to the swiftness of the pigeon. On the lowest computation I think the number could not have been less than a hundred millions; and we

248

were thence led to believe that there must be, in the large bight, one or more uninhabited islands of considerable size.

A footnote is added:

> Taking the stream to have been fifty yards deep by three hundred in width, and that it moved at the rate of thirty miles an hour and allowing nine cubic yards of space to each bird, the number would amount to 151,500,000. The burrows required to lodge this quantity of birds would be 75,750,000; and allowing a square yard to each burrow, they would cover something more than 18½ geographic square miles of ground.

A writer nearly half a century later records of the sooty petrels, more commonly known as mutton birds:

> In sailing from Port Albert to the Melbourne Heads in 1844 our vessel was continually amongst flocks of from two miles to ten in length. These would rise as we approached, making a noise like distant thunder.

Shall we ever again in this world hear the music of feathered wings like distant thunder? Shall we know only the deafening drone of winged engines spilling death and devastation?

The grandchildren and great-grandchildren of such folk as the Mazeres, M'Eacherns, and Brennans have seen flocks of black swans and pelicans at least three miles deep and ten miles wide. Today in that land they still may wake to the music of thousands of magpies or the riotous laughter of kookaburras, or ride the long day through attended, like King Solomon with his hoopoes, by clouds of green and red and purple and rose parrots, and enjoy the glittering tinkle of their conversation. They still may ride through miles of blossoming snow-gums, or blackthorn, or tea-tree, spreading a perfumed canopy of loveliness.

One of the pioneers, still south of seventy, told me here in London that once at dawn he woke from sleep wrapped in his blanket beside a stream in Queensland amid the domed shape of ant-hills and thought the Judgment Day had come, because it seemed that the very earth rose up and moved about him red and beautiful. Kangaroos in hundreds were hopping past, avoiding him in their stride.

Contemplate these things as sustenance to the soul, as we huddle in the great metropolises with the shabby sparrow or ill-tempered pigeon to represent bird life, and the rats and mice that stink and gnaw, or tom-cats libidinously screeching among the soot-shabby aucuba bushes to represent animal life!

The author of the tale of the kangaroos once on the way to Alaska came upon an Oxford Don who was at the last gasp because his man had died on the trail. He was surrounded by supplies of flour, etc., but his culture and education had not fitted him to shift for himself in emergency. The pioneer rescued him, being so educated that he could fashion his own habitation and grow and grind his own corn if put to it, and would not have starved where game abounded. Of the Oxford graduate he sorrowfully exclaimed, "God Almighty! To think that the Lord could allow such a jackass to be created."

We are threatened by standardisation and specialisation, with Big Business cracking the whip of mechanical efficiency, in an era in which graded mediocrity will be divided into gangs each set to a simple movement of a complex operation, and fit for little else. The old pioneer life, with each person able to fend for himself completely, cannot be recalled. It is too cumbersome, too extravagant of time and material. But humanity, if it is to retain its present nucleus of a soul and develop it further, must before long wholesomely react and live life more in the whole. An educated sense of values will recapture and adapt old pioneer experience. No man will be considered properly manly or cultured or aristocratic and capable of dignity who is unable to shift for himself to a certain degree. No woman will be able to assume superiority of refinement, sensitiveness or breeding, by boasting — as some Mayfairites and their imitators do today — "I don't even know how to boil water."

Thus to the Old Hands at home and abroad — old enough to be cultured by contact either with nature or with humanity's stored knowledge — this yarn is an offering. I don't care what folks who are artists in literature rather than in life, or who substitute sophistication for wisdom, think or don't think about it. Those precious ones who are thrilled each spring by the return of the cuckoo and primrose or the finding of the fritillaries, would dither with enjoyment to yarn with the Old Hands up the country, so if they wish they are hereby invited within the dedication; and if only half a dozen genuine old pioneers commend the verisimilitude of their story as here writ down, I shall be rewarded extravagantly in excess of my deserts.

BRENT OF BIN BIN

S. 9, Reading Room,
    British Museum,
        June 1927